About the Underground G

MW01119786

Welcome to the underground!

Are you tired of all the fluff—books that tell you what you already know, ones that assume you're an idiot and treat you accordingly, or dwell on the trivial while completely ignoring the tough parts?

Good. You're in the right place.

Series Editor Woody Leonhard and Addison-Wesley bring you the Underground Guides—serious books that tackle the tough questions head-on but still manage to keep a sense of humor (not to mention a sense of perspective!). Every page is chock full of ideas you can put to use right away. We'll tell you what works and what doesn't—no bull, no pulled punches. We don't kowtow to the gods of the industry, we won't waste your time or your money, and we *will* treat you like the intelligent computer user we know you are.

Each Underground Guide is written by somebody who's been there—a working stiff who's suffered through the problems you're up against right now—and lived to tell about it. You're going to strike a rich vein of hard truth in these pages, and come away with a wealth of information you can put to use all day, every day.

So come along as we go spelunking where no book has gone before. Mind your head, and don't step in anything squishy. There will be lots of unexpected twists and turns . . . and maybe a laugh or two along the way.

The Underground Guide Series

Woody Leonhard, Series Editor

The Underground Guide to Word for Windows™:
Slightly Askew Advice from a WinWord Wizard
Woody Leonhard

The Underground Guide to Excel 5.0 for Windows™:
Slightly Askew Advice from Two Excel Wizards
Lee Hudspeth and Timothy-James Lee

The Underground Guide to UNIX®:
Slightly Askew Advice from a UNIX Guru
John Montgomery

The Underground Guide to Microsoft® Office, OLE, and VBA:
Slightly Askew Advice from Two Integration Wizards
Lee Hudspeth and Timothy-James Lee

The Underground Guide to Telecommuting:
Slightly Askew Advice on Leaving the Rat Race Behind
Woody Leonhard

The Underground Guide to Computer Security:
Slightly Askew Advice on Protecting Your PC and What's on It
Michael Alexander

The Underground Guide to Microsoft® Internet Assistant:
Slightly Askew Advice on Mastering the Web with WinWord
John Ross

The Underground Guide to Color Printers:
Slightly Askew Advice on Getting the Best from Any Color Printer
M. David Stone

The Underground Guide to Windows® 95:
Slightly Askew Advice from a Windows Wizard
Scot Finnie

The Underground Guide to Troubleshooting PC Hardware:
Slightly Askew Advice on Maintaining, Repairing, and Upgrading Your PC
Alfred Poor

The Underground Guide to

Troubleshooting PC Hardware

Slightly
 Askew
  Advice on
   Maintaining,
    Repairing,
     and Upgrading
      Your PC

Alfred Poor

Series Editor Woody Leonhard

ADDISON-WESLEY PUBLISHING COMPANY

Reading, Massachusetts • Menlo Park, California • New York • Don Mills, Ontario
Harlow, England • Amsterdam • Bonn • Sydney • Singapore • Tokyo
Madrid • San Juan • Paris • Seoul • Milan • Mexico City • Taipei

Many of the designations used by manufacturers and sellers to distinguish their products are claimed as trademarks. Where those designations appear in this book, and Addison-Wesley was aware of a trademark claim, the designations have been printed in initial capital letters or all capital letters.

The author and publisher have taken care in preparation of this book, but make no expressed or implied warranty of any kind and assume no responsibility for errors or omissions. No liability is assumed for incidental or consequential damages in connection with or arising out of the use of the information or programs contained herein.

Library of Congress Cataloging-in-Publication Data

Poor, Alfred E.
    The underground guide to troubleshooting PC hardware : slightly askew advice on maintaining, repairing, and upgrading your PC / Alfred Poor.
       p. cm. — (The underground guide series)
    Includes index.
    ISBN 0-201-48997-X
    1. IBM-compatible computers—Maintenance and repair—Handbooks, manuals, etc. 2. IBM-compatible computers—Upgrading—Handbooks, manuals, etc. I. Title. II. Series.
    TK7887.P66 1996
    621.39'16—dc20
                                       95-48225
                                         CIP

Copyright © 1996 by Alfred Poor

All rights reserved. No part of this publication may be reproduced, stored in a retrieval system, or transmitted, in any form or by any means, electronic, mechanical, photocopying, recording, or otherwise, without the prior written permission of the publisher. Printed in the United States of America. Published simultaneously in Canada.

Sponsoring Editor: Kathleen Tibbetts
Technical Editor: Ed Perratore, Contributing Editor, *Computer Shopper*
Project Manager: Sarah Weaver
Production Coordinator: Erin Sweeney
Cover design: Jean Seal
Text design: Kenneth L. Wilson, Wilson Graphics and Design
Set in 10 point Palatino by Pre-Press Company, Inc.

234678910 MA 0099989796
Second printing, May 1996

Addison-Wesley books are available for bulk purchases by corporations, institutions, and other organizations. For more information please contact the Corporate, Government, and Special Sales Department at (800) 238-9682.

Find us on the World-Wide Web at:
http://www.aw.com/devpress/

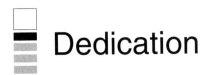

Dedication

Gratitude is the heart's memory.

French proverb

To my father, for teaching me how to troubleshoot everything from boat engines to missile policies, for helping me learn the value of all sorts of important things, and for giving me all those clocks to take apart when I was very small.

With my love and appreciation,

George #3

Contents

Foreword

Welcome to the one indispensable guide to what's going on in your PC.

With all the confounding questions floating around about PCs—is 16 bit really different from 32 bit? why do you need so much main memory? how do you get a sound board to work with a CD drive?—and danger at every turn, it's more important than ever before to understand what's happening within that beige cage.

Alfred Poor, one of the world's foremost authorities on PC hardware (and not coincidentally one of the funniest and most informative writers in the PC industry), takes you on a guided tour of your PC, from the often-misunderstood central processor chip to the outer limits of peripherals and add-ons, and everywhere in between. He'll have you understanding the most crucial concepts in minutes, then show you step-by-step how the theory translates into nuts-and-bolts silicon on your machine.

Every page of this Underground Guide is packed with the kind of detailed know-how that can only come from an expert who's wrestled with PC demons, and survived to tell about it. Whether you're choosing a new PC or upgrading an old one, trying to parse obtuse marketing hype for an add-on, or just trying to make the bloody thing *work*, this book is your reference of first resort. Concise, accessible, and authoritative, if you have a question about PC hardware, this is the place to look for down to earth answers.

And have a little fun while you're at it.

Enjoy!

Woody Leonhard
Series Hack

Acknowledgments

Behind an able man there are always other able men . . .

    Chinese proverb

. . . and women.

This is the most dangerous section of all to write. The rest of this book is risky enough; if I'm wrong, somebody might toast a piece of expensive equipment. But here, if I leave someone out, they may get the idea that I have omitted them on purpose, which certainly is not the case. (If I want to offend you, I'll be very open about it!) So here is an attempt to cover all the bases, and I hope that you'll forgive me if I have missed anyone.

First on the list is Kathleen Tibbetts at Addison-Wesley. I know how hard it can be to get me to do something, and her persistence, patience, and enthusiasm are the reasons that this book came to be.

Woody Leonhard comes right after Kathleen. His wacko writing has opened a door for the rest of us who want to try to write computer books with personality and attitude, yet deliver solid information without talking down to the readers or treating them like dummies. Without Woody, there would never have been an *Underground Guide* series, and I would have missed the chance to have all this fun. He has set a high standard for this style of writing, and I hope that my efforts measure up. Woody also was one of the biggest cheerleaders for this project, even before I turned in the initial proposal; that helped more than he knows.

Carol Mann, my agent, took care of dotting the i's and crossing the t's and working out the finances (which are all the things that I don't do well) so I could stay focused on the writing (which is something I do a bit better). It's great having someone like Carol watching your flank so you don't have to worry about that side of the project.

The book you hold bears only a slight resemblence to the words that originally crawled across my screen. A small army of people worked hard to clean it up and make it presentable—I have never met most of them, nor do I even know many of their names. I do know Edward Perratore, who did the technical read on the manuscript, and his thoughtful comments and questions improved the final result. Sarah Weaver and the folks at Addison-Wesley are the ones responsible for the final edits, the design and layout, and all those other nitty-gritty details that can be really boring to do, but you'd know if they weren't done because the book would not look as nice or read as well.

One part that Addison-Wesley didn't do was create George. As you'll read in the following introduction, George is my marginal character who helps flag different topics throughout the book. When I decided to "let George do it," as it were, I needed someone to bring him to life. Louise Max of Max Design in Doylestown, Pennsylvania, is the talented artist who was able to take my sketches and descriptions, mix in her own clever ideas, and come up with what it was that I was talking about all along—only better. Her drawing talent is matched only by her ability to listen, and I am grateful for her unique contributions to this project.

I would also like to thank all the vendors who helped make this book possible. Lots of them provided evaluation units or copies of programs for testing or reference, and there are too many to name here. I do want to single out Gateway 2000 for providing a Windows 95 testbench computer system, and ViewSonic for providing a monitor to use in Plug-and-Play tests. I also want to tip my hat in the general direction of all the technical and public relations workers at all the computer product companies. Their press releases, product sheets, white papers, and answers to telephone calls make it so much easier to do my part of the work that I probably wouldn't even have tried if they weren't there. These are jobs that are too often taken for granted, and they deserve some recognition. So here it is: I really appreciate your help on this and all my other projects.

Then there are all the people who helped me get to the point where I could even write a book like this. Ted Sage introduced me to BASIC and computers about 28 years ago. Joe Sproule was my boss in a public school district in Connecticut who encouraged me to explore ways to use computers to help me do my job. Bo Shmorhay gave me my first assignment at *PC Disk Magazine*, which led to my introduction to Mike Edelhardt and my first assignment at *PC Magazine*—so you can blame those last two folks for my name appearing in print since then.

Over the years, I have learned just about everything I know about computers through my work with the great people at the various Ziff-Davis magazines. Robin Raskin, Trudy Neuhaus, and Sharon Terdeman deserve special mention and appreciation for giving me the chance to write the hardware portion of the "Solutions" column in *PC Magazine* since it started a few years ago. And John Blackford, Oliver Rist, and Mark Weitz deserve similar credit for taking a chance with the "Alfred Poor's Computer Cures" question and answer column in *Computer Shopper*.

The folks from PC Magazine Labs over the years also deserve special mention: Bill O'Brien, Bob Kane, Charles Rodriquez, Wendy Dugas Perez, Mike Zulich, Lori Grunin, Steve Plain, and all the other project leaders, lab technicians, and other people there who have taught me so much over the years. I am especially grateful to John Dickinson for his support and encouragement over the years, starting with that first fateful Printer Project a dozen years ago, and continuing in spite of his changes in titles and magazines since then.

There are editors who have given me the chance to learn about all these great toys. Bill Machrone certainly tops the list, with a long list following—Robbin Juris, Don Wilmott, Gus Venditto, Mitt Jones, Dan Rosenbaum, Alice Hill, Barbara Krasnoff, Stephanie Stallings, Mary K. Flynn, Brian Nadel, Carol Levin, Leon Erlanger, Tom Mace, Lance Ulanoff, Rock Miller, Jim O'Brien, Tami Peterson, Vicky von Biel, Patty Ames, Steve Schwartz, and . . . oh boy, I've done it now; this could go on for pages! Either I stop here, or I pull out all the back issues of all the magazines I have written for and just copy the masthead listings for you. There are a lot of these people, and it is the review assignments of new products that keep this work fresh and appealing for me. Without those articles, this book would never have happened. And if I haven't included someone's name in this short list, it's not an intentional omission, I promise.

The free-lancer's lot can be a lonely one; you typically work at home, more or less in isolation. In spite of this—or maybe because of this—I have grown to appreciate the camaraderie and collegial exchange with the other writers at *PC Magazine* and the other Ziff-Davis magazines. I find that they are always available to discuss finer technical points or to explain an issue. Again, the list could go on for pages, but I especially want to mention Luisa Simone, John Quain, Ed Mendelson, and Joe Salemi, for I value them as friends as well as colleagues. Thom O'Connor took the time, over the years, to share some of his photography tricks, which made it possible for me to attempt to take the pictures for this book. And special mention goes to M. David Stone, fellow *Underground Guide* author and erstwhile co-author, because we have managed to remain on speaking terms despite working on three (large) books together and because we count on each other as a critical and educated sounding board for all sorts of technical issues.

Then there's Bruce Brown, my co-worker "down the hall," even if he's three states or a continent away. He's never too busy (well, almost never) to chat and discuss computers or anything else. His support and friendship helps me ward off the cabin fever that can threaten when I've been behind the keyboard for too long.

I also want to thank you and everyone else who buys computer books and magazines. A writer is a performer whose stage is the printed page; I have the privilege of lecturing at considerable length in front of millions of people. Without your support, I would not have been able to do it for all these years. There is nothing so fortunate in this world as people who love what they do for a living, and I count myself among that lucky number. So thanks for letting me work at something I enjoy so much, and I hope that you'll continue to give me the chance to do so in the future.

And finally, there are three other people for whom I do all this, and without whose help none of it could happen. My wife Bebe, daughter Anna, and son Alex mystify me in their unconditional support of my work—especially when it comes to books. "You're writing another book? Why!? Have you lost your mind? Don't you remember how it was last time?" But once they realize that I'm serious about it, they get behind it all the way and understand when I work late into the night or sneak away early in the morning on weekends to try to catch up on delivery schedules that inevitably fall into shambles sooner or later in spite of my efforts. And they mean it when they ask me how it is going—making encouraging noises when it goes well, shaking their heads in commiseration when I hit a sticky section, and joining in sincere celebration when the final pages are sent off to the publisher. So if not for their love and ecouragement and support, this book would never have reached you.

I hope you will appreciate the contributions of all these people, at least a little. I sure do.

Introduction

Oh, No! Another Hardware Book?

As machines become more and more efficient and perfect, so it will become clear that imperfection is the greatness of man.

Ernst Fischer
The Necessity of Art, 1959

I'm a man on a mission.

I get stacks of letters and disks of electronic mail each month from people with computer problems and upgrade questions. And these people are not dummies or idiots—these are intelligent, educated folks who are simply stymied by the complexity of the issues. But who can blame them for being stumped when the CPU makers use overlapping and confusing names for their products, and when Microsoft Windows gives error messages that have nothing to do with the cause of the problem, and when there's a Tower of Babel standing between the graphic adapters and monitors of our computers?

The fact is that the average computer user is quite capable of diagnosing a wide range of common problems and, in many cases, fixing these problems without outside assistance. This same user is just as capable of determining when certain parts of a computer system can be replaced to get a cost-effective upgrade, and when it makes more sense to simply start over with a new system.

We're not talking rocket science here (because that stuff really is difficult—I know, because my dad is a rocket scientist!). These are issues that you can deal with on your own. All you need is the information.

If I were the betting type, I'd bet that you already have a stack of books about hardware sitting on shelves, in desk drawers, or packed away in boxes. Even if you haven't bought such a book, consider all the manuals you got along with your computer, monitor, printer, modem, and other pieces of hardware that make up your computer system. And I also suspect that there have been times that these resources have been less than sufficient in helping you solve a problem. **You've got books already**

There are also lots of books in the bookstores that cover hardware. Some of them are pretty good; I know, because I have a rather extensive collection of books about hardware, and I've even written a couple of them. But they're all flawed in one way or another.

Some books are just compendiums of tables and details extracted from technical manuals. (Who would ever really need to know what each pin on an ISA edge connector does?) Others talk down to the readers as if they can't be trusted to understand complicated details. Yet others assume that you already know what needs to be fixed or upgraded, and they just stick to the easy screwdriver-and-wrench steps.

WHY THIS BOOK IS DIFFERENT

> Give a man a fish, and he'll eat for a day. Teach a man to fish, and he'll eat for a lifetime.
>
> Chinese proverb

Part of my mission is to teach you what you need to know to fix your hardware problems and solve your upgrade questions now. The editors have only given me a limited number of pages in which to accomplish this task, so I can't cover every possible topic in as much depth as I'd like to, but that doesn't really matter because this would still just be giving you fish.

The other part of my mission is to give you the strategies and the technical knowledge that you need to be able to tackle the problems that aren't covered directly in these pages. To keep going with the analogy, I also want to show you how to decide what lure to try and how to decide where to cast first when you need to catch a new kind of fish.

How Much Do You Know About Fishing?

> Everyone is a beginner for at least the first 30 minutes.
>
> Bill Machrone, former Editor of *PC Magazine*

I've also set myself an ambitious goal, but I'll need your help in pulling it off. I want this book to be useful to you for a long, long time. If I were to write just for the experienced, knowledgeable, power users, that would shut out the beginners. But if I write just for beginners, it would be of little use to experienced users.

From beginners to experts   Because I'm the kind of person who isn't convinced that something can't be done until I see proof, I'm going to try to write this book for both ends of the experience spectrum, and for everyone in between. If you're a beginner now, you won't be one forever (especially after you've spent some time with this book), and I want you to get your money's worth. If you already know a lot about computers, you'll find lots of tips, tricks, and secrets that you can use now and in the future. There's even a chance that you'll find some information in the more basic sections that can fill some gaps in your knowledge.

Not content with that ambitious goal, I have also complicated matters by trying to tackle two kinds of problems at once. I want to help you solve problems with your existing system and get everything working again as quickly and cost effectively as possible when something goes bump in the night. On the other hand, you will also have questions about upgrades—if not today or tomorrow, then someday, and probably sooner than you might think. So I also intend to help you make sense out of the nearly infinite universe of upgrade choices that confront you. To make this work, I need your help. I need you to be a smart reader so you don't get bogged down in the parts that you don't need at the moment.

Repairs and upgrades

HOW THIS BOOK IS ORGANIZED

> Order is Heaven's first law.
>
> Alexander Pope (1688–1744)
> *An Essay on Man*

I've done my best to arrange the information you need so that you can find it quickly. Let's face it, this is not going to be the kind of book that you're likely to read all the way through at one sitting (though you might want to spend an afternoon or evening skimming it to get an idea of what's in here, and to find all the funny bits). No, it's more likely that something will break or you'll finally get fed up with the performance of one component or another, and then you'll want to find the answers right away! So here's where I've stuck everything (or as much as I could fit).

Find it fast!

Let's start with the chapters. Each one covers a different set of components or subsystems. I've started from the inside—the computer's brains—and worked my way out. Here's the chapter line-up:

1. CPUs and Motherboards

2. Memory

3. Storage

4. Displays

5. Printers

6. Multimedia Stuff

7. Input Devices: Keyboards, Mice, Joysticks, Scanners

8. Portable Stuff

In the back of the book, you'll also find a bunch of interesting and possibly useful lists and tables that actually might come in handy some day. You probably won't want to jump there first, but do plan on browsing the appendices at some point, just so you know what is there. (And they're not just stuffing—my biggest problem with this book was deciding what material to leave out, not trying to stretch to fill pages!)

That's certainly straightforward, but that's not enough. I have also structured the chapters so that they all follow the same format. Each chapter has the same three major sections: Need to Know, @#%$%@!, and Upgrading.

Need to Know

The first section of every chapter covers the basics. This is where you can find definitions of different terms and concepts (such as what the heck an L2 cache is and why you should care), as well as a little historical perspective.

I expect that this section will be most useful to beginners who may be a bit baffled by the technobabble, but I also expect that more experienced users may find some nuggets of information that they may find useful or intriguing. (Besides, it's lots of fun to find points where you think I'm all wet—there's lots of room for opinion even in a topic that seems as cut and dried as computer memory!)

So if you're interested in a specific chapter, skim the Need to Know section at the very least. That way you'll know what I mean by certain terms.

@#%$%@!

When bad things happen to good computers, this is the section you'll want to read next. I'll cover many of the most common problems and help you troubleshoot them to determine the exact cause. Because computers are so complex these days (and the software tries to hide this complexity from you as much as possible), the cause of the trouble may appear to be unrelated to the symptoms you observe.

You'll also learn strategies that will help you troubleshoot problems that I don't describe in specific detail. By the time you've worked your way through a few of the chapters, you'll be a master of the classic "A-B" test method (though there are some important caveats to this technique to keep in mind).

Upgrading

This section really serves two functions. If you're not happy with the performance you're getting from a subsystem, you can come here to find out which upgrades are worth considering, and which are a waste of time, money, or both.

This section also has a second purpose. If you have worked through the middle @#%$%@! section of a chapter and find that you need to replace a busted component, the Upgrading section will help you choose the right replacement part, as well as help you decide whether you should use the opportunity to upgrade that component while you're at it.

UNDERGROUND CHARACTERS

> Friends . . . are the only real means for foreign ideas to enter your brain.
>
> Nicholson Baker
> *U And I: A True Story,* 1991

The chapter structure should help make it easier for you to go directly to the information you need, but to make it even easier, I've also enlisted the help of a friend of mine.

Other books in the *Underground Guide* series use a little bug and a magic wand in the margins. Those other titles deal largely with software, so bugs and magic tips play an important role in helping you understand the content. But this book is about hardware, and the problems and tips fall into a broader range of categories. As a result, I've called on my friend George to help flag some important tidbits scattered throughout the book. George likes to dress up, so he wears a different outfit depending on the kind of information. He plays five different roles:

The Professor

He's only nerdy at first glance—sure, he knows the technical details, but he does not always follow the conventional wisdom on what those details mean!

The Lifeguard

When you're sinking fast, you want to to be rescued . . . and right away! The Lifeguard will help keep you afloat, and if he can't fix the problem on the spot, he can at least get you standing on dry land until you can get expert assistance.

Dr. Frankenchip

He's a cross between a mad scientist and a driveway mechanic—he simply wants to get the pieces together in the easiest, most reliable, and cheapest way that he can.

The Spy

If it's slick secrets you seek, turn to the spy for the little-known intelligence that can get you out of a tight spot.

Baby 95

Let's face the fact that Windows 95 is here, and and if you don't have it yet, you will be running it sooner or later. It's going to have an impact on all sorts of hardware issues such as monitors and graphics adapters that are supposed to be able to configure themselves to work together, automatically and without your help. This youngster will flag the points about Win95 so you can find them faster.

THE NEXT STEP

It's up to you.

You can now decide that this book is what you need, stick it on a shelf near your computer, and wait until there's a problem before you go directly to the section that has the information you need.

Or you can decide to spend an hour or two getting introduced to the material inside here. Browse a few chapters, dive into a few sections that catch your eye, learn the lay of the land so to speak. You will probably find some good information that you can use right away, and I'd hope that the experience would turn out to be enjoyable as well.

Either way, the book is ready to be your companion, awaiting your beck and call, standing ready to help out with hardware problems and questions.

One thing you might want to do right now, before you even get started, is make an Emergency Boot Disk. You'll find it discussed in more detail in the middle of Chapter 3, but here are some quick steps to follow now, just in case:

- Format a floppy disk for your floppy disk Drive A.

- Make it bootable; at the DOS prompt, type SYS A: and press Enter.

- Copy your CONFIG.SYS and AUTOEXEC.BAT files from the root directory of your hard disk to the floppy disk.

- Reboot your computer with the disk in Drive A and make certain that you can access your hard disk after it boots.

- If the Emergency Boot Disk works, label (and date) it clearly and put it in a safe place where you can be sure to find it when you need it.

If the Emergency Boot Disk doesn't work, you may need to add some files to it,

such as some driver files from your hard disk. Check the section in Chapter 3 for more information.

See? There's one useful tip that could save you hours of anguish later on, and you haven't even started Chapter 1 yet! And there's lots more to come as soon as you turn the page.

Get ready to have some fun!

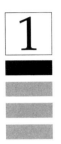

1 CPUs and Motherboards

God has placed no limit to intellect.

Francis Bacon (1561–1626)

Although it may not be possible to prove Bacon's theological theory, there is strong empirical evidence that there is no limit to how many different microprocessors Intel and its competitors will produce for the microcomputer market. This open-ended string leaves us with at least two certainties:

- No matter what kind of brain may lurk inside your computer, eventually it will be obsolete—and almost certainly sooner than you'd like.
- You will face unending frustration and confusion as you grapple with the issue of when to move up to a more powerful processor.

The frustration and confusion are intensified by the lack of absolute measures. What is "fast enough" for a car buyer, or "enough closet space" to a home buyer, or "enough research" for a doctoral committee? It's all relative, especially with computers; a processor that can handle one application without a problem might perform at a glacial pace on another.

The chip makers don't help matters, however, as we'll discuss in a minute. Just because two processors have "386" or "486" in their names doesn't mean that they will have anywhere near the same performance, even when installed in otherwise identical systems.

She's somebody's mother, boys, you know,
For all she's aged and poor and slow.

Mary Dow Brine
Somebody's Mother

It's nearly impossible to discuss a computer's processor without also paying attention to the motherboard on which it is installed. After all, CPU is a TLA for

Motherboards

Central Processing Unit, and if the CPU is at the center, there must be some other important stuff around it. (TLA stands for Three-Letter Acronym, which means that TLA is also a TLA. Ooh, this self-reflexive stuff makes my head hurt sometimes.) As you'll see, having a motherboard that cannot take advantage of a processor's features can limit performance just as much as using a processor of lesser ability would.

To avoid all this frustration and confusion, you must consider both the processor and the motherboard. Fortunately, you should be well immunized against the dreaded "Processor Befuddlement Virus" by the time you finish Chapter 1. Granted, you may need a booster in the future as the new chips appear on the market in an attempt to confuse you, but this chapter will give you a solid base of protection.

You'll learn about the various processors on the market today and how their capabilities relate to motherboard design. You'll be able to diagnose and deal with many common problems that you may encounter with CPUs and motherboards, and perhaps most important of all, you'll be able to make informed decisions about just what types of upgrades are cost effective in terms of time, performance, and money.

NEED TO KNOW

If you want to find out about the origins of the microprocessor, you can find the history detailed in dozens of books. The short story is that a bunch of engineers designed an electronic calculator and realized that it was easier to "teach" it instructions than it was to build the instructions into the semiconductor chips. A few forward-thinking folks realized what this could mean in terms of inexpensive and small computers, and a bunch of pioneer companies became very famous by building the first generations of mini- and microcomputers. Most of those companies have long since disappeared.

Apple made a lasting contribution with the Apple][, offering such innovations as expandable memory and slots that third-party manufacturers could make cards for to add new features and functions. But it wasn't until IBM weighed in with a computer that improved on Apple's design that the microcomputer took off. (Oddly enough, Apple abandoned the "open" system philosophy when it built the Mac, and only recently has the company changed its direction.) IBM didn't choose the most powerful processor available at the time—but the one it chose was powerful enough for the moment.

And we've been upgrading our CPUs ever since.

Different CPUs

> There is only one difference between a madman and me. I am not mad.
>
> Salvador Dalí
> *Diary of a Genius,* 1966

There are lots of ways that microprocessors are different. Some differences are esoteric, such as the different instruction sets that they support, while others are kinda obvious, such as speed ratings. But the one thing that is really the most important of all is the data paths.

In order for your computer to do anything at all, it has to move data around. In fact, because a computer can really only take a series of bits of data and combine them, at heart it's just a really fast light switch—well, a bunch of light switches, actually. The more light switches you can turn on and off at a time, the more information you can process at one time. (More switches mean more bits, which means that the processor can process higher numbers in one pass; with fewer switches, you would have to break the problem up into smaller numbers and then combine the results—which would take more steps, and thus more time.)

The number of light switches inside a processor is really a measure of the chip's internal data path—how much information can it hold in its tiny brain at a time? Like most of the microcomputers of that time, the Apple][processor was an 8-bit processor. It could process numbers as high as 256 at one time. The IBM PC came along and gave us a 16-bit processor in our computers, and the extra power was immediately obvious. Since then we have grown to use 32-bit processors, and now 64-bit powerhouses. But there's more to the story than just the internal data path.

The System Data Bus

> Either you're on the bus or you're off the bus.
>
> Ken Kesey (quoted by Tom Wolfe)
> *The Electric Kool-Aid Acid Test,* 1968

Processing chips essentially can't remember anything. In order to have something to think about, the processor has to get data from somewhere. And once it has thought about it, it has to have a place to put the answer. The place where this data sits before and after the processor has thought about it is the system memory. (In general, this is memory on your computer's motherboard, but on some computers it may be on a separate expansion card.)

Now, think of the CPU as being connected to the memory by a hose. If the hose is too thin, the processor may have to wait while new data arrives for crunching, or for the results to get squirted out to be held by the memory.

The original IBM PC was derided by some pundits at the time of its release because its 8088 chip (Figure 1.1) only had an 8-bit-wide "hose" to its memory, even though it could think in 16-bit chunks. As it turned out, it was powerful enough to dominate the market and establish a course of microcomputer evolution that few could have imagined back then. When the IBM AT came along, it used the Intel 80286 chip, which had a 16-bit data bus to match its internal data path.

Figure 1.1   Intel's 8088: The chip that launched a million PCs.

The Intel 80386SX has a 16-bit data bus path, but a 32-bit internal path. The Intel 80386DX and 80486DX both have 32-bit width internally and to memory. The Intel Pentium is a bit different from any of the prior chips in that the data bus is wider than the internal path; it is a 32-bit processor, but it has a 64-bit data bus path. So along with a wider internal processing data path, you'll get better performance from a CPU that has a wider path to the system memory.

In Chapter 2, we'll get into more detail about memory issues, but for the moment, just know that the DRAM (Dynamic Random Access Memory) used for system memory is usually configured with chips that are relatively slow but inexpensive. There are faster kinds of memory, such as SRAM (Static RAM), but they cost more, so you rarely find them used as system memory.

Memory speed is important, however. You've got a happy little processor, chugging away, grabbing data from memory and processing it, and spitting out answers. When working with complex processing, or when repeating the same step over and over with different data, the processor frequently reaches for the same data that it reached for or spit out just a few cycles before. But because the memory is slow, the processor sometimes has to wait . . . and wait . . . until the memory is ready to hand over the data, even though it is data that the processor had recently used.

Cache and carry   System designers realized that a little fast memory could be used to hold the most recently used data and instructions, so the processor wouldn't have to wait when it needed them again. This bit bucket is called a *cache.* A system memory cache became a popular way to improve the performance of 80386-based motherboards, and soon systems needed to have one in order to be competitive.

Then Intel got the idea that instead of making manufacturers add the extra memory for a system cache on the motherboard, the cache could be built right into the CPU chip itself. So when the 80486DX first appeared, an 8KB cache was included in the chip. As it turns out, this cache provided a performance boost, but it wasn't large enough to provide all the benefits you could get from caching. So motherboard manufacturers again started adding fast memory as a system memory cache.

To distinguish the two caches, the one on the chip is called the **internal,** or **Level 1,** cache, and the one on the motherboard is called the **external,** or **Level 2,** cache. The Level 2 term is often abbreviated as L2 in system specifications.

And now the Intel Pentium (Figure 1.2) has a 16KB internal cache. Actually it's two separate 8 KB caches: one for data and another for instructions. And still performance is boosted sufficiently that it pays to invest in the extra cost of an L2 cache.

Figure 1.2 The Intel Pentium has become the current standard for PC CPUs.

Math Coprocessor

> It is wonderful when a calculation is made, how little the mind is actually employed in the discharge of any profession.
>
> Samuel Johnson (quoted by James Boswell)
> *Life of Johnson,* 1791

We tend to think of computers as experts at calculating numbers, when in fact, they really work best with relatively small, whole numbers. When faced with a problem involving messy fractions or very large values, even the most powerful processors have to start carving up the problem into manageable parts. These types of calculations are called **floating-point calculations** because the decimal point has to float around, away from its cozy home at the far right of the digits where it is found on whole numbers.

Intel realized early on that some programs—like CAD (computer-aided design) and some scientific calculations—needed some extra horsepower in order to get problems done in an acceptable length of time. So the company came out with **math coprocessor** chips: processors that took over from the CPU for certain types of problems. So for the 8088, you could add an 8087, or an 80287 to an 80286, or an 80387 to an 80386. Engineers and scientists were happy to pay the extra to cut processing time in half or more for some of their calculations.

Then Windows 3.0 took off, and average users started running programs like Word for Windows and Excel that could take at least a small advantage of a math coprocessor. So Intel decided to stuff floating-point coprocessing circuitry into the 80486DX chip as well. But then they came out with an 80486SX chip that didn't have the math coprocessor support, as a lower cost alternative to the 80486DX, and for most people, the performance was negligibly slower.

How Chips Are Named

> Chaos is a name for any order that produces confusion in our minds.
>
> George Santayana
> *Dominations and Powers,* 1951

You'd think it would be easy to come up with a simple way to name CPUs so that the buyer could tell instantly what the chip's capabilities were. Intel had a nice pattern going for a while with the 80x86 CPU and the 80x87 math coprocessor, and the company also tacked on the rated operating speed at the end. So an 80286-12 was an 80x86 CPU designed to run at 12 MHz.

Then they had to go and create that 80386 chip with the crippled data path: the 80386SX. And that meant that the "regular" 386 needed a different name, so it became the 80386DX. So "SX" means "narrower data bus," right? Not always! In the 80486 series, the DX version was the complete chip, but the SX version had the same width data bus; the difference between the two was that the SX version didn't have the math coprocessor.

Then Intel started making hot rod chips that ran faster. They still interacted with the system memory bus at familiar speeds, but they ran twice as fast when processing data internally. So the 80486DX2-66 (Figure 1.3) was able to go in a motherboard designed for an 80486DX-33 but with a significant performance boost. (Performance is not actually doubled precisely, because not all the processor's operations can be run at the 66 MHz speed, but depending on your application, it's still a big boost.)

Figure 1.3   The Intel 80486DX2 was the first CPU to make clock-doubling a popular feature.

So the number after the DX and before the speed tells you how many times faster the chip runs internally than externally, right? Wrong. Intel's DX4-100 is actually a clock-*tripled* chip, so it talks to the system bus at 33.3 MHz but operates internally at 100 MHz.

Confused yet? Well, then there were the Intel 486SL chips, which had special power-management features built in so system designers could put the CPU "to sleep" when it had nothing to do; this helped engineers design battery-powered notebook computers that would draw less power. But now those energy-saving features are built into all the 486 chips, so the SL designation is no longer used.

What really threw a spanner in the works for naming CPU chips was the development of Intel-compatible chips by Cyrix, AMD, and other sources. For example, Cyrix created the 486SLC. Although all the Intel 486 chips have 32-bit wide system data buses, this chip only has a 16-bit wide path. And although the Intel 486 chips have 8 KB internal caches, the Cyrix 486SLC only has a 1KB cache. And where the Intel 486DX series includes a math coprocessing for floating-point calculations, the Cyrix chip only has some circuitry to speed up simpler integer math calculations.

There are now CPUs being made by IBM, Texas Instruments, Cyrix, AMD, and other manufacturers, all with similar names. Is it any wonder that Intel chose to call the 80586 the Pentium, something that it could control? And it should come as no surprise that most computer users do not know and understand the differences within the Intel line of chips, let alone all the competing products with confusing, sound-alike names.

As it turns out, however, understanding these differences is important when it comes time to decide about fixing or upgrading or replacing your current computer system, as we'll see later on in this chapter.

Motherboards and Different Buses

> Art has to move you and design does not, unless it's a good design for a bus.
>
> David Hockney, quoted in the *Guardian* Oct. 26, 1988

Perhaps the only other feature about a computer system that is as confusing as the way its CPUs are named is the whole issue of expansion buses. Fortunately for us, IBM decided to build the original PC so that it could accept expansion cards to add new features and capabilities. Unfortunately, a number of different kinds of buses have grown from that original PC, leaving us with a bunch of choices.

The first change came about when IBM developed the AT. The 80286 processor had a 16-bit data bus compared with the PC's 8-bit width, and so it could move data to and from peripherals twice as fast because it could send twice as much in a given time. This made it possible to get data to and from a hard disk much faster, for example. The problem, however, was that the PC slots could only handle 8 bits of data, so in order to design a 16-bit-wide hard disk controller, a new kind of slot had to be invented for it to fit. But IBM designers also wanted users to be able to fit existing 8-bit PC cards in the same slots.

This was the beginning of what has since evolved into the **ISA (Industry Standard Architecture) slot.** The problem is that there never really was a formal specification for this design. IBM added on an extra edge connector next to the original PC slot and came up with a slightly clumsy way for the computer to know whether it was talking to an 8-bit or a 16-bit card. It also ran the expansion bus at the same speed as the system clock for the CPU—6 MHz in the first IBM AT, and 8 MHz in the second version of the computer.

Not many people realize it, but 16-bit cards may automatically "dumb down" when there is an 8-bit card installed and configured so that the two cards are in the same memory segment. When initiating a transfer to one of the cards, the CPU first sends out an interrogating signal to see if the card can handle 16-bit transfers. The question is sent to a wide range of memory addresses at one time, however, so an 8-bit card may respond that it can't handle 16 bits, even though the transfer is intended for a different card that can handle the extra width. But all the CPU hears back is that 16-bit transfers won't work, so it proceeds to make the transfer only 8 bits at a time. The only solution—aside from switching to a different bus—is to reconfigure the cards so that the 16-bit card is not configured for the same memory segment as an 8-bit card. Check your display adapter card's manual for more details on how to configure the card.

Problems arose for the AT-style bus when clone system makers started running their CPUs faster and faster to get a performance edge on the competition. Around 12 MHz, some expansion cards started to be unreliable, especially communication cards like modems and network adapters.

Eventually system designers agreed that they wouldn't run the 16-bit bus faster than the AT's 8 MHz speed. And now almost all systems run their ISA slots at 8 MHz.

The next problem came with the 32-bit processors, such as the 80386DX. These had 32-bit-wide data buses and so could transfer twice as much data at a time as processors with 16-bit data buses but the ISA expansion bus could only handle 16 bits at a time. Initially each manufacturer came up with their own 32-bit expansion slots—usually limited to just memory expansion—but then two other standards appeared. **EISA,** or **Extended ISA,** was developed so that it could take either standard 8- or 16-bit ISA cards, as well as newer 32-bit cards, using a single design for the expansion slot. IBM created the **MicroChannel** for most (but not all) of its first computers in the PS/2 line, with the intention that the one slot would serve all needs. The MicroChannel slot design has 16- and 32-bit versions, plus special versions for graphics adapters and memory.

The 32-bit expansion slot didn't really take off, however, until the development of the **VESA (Video Electronics Standards Association) local bus,** which came to be known as the **VL-Bus** (Figure 1.4). It adds a short slot to the ISA 16-bit slot, and so you can use most older cards in the same slots. The VL-Bus is designed to be wired directly to the CPU data bus and is specified for speeds up

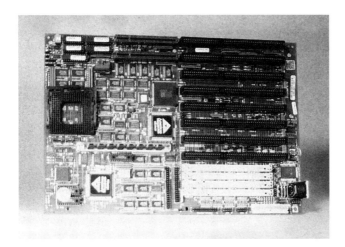

Figure 1.4 This motherboard has eight 16-bit ISA slots, two of which also have 32-bit VL-Bus local bus extensions.

to 33 MHz. (There are provisions to run the VL-Bus connections at speeds higher than 33 MHz, but these require either direct connections without using an expansion slot or buffering, which essentially creates a separate connection between the CPU and the bus, which reduces performance.) The 33 MHz limit is significant; it means that the VL-Bus is well matched for the 80486DX-33, 80486DX2-66, and 80486DX4-100, which all have 33 MHz data bus speeds.

The arrival of the Pentium processors marked the ascendance of another local bus design, **PCI (Peripheral Component Interconnect).** This bus is designed to work with high-speed processors because the PCI bus and the processor data bus are separate and can run at different speeds.

As a rule of thumb, ISA-only motherboards are not appropriate except for CPUs that have a 16-bit data bus; if you have a more powerful processor, you should plan on using one of the two local bus designs. VL-Bus motherboards are generally less expensive than PCI motherboards and are best suited for 486-level processors. For a Pentium processor, the PCI bus is the best way to go.

I/O ports   Many newer motherboards have less need for expansion slots than older designs because more and more of the features that you would want in a computer are included right on the motherboard.

In the past, motherboards followed the example set by the original IBM PC; you got a keyboard connection and that was it. (Well, the original IBM PC also had a port to which you could connect a standard audio cassette recorder so that you could save and load programs, but that's another story . . .) Now, a typical motherboard also includes two serial ports, a parallel port, a mouse port, a graphics adapter, and connections for hard and floppy disk drives. For many users, there is no need to add any expansion cards at all.

There are advantages and disadvantages to this approach. On the plus side, this high level of integration lowers costs for the manufacturer and makes it easier to put together a system. On the down side, however, you can run into problems when something breaks or you want to upgrade one component of your system. You need to have a way to disable the feature on the motherboard before you can install the replacement; you may not always be able to disable a component.

BIOS and   The final main difference among motherboards is the **BIOS (Basic Input/**
CMOS settings   **Output System).** If the CPU is the brain, the BIOS holds the computer's personality: the basic programs that let the system "wake up" when you turn on the power, and that keeps track of how the system is configured, such as how much memory and what disk drives are installed.

In the early days of microcomputers, users had to write their own BIOS depending on what components they used to assemble their systems. (This was particularly true of expansion card–based computers that used a design called the S-100 bus and ran the CP/M operating system.) Today there is a booming market in IBM-compatible BIOS code, with companies such as Phoenix, AMI, and Award providing most of the BIOS code used in popular computer systems and motherboards.

The BIOS is stored in ROM (Read Only Memory), so it is not lost when the power is turned off. The BIOS also needs to know some basic information about your computer system, however, and this must be stored in memory that is not lost either when you hit the power switch. These settings are stored in **CMOS** memory (which stands for Complementary Metal-Oxide Semiconductor, and I only mention that because I've spelled out all the other acronyms so far but there's really no reason why you'd ever need to know this since nobody ever uses anything but the acronym to refer to it).

Any IBM PC-compatible BIOS has configuration settings for the time and date, the hard and floppy disk drives that are installed, and type of display adapter. Figure 1.5 shows the information for a typical BIOS version from Phoenix.

```
                         Dell Computer Corporation
 Page 1 of 2             System OmniPlex 590 Setup          BIOS Version: A10

 Time:  15:52:53  Date: Mon  Nov 13, 1995    This category sets the time in
                                             24-hour format (hours:minutes:
    Diskette Drive A:    3.5 inch, 1.44 MB   seconds) for the internal clock/
    Diskette Drive B:    Not Installed       calendar.
    Drive A Location:         Top
                                             To change the value in a field,
 Hard-Disk Type Cyls Hds  Pre  LZ Sec Size   enter a number or use the left-
 Drive 0: None                               or right-arrow key.
 Drive 1: None
                                             Changes take effect immediately.
      Base Memory:        640 KB
     Board Memory:        640 KB
   Fast Video BIOS:         Off
   Extended Memory:       7168 KB
                                             Microprocessor: Pentium-90
            Cache:          On               External Cache: 256 KB
        CPU Speed:        90 MHz               Video Memory: 2 MB
         Num Lock:          On               System Memory: 8192 KB
          Speaker:        High                 Service Tag: 3L6LV

 Tab,Shift-Tab change fields|←,→ change values|Alt-P page|Esc exit|Alt-B reboot
```

Figure 1.5   The BIOS configuration settings are stored in CMOS memory.

Many versions of BIOS have advanced settings, which you change on a separate screen, as shown in Figure 1.6. In general, you don't want to change these unless you have a good reason. The one exception is the Shadow Video BIOS setting, which we will cover in Chapter 2. For most of the others, you may stand to get only minimal performance gain, while there is a real chance of putting your system in a state where it won't boot at all until you restore the CMOS memory to its default settings.

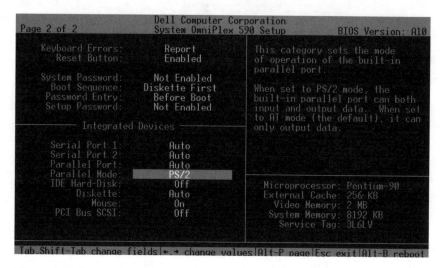

Figure 1.6   Most users won't need to change any of their system's advanced BIOS settings, if the system has them.

CMOS memory still needs power to keep it from forgetting what it knows, but it needs less power than regular memory. As a result, a little battery can be enough to keep the system configuration information for years. Some systems even use rechargeable nicad (nickel-cadmium) or lithium batteries, which get recharged whenever you run your computer. When the battery runs out, however, the computer will forget all its settings, and you will need to restore the settings before you can get the computer to work again. (We'll go into more detail about this in a moment.) To save yourself some future aggravation, however, you should make sure you have a handy record of all your CMOS settings.

I'd put this tip in the next section, but it's really a preventative tip, and the last thing you'll want to read when you've got a problem is how you could have prevented it by doing something earlier. So I'll put it here. Run your computer's configuration (or setup) program and write down all your computer's CMOS settings. (Different computers run their configuration programs in different ways; check your system's manual for instructions on how to run yours.) While you're at it, you might also want to document any jumper settings, IRQ assignments, and other configuration details. Put all this information in a plastic bag (the kind that zips closed) and tape it to the bottom of your computer case; make sure you don't block any ventilation holes. Then you'll have all the essential information you'll need if something drastic goes wrong and you have to reconfigure your system. You might also want to put an emergency boot disk in the plastic bag, too. (See Chapter 3, Storage, for details on what to put on your emergency boot disk.)

@#%$%@!

> The nearer any disease approaches to a crisis, the nearer it is to a cure.
>
> Thomas Paine

The good news is that your CPU and motherboard are probably the most reliable components in your whole system. There are few moving parts, if any, and they are generally overengineered in favor of long-term reliability. But that's because of the down side—if your CPU goes, you're cooked until you get it fixed. And the same goes for your motherboard, more or less (though there may be steps you can take to get a motherboard going again).

You're also not likely to repair a broken CPU or motherboard; it's more cost effective to replace it. And when you replace either of these components, chances are excellent that you'll want to upgrade to something with better performance. So all in all, your CPU and motherboard will probably run just fine for longer than you want them to. Of course, there are exceptions, which is why there is the following section.

CPU Problems

Problems with CPU chips (and related components such as math coprocessors) tend to be pass/fail propositions. Either the chip works, or it doesn't. You don't often find intermittent problems (like you get too often with disks and memory) or a situation where a CPU works okay with one application but not with another. When a CPU dies, you replace it or upgrade—a decision that is covered in the last part of this chapter.

Sometimes the CPU will be working fine at first, however, and then it goes south (your computer hangs, spontaneously reboots, or behaves in some similar, unproductive manner). Or you may find that you turn your computer on, and it doesn't boot at first. Instead, you have to try pressing the reset button or cycling the power after a minute or two before the system seems to "catch" and start running. In a way, these two problems are flip sides of the same coin.

Here is *George's First Rule of Hardware Troubleshooting*: **Cold failures are mechanical, hot failures are silicon. In other words, if something fails when you first turn it on, before it has had a chance to warm up, the first places to check are the mechanical connections: cables, cards, socketed chips, and so on. The reason the problem "fixes itself" after the unit warms up is that the metal in the connections expands with the heat and may squeeze together to make a better contact than when cold.**

On the other hand, if the problem seems to appear after the system has been powered up for a while, the problem is more likely to be a chip that has become too hot. Heat is one of the main enemies of semiconductors and can cause them to perform unreliably. Too much heat can permanently damage a chip.

Heat Problems

Today's CPUs are more and more prone to heat problems. If your computer starts behaving erratically after running a while, heat could be the cause.

One way to determine whether or not heat is the problem is to simply take off the cover of your computer case and run the computer with the case open. This may be inconvenient, especially if you normally have the monitor sitting on top of the case, and you may also find that your case's cooling fan and hard disk are a lot louder than when the case is closed up. But if the problem goes away, heat may well be the cause. (Note that when you run your computer with the case off, however, it will emit a lot more radio wave interference since most rely on the case to shield these waves. This could interfere with your radio or television reception when you're running the computer.)

If you suspect heat is giving you troubles, it is possible that the CPU or other semiconductor component has gone bad and needs to be replaced. It is also possible that the components are okay, so there are other causes that you should investigate first.

Check cooling fan
One item to check is the cooling fan on the computer's power supply. These are mechanical devices, and even though they are designed to be run for long hours at a stretch, they do give out eventually. If your power supply is assembled with screws and you're mechanically adventurous, you may be able to remove a failed fan from the power supply and find a replacement at a local Radio Shack or other electronics store. These fans typically come in square housings and are commonly referred to as **muffin fans.** Make certain that the replacement fan is designed for the same power (AC or DC, and the correct voltage) and has at least the same capacity specification, which is usually stated in terms of CFM, or cubic feet per minute.

On the other hand, if your computer case is a standard size, you can get a replacement power supply for less than $50, and it's relatively easy to remove the old power supply and install a new one. Depending on what your time is worth to you, this may be a less expensive solution than figuring out how to open your existing power supply and finding a match for its fan.

Check for dust
Another cause for heat problems with a CPU (or other chips on the motherboard, for that matter) is dust. The reason that there's a big fan on the power supply is so that it can pull cooler air through the system case and remove excess heat that is generated by the chips. If you put an insulating blanket over the chips, this

airflow will do little to help cool them off, and their temperature will rise. If you've never opened the case of a four or five year old computer in an office environment, you might be startled to see how much dust can settle inside. (Think about that stuff you find under the refrigerator at home, and you'll get the idea. You *have* cleaned under your refrigerator, right?) And if you're in one of those rare offices where the occupants still smoke tobacco, be prepared to see an amazing blanket of dust; smoke is dust, after all. So get out your little hand vacuum cleaner and get rid of that insulating blanket.

A third cause of restricted air flow is less obvious. Some people run into flaky system performance after they add a new expansion card to their system. The problems could be caused by a hardware configuration conflict, but it is also possible that the new card simply has disrupted the cooling air flow patterns within the case and the CPU is not getting sufficient ventilation. One solution is to try shuffling cards around so that the airflow is less restricted, or at least, is improved over the CPU. If this fails, you can add a heat sink—or even better, a small fan as shown in Figure 1.7—mounted directly on top of the CPU chip to help keep it cool. This can cost you $20 or less. Remember, however, that only helps the CPU and does nothing to help the other chips on the motherboard.

Improve air flow

Figure 1.7 A small fan mounted directly on the CPU can help it keep its cool.

Finally, you can have heat problems in your system simply because the air cannot flow through the case. Have you ever noticed the little louvers and holes across the front of some cases? They are more than a design statement; they have a functional purpose as well. So if you encounter heat problems, make certain that the holes are not clogged with dust, obstructed by Post-Its, or simply covered with a clever bumper sticker. (I have even seen well-intentioned folks who tried to run their computers with vinyl dust covers in place . . .)

Check for blocked air holes

If you have the opposite problem—the computer works okay when hot, but not when cold—mechanical connections are the likely culprit. The CPU and other chips are mounted on the motherboard in sockets. The repeated heating and cooling cycles as the computer is turned on and off cause the metal in the chips' pins and in the sockets to expand and contract repeatedly, and in some cases, can actually cause the chips to "walk" out of their sockets.

One computer stands out in history as being the ultimate for this problem. Apple Computer built the Apple /// as a successor to the Apple][, targeted for business users. Unfortunately, the chips would work loose on a regular basis, and some users reported taking out the motherboard and standing on it every month, just to reseat the chips.

Don't resort to the Mexican Hat Dance to fix this problem, should you encounter it. Instead, press down firmly with your thumb on the CPU (and any other socketed chips on the motherboard). You should hear a distinct "scrinch" sound, and the chip will give slightly in response to the pressure as it slides back into the socket. If the chips are seated tightly, you won't hear anything, but a firm push on the chips won't damage them if they are already in place.

Although this doesn't relate to the CPU, you might also want to remove and reinstall all expansion cards, and disconnect and reconnect all cables, to make sure that they are thoroughly seated on their connections. Be careful as you do this however, and keep careful track of what is connected to where, so that you can put it all back together again.

Pushing the CPU

Another reason that CPU chips fail to operate properly is that the CPU is run outside of the limits specified by the manufacturer. This practice is known as "pushing" the processor. It is at least as old as microcomputers themselves, but it didn't really catch hold with end users until the advent of the original IBM AT.

The AT used a single crystal to provide the timing signal for the CPU and the system bus. IBM shipped the computers with a 6 MHz crystal, but some sharp-eyed hackers noticed that the crystal was mounted in a socket, instead of being permanently soldered to the motherboard. So these enterprising pioneers experimented with putting faster crystals in to see what would happen. As it turned out, they were able to greatly increase performance for a few dollars—the price of the crystal. They discovered that some systems could run faster than others, but that there were limits to how fast a given system could be accelerated. When you used a crystal that was too fast, you either got unreliable performance, or the system would refuse to boot at all.

Soon, there was a booming industry selling sets of crystals for IBM ATs. You'd plug in the next fastest one until you found the one where the system wouldn't work any more, and then go back to the next-slowest speed. When IBM brought out an upgraded version of the AT, it raised the clock speed to 8 MHz (to compete with clone makers who were running at that speed or faster) and the crystal was soldered to the motherboard (to prevent any further end-user speed experiments).

Modern motherboards are designed to work with a wide range of CPU chips that are designed to run at system bus speeds from 20 to 50 MHz. Instead of an array of crystals, however, these motherboards use a single crystal and mathematically synthesize any specific timing signal that is needed. Today's enterprising end users and system configuration vendors have discovered that you can save a few bucks and get a bit better performance by setting the motherboard's timing jumpers for a speed faster than the rated speed of the processor. So, for example, a 486DX-33 run at 40 MHz gives you nearly a 25 percent boost in processing speed, for no more money.

Your CPU's rated internal speed is marked on the chip itself; the rating is a two-digit number separated from the chip model number by a hyphen. Remember that for clock-multiplied chips, you have to divide this number by the multiplier. So for an 80486DX2-66 clock-doubled chip (Figure 1.8), the system bus speed is one-half the 66 rating.

Figure 1.8   The CPU chip is marked with its maximum rated operating speed; exceed this specification at the risk of your data.

The proponents of this practice say that the risk of problems is small and outweighed by the benefits. After all, Intel and the other CPU manufacturers overengineer their products to a degree, and most chips should be able to run faster without a problem.

I disagree. The dollar savings over the cost of the correctly rated chip is small, and the risks are higher than I think most users are willing to accept. First and foremost, pushing a chip causes it to run hotter, which in turn increases the chance of having a heat-related problem. More than that, when the CPU just can't quite keep up with the accelerated pace, timing errors could cause subtle problems. Not only can these problems cause frustrating errors, it can be difficult to identify their cause.

If you bought your computer from a reputable, major manufacturer, you shouldn't have to worry about having a pushed processor (unless, of course, you pushed it yourself). Some smaller companies resort to pushing to gain a small competitive advantage, so beware. Make sure you can inspect the markings on the CPU—if the speed rating has been scratched off or covered by a heat sink that has been permanently glued on top, you can't be certain of what you're getting.

Just plain slow   The reason that people resort to pushing is that they become dissatisfied with their system's performance and want to give it a boost. The fact is that no matter how fast your computer may be today, there will come a time—sooner or later—when you'll wish it were faster or more powerful. Your computer *can* start running more slowly all of a sudden if the system's "turbo" button has been pressed, slowing the CPU to 8 Mhz. In general, the only change in performance that takes place over time is more a matter of your perception than of what the CPU is actually doing.

George's Potato Chip Syndrome: **You're never satisfied with just one potato chip, and you'll never be satisfied with one computer's performance. If a task takes 2 hours to do by hand, and you get a computer to do it in 20 minutes, the time will come when you long for a computer that can do the same task in 2 minutes.**

So the most likely reason that you'll have for doing something to your CPU (or motherboard) is not because it fails, but because you want more than it can deliver. We'll get to upgrading your CPU in a moment.

Motherboard Problems

The most common motherboard problems have already been covered. If it fails hot, the cause is probably a chip; if it fails cold, the cause is probably a mechanical connection. For hot problems, check for obstructed ventilation and dust build-ups. For cold problems, check that socketed chips, expansion cards, and cables are all seated snugly.

Playing the slots   There's another, less common problem that you might encounter, in which an expansion card (graphics card, hard disk controller, network interface, or whatever) is not working correctly or not working at all. It is possible—even likely—

that the problem lies in the card and not the motherboard, but if you are fairly certain that the card is okay, you might be right in suspecting the motherboard.

Try putting the card in a different expansion slot on the motherboard. It is possible that a bit of oxidation or dust in the edge connector for that slot is interfering with a solid electrical connection, or that a trace on the motherboard leading to that connector has broken, creating an intermittent or permanent break in the connection. You may find that the card works in a different slot.

Note that not all slots are the same in all computers. Though this is not the case with modern motherboards, the IBM XT had one slot that did not have all the signals of the other seven, standard slots. It still worked fine with most expansion cards, but a few did not. This was a poorly documented "feature" that gave XT users troubleshooting fits.

A more serious problem can occur when a trace breaks elsewhere on the motherboard. A trace is like a wire, embedded on a printed circuit board. The board is made of plastic, and if the board is flexed, it is possible that one or more of the fragile traces may crack. When this happens, the electricity does not flow along that "wire" reliably, causing intermittent or permanent failures.

A trace of trouble

You can go nuts trying to isolate such a problem. With a continuity tester, volt meter, schematic of the motherboard, and a lot of time, you might be able locate the problem, and then possibly fix it with a bridge of solder or a jumper wire. If your time is worth anything—or if you're paying a technician to perform this hunt for you—chances are excellent that it will cost you far more than it would to simply buy a new motherboard. Without a CPU and memory (assuming that these components on your existing board are okay), a new motherboard can cost $100 to $200 depending on features. As a result, you will probably be better off just replacing the motherboard than trying to repair it.

> He who has great power should use it lightly.
>
> Lucius Annaeus Seneca (c. 5 BC–AD 65)

Without electrical power, not much good is going to happen in your computer. And one of the most ignored components in a computer system is the power supply. We have already addressed the problem of a failure in the power supply's cooling fan, but what if the whole unit goes south?

Power problems

The dead give-away is when you turn on the power switch and nothing happens; no cooling fan noise, no lights, no clicks, no buzzes—nothing. Smoke pouring out of the power supply is also a pretty good indicator of a failed unit.

Some failures are more subtle, however. A power supply must produce a number of different voltages for different parts of your computer system, and although unlikely, it is possible that one part will fail while others continue to function. As a result, your hard disk might spin up, but you don't get any other action from your system.

If you suspect that your power supply is not working correctly, all you need is a voltmeter to check it. This is a simple procedure that requires little technical aptitude, and as long as you take simple precautions, it is no more dangerous than changing a light bulb.

Start by disconnecting the power supply from the motherboard, disk drives, and any other peripherals that are connected to it. Note that the motherboard has two connectors, side by side. Take care to note which one goes where. On the typical system, a black wire is at one end of one connector, and a black wire is at the opposite end of the other connector; the connectors attach to the motherboard so that these two black wires are next to each other. Table 1.1 lists the typical system's motherboard connectors and the voltages they should produce.

Table 1.1   Voltages for the motherboard power connectors.

Connector	Wire Color	Voltage
1	Orange	Power-Good signal (+5 VDC)
	Red	+5 VDC
	Yellow	+12 VDC
	Blue	-12 VDC
	Black	Ground
	Black	Ground
2	Black	Ground
	Black	Ground
	White	-5 VDC
	Red	+5 VDC
	Red	+5 VDC
	Red	+5 VDC

Plug the voltmeter's common or ground probe to one of the ground leads (black wire) on the connectors, set the voltmeter to a DC (direct current) scale that goes at least to 15 volts, and check the orange, red, and yellow wires that have positive voltages with the positive probe. Then remove the common probe from the ground lead, and connect the positive probe to a ground lead. Then use the common probe to test the remaining white and blue leads that have negative voltages.

If your power supply checks out okay, repeat the checks using the other ground lead; it is possible that one is not good. Then check the voltage in the peripheral power connectors (the ones that connect to the disk drives). Table 1.2 lists the four wires and their voltages.

Table 1.2 Voltages for the peripheral power connectors.

Wire Color	Voltage
Red	+5 VDC
Black	Ground
Black	Ground
Yellow	+12 VDC

Again, connect the common probe to the black ground wire and test the positive voltages with the positive probe. If your power supply has failed and your case uses a standard power supply, your best bet is to replace it rather than try to repair it. Since you can buy a replacement for $50 or less, it generally isn't worth trying to find what's wrong and fix it.

Another reason to replace your power supply rather than repair it is that it may have failed because it wasn't powerful enough. Everything that you plug into the power supply adds to its load, and like all electrical devices, a power supply has a finite limit to how big a load it can handle. If you have a minimal configuration (a small hard disk, 8 MB of memory, and no extra expansion cards), the power supply that came with your system is almost certain to be big enough. But if you load up with maximum memory, fill your expansion slots, and add a few extra hard drives, a CD-ROM drive, tape backup, and more, you may well be taxing your power supply to its limit.

Sizing the power supply

How big a power supply do you need? That's not easy to answer, simply because it's not always easy to get all the information you need. Also, power supply capacity is typically rated in watts, but the power consumption of components is typically rated in amps. As a rule of thumb, multiply the amp rating on a device by 110, and you will be close to how much power it draws in watts. Still, you should consult your documentation to find the amp ratings for all your devices to calculate the total power draw, convert to watts, then round up to the nearest 50 watts to give a margin for error and future expansion. The result should be at least as large as the rating on the power supply you are replacing.

Today's components are far more energy efficient than older components, so you may well need less power in a new system than in an older design. If you don't want to go through all the research and calculations to figure out what your system needs or you can't find all the specifications for your components, simply get a power supply that is rated at least 50 watts more than the one you are replacing, and it will likely work fine.

> I regret often that I have spoken; never that I have been silent.
>
> Publilius Syrus

Cool and quiet There's one more reason to replace your power supply, even if it is working fine now. Some people find that the cooling fan on the power supply is too noisy in a small working environment. (A friend of mine stuck with an outdated Televideo PC for years and put up with all sorts of incompatibility and repair aggravations simply because it was designed so that it did not use a cooling fan and he had grown accustomed to its silence.) Some companies make power supplies with ventilation fans that are quieter than others; one of the leading sources of quiet power supplies is PC Power & Cooling, Inc. (For the address, see Appendix A.)

> We must have old memories and young hopes.
>
> Arsène Houssaye

Batteries included The final problem we'll cover here is what to do when your computer starts becoming forgetful. It may be as innocuous as forgetting the date and time, or as serious as forgetting that it has a hard disk installed. As covered earlier in this chapter, these and other essential configuration settings are stored in the CMOS memory of your computer. And as suggested earlier, the time to make a record of what those settings are is *before* your computer forgets them.

If your computer should forget your CMOS settings, you should still be able to boot from a floppy disk—we'll discuss what to put on an emergency boot disk in detail in Chapter 3, Storage. As a result, you should be able to get into your computer's CMOS configuration utility and restore the correct settings. If you don't have a record of the settings, you will need to re-create them. Some of them will be straightforward, such as what floppy disk drives and how much memory you have installed in your system. Others are more difficult, such as the correct settings for the hard disks that you have installed. You may need to call the technical support line for the company that built your computer to get the details you need.

The main reason that your computer will forget its CMOS configuration settings is that the battery that powers the memory while the computer has been turned off has run down.

If your computer's CMOS batteries have run down, and you can't get replacements right away, you can continue to work without any problems. The configuration settings will not go away unless you turn off your computer. So simply power up the computer, reconfigure the settings, and then leave the computer running until you can get a new battery. It is okay to leave a computer running day and night, though you will probably want to turn off the monitor overnight to save power and to reduce the chance of burning in an image on the screen. (We'll discuss monitors in more depth in Chapter 4, Displays.)

Different motherboards use different types of batteries to power the CMOS memory. Some use little disc batteries, others use barrels, others have batteries in a chip-style DIP (a TLA for dual in-line pin) package, and still others use an external battery pack that connects to the motherboard with wires. With so many variations and locations, it is not possible to provide generic replacement instructions that will work in all cases.

You may be able to determine what kind of battery your system uses and where it is located by referring to the documentation that came with your motherboard. It is also likely that you won't have this information in any of your manuals. Your next best bet is to try calling the manufacturer of your system. If this fails, you can try taking your system to a local computer repair service; they may have a technician who can identify and replace the battery easily.

If you can't find the battery on the motherboard, and you can't get any help or information, you may be able to work around the problem. Look on the motherboard for two to four pins that are marked "Battery." Pin 1 typically gets a +6 VDC, and pins 3 and 4 are grounded (pin 2 is not used). You can buy a little battery pack that takes four AA penlight batteries for about $5 from Radio Shack, and then a connector that will match up with the pins on your motherboard. Fill the pack with alkaline batteries (they last the longest), connect the plug so that the red wire attaches to the positive pin (pin 1) on the motherboard, and mount the pack on a convenient part of the case with some double-sided tape.

UPGRADING

Old houses mended
Cost little less than new before they're ended.

Colly Cibber (1671–1757)

Whether your CPU or motherboard has broken down, or you simply have grown impatient with their performance, there will come a time when you will consider upgrading your existing configuration. The replacement of a failed part with one faster than the original often comes at such a small increment in cost that it hardly seems worth it not to upgrade.

The problem with upgrading is that you soon encounter a mind-numbing spectrum of choices, starting with a simple replacement and ending with a totally new system with vastly greater capacities than what you have now. The one thing that makes this problem so difficult is that the increase in cost from one step to the next is just $100 or so, making it nearly impossible to know where to draw the line.

There is no one "right" answer; personal budgets and preferences play an important part in the decision process. And a spouse or partner adds a whole new dimension to the equation. Still, there are some objective factors that can be considered (and there's also room for some informed opinion, which I am only too happy to offer), which may help you narrow your range of choices a bit.

Upgrading Your CPU

> The true, strong, and sound mind is the mind that can embrace equally great things and small.
>
> Samuel Johnson (as quoted by Boswell)
> *Life of Johnson*, 1791

The fastest and easiest way to get a significant performance boost in your system at a reasonable cost can be a CPU upgrade, but the biggest waste of money can also be a CPU upgrade. The trick is understanding when it makes sense, and when it doesn't.

The most important factor is the location of the bottlenecks that limit your system's performance. Local bus expansion slots are a lot faster than ISA slots; 32-bit access to system memory is a lot faster than 16-bit. If your applications take significant advantage of it, floating-point math coprocessor support is a lot faster than running without it.

The fact is that just dropping a hyper-active CPU into an old PC that has other serious limitations is a waste of money. For about the same cost, you can often get a complete replacement motherboard with an equally powerful CPU that will give you much better performance than you'd get with the upgrade.

No silk purse

Some CPU upgrade products on the market promise to turn your AT-level 286 or 386SX computer into a 486 system. The ads aren't lying, but they're not telling the whole truth, either. They do give you a CPU that executes 486 commands, but that's not all that significant. The processor also runs faster than the CPU it replaces, and that helps some. But the fact remains that communications between the replacement CPU and the rest of the system's components—system memory and expansion slots—are conducted at 8 MHz, and at only across a 16-bit-wide data path.

Compare this with a true 486 motherboard, which accesses system memory at the system bus speed—probably at 33 MHz—and at the full 32-bit data bus width. As a result, about *eight times* as much data will move between the 486 on the new motherboard and its system memory, compared with the 486 added to the old motherboard. And if the new motherboard has local bus expansion slots, you'll get eight times more data transferred between the system and a local bus graphics adapter or disk controller than you would with an equivalent ISA card.

So adding a 32-bit processor to a motherboard with a 16-bit system data bus is like building a 20-acre parking lot at the end of a two-lane road; things may move more quickly once they get there, but you're still going to have a slow traffic jam leading to and from it.

And the same holds true for adding a Pentium to a 486 motherboard.

So when *does* it make sense to upgrade the CPU? The most cost-effective upgrades are the ones that give you additional processing speed and a motherboard capable of taking full advantage of what the processor offers. **When to upgrade**

The best upgrade is switching from a single clock speed CPU to a matching clock-doubled or -tripled chip (or a faster one, if your motherboard supports it). If you have an 80486SX or 80486DX processor, you should be able to pull it and replace it with an 80486DX2 or 80486DX4 chip. If your CPU currently runs at 33 MHz or less, your replacement should be easy. If your CPU is running at 40 MHz, you will have to change the system clock speed on your motherboard to slow it down for a DX2-66 or DX4-100 chip. (If your current CPU is running at 20 or 25 MHz, remember that the motherboard may be able to run at a faster speed; check your documentation to see if there are jumpers you can change to work with a 33 MHz CPU.)

The only reason to replace the whole motherboard and not just the CPU in this instance would be if your existing motherboard does not have local bus expansion slots. The performance gained through local bus is enormous, and even if you don't upgrade your graphics adapter or hard disk controller right away, adding a motherboard with local bus slots gives you an inexpensive avenue to further performance improvements in the future.

The second-best upgrade bet is adding a clock-doubled or -tripled 486 replacement for an 80386DX CPU. Few 386 systems have local bus slots, so a motherboard replacement will be less limiting. However, if you're looking for a bargain boost and have no intention of ever upgrading the graphics adapter or disk controller, this is a reasonable way to go. You get a faster CPU in a motherboard that can most likely take advantage of most of its capabilities. Some 386 motherboards are set for 20 MHz operation, however, so you'll get about two-thirds the performance you'd get from a motherboard designed to operate at 33 MHz.

Shift to OverDrive

Intel has a special line of 486 CPUs called "OverDrive" chips. These are designed to fit in special sockets on some motherboards; these sockets were a feature that was intended to make future CPU upgrades easier at a time when the CPU development cycles were just starting to hit a frenzied pace and buyers had their knickers in a knot, worried about instant obsolescence. The fact is that these sockets are more of a convenience gimmick than anything else.

You can buy a 486DX2 chip in either an OverDrive version or a regular version that drops right into a 486DX CPU socket. When you put an OverDrive chip in a socket designed for it, it essentially turns off the original CPU. Thus there's little difference between adding an OverDrive and simply replacing the original chip.

Socket to me

The key is to get the right chip to match the socket on your motherboard. There are a variety of different packages for 486 chips, and you have to get the right one for your system.

Caution: Just because you can find a CPU chip that fits the socket on your motherboard and that operates at a speed that your motherboard can accommodate, this doesn't mean that the chip will work in your system. The first place to check is your computer's manufacturer; they should know if there are problems using that particular chip in your system. If they can't tell you (or the company can't be found), contact Intel at 800-321-4044. They maintain a list of systems that have been tested for compatibility and should be able to tell you if you will have any trouble.

Some motherboards have a special type of CPU socket designed to make upgrading the CPU much easier. It is called a **Zero-Insertion Force** socket, or **ZIF**, and it has a lever along one side. When you lift the lever, the pressure on the CPU's pins is released, so you can remove the chip easily. You can then drop the replacement into the socket, and when you push the lever back down, the pins are clamped to make a tight, reliable connection.

If your motherboard does not have a ZIF socket, removing and installing a CPU chip can be a bit more difficult. You need to carefully pry the chip up from the socket. Perhaps the easiest way is to use a thin, flat-bladed screwdriver. Insert the blade in the crack between the CPU and socket and twist the screwdriver. This makes the width of the blade act as a tiny lever and lifts the CPU just a tiny distance. Move the screwdriver to another side of the CPU, and repeat the process. If possible, repeat on all four sides until you have lifted the chip as much as possible with this method. If the chip is not yet loose, put the screwdriver along one side and lift gently, then repeat on the opposite side. Don't lift one side too much more than the other so that you don't bend any pins.

When you go to insert the replacement CPU, one corner of the chip will be cut off or one corner will have a dot. The socket will also either have a cut-off corner or a dot. These marks indicate the location of the first pin on the chip and the socket. Make sure that these marked corners line up when you insert the chip in the socket. If the motherboard doesn't have a ZIF socket, make certain that all the pins are lined up with the holes in the socket, and then press down firmly in the center of the chip until the CPU is pushed all the way into the socket.

Replacing the Motherboard

> A feeble body weakens the mind.
>
> Jean-Jacques Rousseau
> *Èmile,* 1762

If you're considering an upgrade to your CPU, chances are good that you'll end up replacing the entire motherboard. In addition to all the performance advantages already described, it often is simply easier than a CPU upgrade and can cost little more.

Before you can proceed with a motherboard replacement, however, you must make certain that it will fit your existing computer case. Most desktop systems use a full- or mid-size case, designed to sit either on the large surface as a desktop or on one edge as a tower. In general, these cases will all take a standard motherboard, which comes in AT and Baby AT formats. The mounting holes are more or less standardized, making it fairly easy to install a replacement using the mounting points in your existing case.

Making a case

Some of the IBM PS/2 computers are exceptions; their unique modular designs do not accept a standard motherboard. Also, some motherboards have integrated I/O ports—such as serial, parallel, and graphics adapter—that have connectors along the edge of the motherboard; you may not be able to find a replacement that matches the placement of these connectors.

Some desktop systems use a low-profile case, which system reviewers often refer to as a **pizza box.** You can tell if your system falls into this category by looking at the back of the case. If the expansion slots are arranged horizontally on a desktop system (pizza boxes are almost never used for a tower configuration), you've got a pizza box. The problem with these systems is that they use a riser card—a special expansion card with expansion slots on it—to provide the slots for cards. The reason for this approach is that the case is not tall enough for most expansion cards, so they have to be mounted sideways.

Although you can find replacement motherboards that use riser cards, there is less standardization about dimensions and mounting points for these boards than with AT-style motherboards. You may have a difficult time finding a board to fit your particular case.

Don't be discouraged if you can't find a motherboard that fits your particular case. You can buy a new case for $100 or less, including the power supply. (You can spend a lot more for a case, too, depending on its size and features.) So if you have a pizza box system and want to upgrade the motherboard, it may cost less in time and money to simply get a new case at the same time. You also might want to buy a new case to change from desktop to tower configuration, or to get one of those snazzy black cases if you're tired of looking at blah beige all the time.

Reusing Components

> Make new friends, but keep the old.
> One is silver and the other's gold.
>
> Traditional song

When you buy a new motherboard, you get everything but system memory and any expansion cards. In general, the CPU and L2 cache memory are optional. You'll want to get the CPU included with the motherboard, but you may be able to skip the cache.

The first step is to determine whether or not your existing system has an L2 cache, and how much. For most systems, the "sweet spot" that gives the best performance gain for the money is 256KB of secondary system cache. If your existing system has an L2 cache, you'll need to find out what type of chips it uses, and whether these can be transferred to the new motherboard. If they can, but you have less that 256KB, you'll want to get the remainder preinstalled in the motherboard. If they can't, you should get the full 256KB of L2 cache as part of the initial purchase.

The system memory itself is a similar situation. We'll discuss memory in more detail in Chapter 2, but for now, simply keep in mind that you need to check the type and speed of the memory in your current system and see if it can be used in your new motherboard.

If you are upgrading from a 386 or 486 to a Pentium, you may find that you have 30-pin SIMMs (an FLA for single in-line memory module) and the new board requires 72-pin SIMMs. You have three options:

1. Buy special adapters that accept four 30-pin SIMMs and plug into a 72-pin slot.

2. Send out your old SIMMs to a service to be remanufactured into 72-pin formats.

3. Sell your old SIMMs and buy new ones.

Each approach has its advantages and disadvantages. The problem with the SIMM adapters is they end up being very tall (and if you are using two of them, you have to get a "left-handed" and a "right-handed" unit so that they don't stick into each other), and this height may obstruct the installation of some expansion cards. And if your case and motherboard are arranged in such a way that the memory installs under a disk drive housing, you may not be able to use them at all. The remanufacturing approach takes time and money—you'll be without your memory right when you're most anxious to get your new system running.

In general, you should be able to get enough for your used memory to cover most of the cost difference between buying new 72-pin SIMMs and using either of the first two approaches.

A similar situation occurs with expansion cards; you may not be able to use your existing cards, or you may not want to use them with your new motherboard.

It's in the cards.

For example, if you currently have an IBM system that uses MicroChannel expansion cards, you will be hard-pressed to find a replacement motherboard that can use them. If you have EISA expansion cards, you will need to get an EISA motherboard in order to use them.

If you have 8- or 16-bit ISA cards, you can still use them in EISA or VL-Bus expansion slots, but they won't give you optimal performance. For best performance, you'll want to take advantage of local bus connections for your graphics adapter and your hard disk controller, which means getting a VL-Bus motherboard if your new CPU is in the 486 class, or a PCI motherboard if you're moving to a Pentium. (Don't be tempted by one of the hybrid boards that offer both PCI and VL-Bus slots; test results indicate that these designs tend to perform worse than those that exclusively use one or the other local bus specifications.)

You can save some money initially, however, by moving your older ISA cards to a new local bus motherboard and replacing them at a later date when the budget allows.

Making the Swap

Changing a motherboard is relatively easy; it's harder than changing an expansion card, but easier than cooking Beef Wellington.

Start by making sure that all the jumpers and switches are correctly set on your new motherboard. The key settings are for the system clock speed and processor type, but check the others as best you can. Motherboard documentation is not known for its lucidity—my favorite example was the one that described its support for a "match coprocessor"—but take some time to check it out and call the company that sold you the motherboard if you have any questions. It's easier to avoid a problem than to repair the damage after the fact.

Before you start, make sure that you have recorded your CMOS configuration settings and have prepared an emergency boot disk (see Chapter 3, Storage, for instructions). Make sure the power is off to your computer, but leave it plugged into the wall; this helps ensure that your computer case is grounded (though this assumes that your outlet is grounded in the first place).

George's Power Postulate: **Just because your outlet has three holes doesn't mean that you've got a properly grounded electrical connection, especially in an older home or office building. Save yourself some aggravation, and buy a simple AC outlet tester at Radio Shack or your local hardware store. This is a small, three-prong device with a set of little LED lights. You can diagnose a number of wiring problems just by plugging it into an outlet.**

Open your computer's case, remove all the expansion cards, and unplug anything else that is plugged into the motherboard, such as expansion cards and ribbon cables to I/O ports or disk drives. Then the last thing connected to the motherboard should be the power connectors; unplug them, but notice that the black wires at the edges of the two connectors are next to each other.

Next, look for screws holding down the motherboard, and unscrew them. You may also see little plastic pyramids sticking up through the motherboard; these are stand-offs, and you may not have to remove them in order to get the motherboard out.

Once all the screws are removed, try sliding the motherboard to the left. Most motherboards have the plastic stand-offs mounted in slots, and you can release them by sliding the board about a quarter inch to the side. If the board slides, you should be able to lift it up and out of the case. If it doesn't slide, you may have to squeeze the ends of the plastic stand-offs so that they can slip through the holes in the motherboard, and then you can lift the motherboard up and out.

For the next step, I find it helps to make a paper template of the new motherboard, with holes in the paper where the holes in the motherboard are located. This helps you figure out where you want to use stand-offs to mount the replacement, and where you want to use screws.

Don't skimp on the mounting hardware! **It can't hurt to use too many screws and stand-offs, but you can have serious problems if you use too few. Without sufficient support, you may not be able to apply enough force to get expansion cards to seat properly. Plus you run the risk of flexing the motherboard enough to break something. So give the motherboard all the support you can; put something in every hole that matches between your motherboard and your case.**

Once you have the motherboard in place, reconnect everything and put your expansion cards back in. You'll need to set its CMOS settings to configure it for your hard disk, and then you should be able to boot up and go to work. Get ready to enjoy computing in the fast lane.

2 Memory

O memory, thou bitter sweet,—both a joy and a scourge!

Mme. Anne Louise Germaine de Staël

If the CPU is the *idiot savant* that runs the show inside your computer, then the system memory is the scratch paper on which it keeps its notes and frantically scribbles out its answers. Without system memory, your computer could know nothing, and knowing nothing, could accomplish even less.

There were times when 16KB was an enormous amount of memory; now 16MB—roughly 1000 times as much—is considered adequate for a fully configured Windows machine.

And prices have dropped as chip capacities have increased to meet our growing, insatiable demand for more memory. Just 10 years ago, a single 64K-bit chip cost $1. To make a full megabyte (if you had a machine that could hold that many chips) required 144 chips, and cost $144. Today, you can buy a megabyte of memory on one little circuit board that uses just three chips and costs $40 or less. For $144 you can get a 4MB module that uses just 9 chips (ignoring, for the moment, that a dollar was worth a bit more 10 years ago than it is today).

Although it is a bit magical, memory is fairly straightforward to deal with, once you understand a bit about how it is configured and what the various specifications mean.

NEED TO KNOW

We need to cover two main types of memory: system memory and cache memory. System memory is the memory used in all computers, and cache memory is memory used to speed up access to data in the system memory.

System Memory

> The true art of memory is the art of attention.
>
>> Samuel Johnson
>> *The Idler,* 1759

System memory is the main memory in your computer, and most new systems now come with 4MB, 8MB, or 16MB of memory installed.

Almost all computers use a form of memory known as **DRAM,** which stands for Dynamic Random Access Memory. (This makes the phrase "DRAM memory" repetitively redundant, for those William Safire fans out there who collect usage blunders like that.)

The "dynamic" part of the name is important. It refers to the fact that the memory cannot store information permanently, the way that ROM (Read-Only Memory) chips can. Instead, data stored in DRAM is like light from a light bulb; turn off the power, and I don't know where it goes, but it's gone.

To help preserve the information in DRAM chips, the computer has to renew the electrical charges within the chips at regular intervals. This **refresh** process has to be done within a certain time interval or the data is lost. As we'll see a bit later, the specification of this interval can be quite important.

> Memory is like a purse,—if it be over-full that it cannot shut, all will drop out of it.
>
>> Thomas Fuller
>> *The Holy State and the Profane State,* 1642

System Memory Configuration

The original IBM PC was able to address a full megabyte of memory; this means that the CPU could keep track of memory locations with a number sufficiently large to track a million locations.

Actually, a "megabyte" does not equal a million bytes, or at least it's not supposed to. Since digital computers are binary creatures—they do all their thinking in terms of bits that are either "on" or "off"—they tend to use measurements based on powers of 2. So when we talk about 64KB, we don't really mean 64,000 bytes. Instead, it is shorthand for 65,536, which is 64 times 1024. 1024 is 2 to the 10th power, or in binary, 10000000000. So when we talk about memory, 1KB really equals 1024 bytes, and a megabyte is 1024 times 1024, or 1,048,576 bytes. Computer people take great liberties with these terms, however, especially when it comes time to measure disk storage capacities, but that's a different matter that we'll address in Chapter 3, Storage. In any case, the "rounding off" error created by the imprecise use of these terms doesn't amount to much in the grand scheme of things, so you don't really have to worry about it. It's just one of those details that is interesting to know.

On a computer running DOS, the first megabyte of memory is divided into two sections: conventional memory and upper memory. **Conventional memory** is the first 640KB and is where much of DOS, drivers, and your application programs get loaded. When the IBM PC was originally designed, the engineers figured that 640KB would be more than enough capacity for a long, long time; we now know better. Their limited foresight can be excused, however, when you consider that this was 10 times more memory than you could cram into an Apple][, the leading competitor of that era.

Engineers reserved the **upper memory** for other uses, so that sections could be used for system programs and adapters (Figure 2.1). By mapping these to memory addresses, the CPU could find and use the information. For example, the BIOS (Basic Input/Output System) code that the computer needed to run was assigned to the 128KB portion of memory just below the 1MB top. Display adapters got the first 128KB block above the 640KB limit; the monochrome and CGA adapters didn't use all of this area, but many VGA and SVGA cards use this entire section of memory. (Don't worry about the alphabet soup used in that last sentence; we'll get into more detail about display adapters in Chapter 4, Displays.)

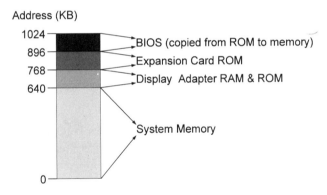

Figure 2.1   This diagram shows how the first megabyte of memory is used in a typical IBM-compatible PC.

Other adapters have their own BIOS code that needs to be addressed by the CPU, such as hard disk controllers, network interfaces, and even some graphics adapters. These were mapped into the middle 128KB section.

Memory addresses in a PC are described in an obscure combination of segment and offset numbers (usually presented in hexadecimal—base 16—numeric format). This can be confusing, but just remember that each four-digit segment refers to a 16-byte block. So C000 refers to a block starting at the 786,432 byte, or at 768KB, which is 128KB above the 640KB limit of conventional memory. Since

adapter cards are often mapped into the middle 128KB range of upper memory, their segment addresses range from C000 to DFFF. For some adapter cards, you need to set jumpers to assign the address. To avoid conflicts when adding new cards, you need to keep a record of which addresses are already in use in your system.

We quickly grew out of the 640KB limit, and with the appearance of the IBM AT's 80286 CPU, the amount of memory that could be addressed by a system grew to 16MB. (Since the arrival of the 80386, CPUs have been able to address gigabytes of memory; I'm tempted to say that this should be enough to handle anything we could throw at it, but past experience leads me to be just a tad cautious about making that kind of statement.)

The next problem was how to use this extra memory. Two different approaches evolved: expanded and extended memory. The differences between these two concepts can befuddle the best of us; a tongue-in-cheek definition that made the rounds of the industry was "expanded memory is memory that's not really there, but you can use it, and extended memory is memory that really is there, but you can't use it."

Expanded Memory

> The difference between false memories and true ones is the same as for jewels: it is always the false ones that look the most real, the most brilliant.
>
> Salvador Dalí
> *The Secret Life of Salvador Dalí*, 1948

Expanded memory grew out of the demands of Lotus 1-2-3 users to support bigger and bigger spreadsheets. Lotus, Intel, and Microsoft teamed up to create the LIM specification, which grew into the expanded memory standard.

Expanded memory works by taking memory above the first megabyte and mapping it in small chunks to addresses in the middle 128KB of the upper memory area. It can then swap data in and out. With IBM ATs, you needed a special board with separate memory that supported this feature, but from the 80386 onward, the CPU is able to use system memory above 1MB for this purpose, with the help of an expanded memory manager such as the EMM386.EXE driver (a standard DOS feature).

Expanded memory isn't really part of the system memory map, which is why the definition says it's not really there, but Lotus 1-2-3 and other programs could make use of it, which is why the definition says you can use it. What the definition doesn't point out, however, is that expanded memory operations are slower than most others because the memory has to be paged in and out of the small upper memory blocks.

Extended Memory

Memory above 1MB in a PC-compatible computer is called **extended memory,** and as I've already mentioned, this can amount to gigabytes. Unfortunately DOS is limited to 16MB and can't use any more.

Furthermore PCs can only use extended memory when operating in something known as protected mode. Until the advent of Windows 3.x, few programs could take advantage of this feature. Windows, however, has made it possible to create multiple "virtual" PCs using different portions of extended memory as if they were separate computers, each running with their own 1MB of memory.

So extended memory does exist in the system memory map, though until the arrival of Windows, we couldn't do much with it. That's the point of the earlier definition.

If you're running Windows, however, you're probably using extended memory all the time, and the process is handled so transparently that you don't even have to know that it's happening.

Windows 95 actually simplifies this whole problem to a great extent. Because 80386 and later CPUs have a 32-bit operating mode, Windows 95 can use a flat, linear memory mode that views all available memory as a single large chunk that can be partitioned more or less in any way that the software needs. This also does away with the DOS 16MB limitation, making it possible for a Windows 95 system to use up to 4GB (gigabytes) of memory.

Furthermore, Windows 95 also has protected-mode drivers for many devices such as CD-ROM drives or network interfaces, which do not require the use of system memory when running DOS applications. As a result, DOS programs running under Windows 95 can have more memory available than they would on a machine that is just running DOS.

Virtual Memory

While we're in the neighborhood, we may as well cover a form of memory that isn't memory at all: **virtual memory.** This is actually hard disk storage that is mapped into the computer's memory system as if it were actually memory chips installed somewhere in the system. This practice originated with IBM mainframes, but was made popular for PCs by Windows 3.x. When you create a swap file in Windows, it is used as extra memory in the event that all the real memory in your computer gets used in a session; this may occur frequently if you have only 4MB of memory in your system or you often open many programs at one time.

In Windows 3.x, swap files may be temporary or permanent. I find that the creation (and deletion) of a temporary swap file every time Windows is started (and closed) creates an annoying delay. As a result, I strongly recommend that Windows 3.x users configure their systems with a permanent swap file. Because the contents of the file must be contiguous, you should defragment your hard disk before creating a swap file.

 Windows 95 has also simplified the problem of configuring your swap file. Although you can still specify the drive location and the size of the file, the program also lets you check "Let Windows manage my virtual memory settings," which is the recommended option. A Windows 95 swap file does not have a fixed size; the program can grow and shrink it as necessary. And the file does not have to exist on an unfragmented section of your disk, which is another advantage.

Memory Specifications

> Variety's the very spice of life,
> That gives it all its flavor.
>
> William Cowper
> *The Task*, 1785

Memory chips come in a bewildering array of capacities, specifications, and packages. It is important to understand the differences because using the wrong memory in your computer generally results in the creation of an expensive doorstop.

Perhaps the best place to start is to provide a key for deciphering the cryptic part numbers found printed on memory chips. As it turns out, you can often puzzle out what a chip does if you know what to look for in its markings (Figure 2.2). Note that these rules of thumb have lots of exceptions, so don't get upset if you find a chip that doesn't conform to the pattern.

Figure 2.2 This close-up of a memory chip shows a part number that you can decipher in order to determine many of the chip's specifications.

In general, you will be interested in the first numeric line. Many chips have two lines, and frankly, I don't know what the second line represents. The first line, however, typically follows this pattern:

xxxNMMMM-OO

The number of characters may also vary, but here are what the different components mean. The xxx part may have letters and numbers and generally is part of the manufacturer's part classification system.

Capacity

Skip over the N digit for the moment, and focus on the last two to four digits before the hyphen, represented by MMMM in the pattern. You may find really old chips where only the last two digits count. These digits represent the number of *bits* stored by the chip, measured in Kb, or 1024 bits. (Some publications are really sloppy about capitalization of units, leading to confusion between KB and Kb. KB is kilobytes, whereas Kb is kilobits, and because there are eight bits to the byte, it takes 8Kb to make 1KB . . . or at least it sometimes does, but we'll get to that in a moment.)

If you have some really old chips, the last two digits before the hyphen may be 16 or 64. In a more modern computer, you are more likely to find 256 on your chips. You may also find 1000 or 4000, which represent 1Mb and 4Mb. Yes, if the chip manufacturers were really sticking to the Kb convention, these should be 1024 and 4096 instead, but someone probably decided that it would be less confusing to simply round the numbers down, so that's what happened. You may also find a letter at the end of this number, before the hyphen, which probably is used to mark design revisions, but you can generally ignore it.

There's more to the capacity than this, however. The bits can come arranged in groups. You can find all sorts of weird configurations, but most commonly used chips have one, four, or eight groups of bits. This is typically indicated by the digit right before the number of bits, represented by the N in the pattern. Some companies have a letter between the N digit and the rest of the number.

As a result, a Motorola chip with a part number of MCM511000-70 would be a chip with one group of one megabits, which would make it a 1Mb chip. Another Motorola chip might be marked with MCM514256A-70, meaning four groups of 256 kilobits, or 1Mb in all. As a result, both chips have the same capacity, though the way the memory is arranged within the chip is different. For the most part, you need only be concerned about the total capacity of the chips.

Rated Speed

The digit or digits to the right of the hyphen refer to the speed of the chip, measured in nanoseconds (ns). The original IBM PC used chips rated for 150 ns, which was truncated on the chip numbers to 15. Most computers today use DRAM rated at 50 to 80 ns. Some companies truncate the speed; others leave the trailing zero. Thus a chip rated at 80 ns might have a part number ending in either 8 or 80.

Packaging

Aside from their capacity and speed specifications, memory chips also differ in the way that they are packaged (Figure 2.3). Some have pins that are designed to fit into sockets, while others are made to be soldered directly onto circuit boards. End users are not expected to assemble their own components, however, so the only time you're likely to see the surface mount chips is when they are already mounted on a memory module.

Figure 2.3   Most computers use either DIP or SIMM memory packages, or a combination of the two.

Most computers now use memory in one of two forms:

- DIP packaging—DIP stands for dual in-line pins and refers to the typical chip package of a black plastic box with two rows of metal legs; they look like high-tech insects (though they have too many legs to be an insect).

- SIMM packaging—SIMM stands for single in-line memory module and is a small strip of printed circuit board with memory chips mounted on top. Typically two, three, eight, or nine chips are mounted on them—sometimes of different sizes—depending on capacity and structure. SIMMs come in two different lengths, with either 30 or 72 pins. The 72-pin modules have a 32-bit data bus and are designed to give better performance for newer CPUs than the older 30-pin SIMMs can.

Parity

It's not the voting that's democracy, it's the counting.

Tom Stoppard
Jumpers, 1972

Why do you find eight chips on some SIMMs and nine on others? Why do most motherboards that use DIP memory have nine sockets? The answer is parity.

The parity question

Essentially parity is a way for the computer to check its own work as it goes along. It takes eight bits to make one byte, but if one of those bits should go wrong, it could mess up your whole day. If it occurs to a piece of data, you can get the wrong answer. If it occurs to an instruction in a piece of program code, you could experience what tech support types refer to as "anomalous performance," ranging from unnoticeable errors to a complete system crash.

The designers of the IBM PC decided that they would prevent this problem by simply adding one more bit to each byte as a way to keep tabs on the other eight. If the sum of the first eight bits is even, the last bit is set to a 1. If the sum of the first eight bits is odd, the last bit is set to 0. Whenever the computer reads a byte from memory, it checks it against the parity bit to see if they agree. If they don't, the computer issues an error—and typically comes to a screeching halt. (We'll talk more about parity errors later in this chapter.)

If your computer uses DIP memory chips, they probably come in banks of nine at a time: eight for data and one for parity. Oddly enough, the Apple Mac does not use parity bits and only uses eight chips per bank. There are proponents for both choices.

If you use a parity bit in your memory design, the computer can detect memory problems before it creates a wrong answer or crashes due to a faulty instruction. This allows for a more or less orderly cessation of activities once the error is detected.

On the other hand, because the computer can't tell what exactly has gone wrong when a parity error is detected, it has to assume the worst and it more or less just stops. Detractors of the parity bit point out, with some justification, that the end result is no different than a system crash because you lose your work in either case. Furthermore, there is a one-in-nine chance that the error has occurred in the parity bit itself, and the other eight data bits are just fine. In this case, your computer crashes because the watchdog ate your data.

Fortunately for us, memory chips are extremely accurate and reliable, and the odds of a true parity error in the midst of a computing session are negligible. So if your motherboard supports a no-parity configuration for its memory and you want to save a few bucks on memory, you can probably run 8-bit memory without taking on a lot greater risk.

How can you identify whether your SIMMs have the parity bit or not? It's easy if eight or nine chips are on the SIMM; eight means no parity and nine means parity. Some 30-pin SIMMs use only two or three chips. A 1MB two-chip SIMM typically has two 4-by-1Mb chips, for 8Mb altogether. A 1MB three-chip SIMM typically has the same first two chips and adds a single 1-by-1Mb chip for the parity bits.

In a similar manner, 72-pin SIMMs come in two configurations: 32-bit versions without parity and 36-bit versions with parity. At current prices, you can save as much as 15 percent by going with the non-parity versions, provided that your motherboard supports the use of this configuration.

It's not widely known, but you may be wasting money if you put 9-bit SIMMs for parity in some Pentium systems. The documentation for many of these systems indicates that the motherboards can support either parity or non-parity memory, but some neglect to point out that they will not use the parity bits even if they are present on the SIMMs. In cases such as this, it makes no sense to spend the extra for parity SIMMs because the computer will operate in exactly the same way with non-parity memory.

L2 Cache Memory

As discussed in Chapter 1, another kind of memory—SRAM (Static Random Access Memory)—is used for a system cache so that the CPU can have a fast "scratchpad" where it can store recently used data and instructions.

Static RAM does not need to be refreshed the way DRAM does, and so it can be accessed much faster and more frequently. DRAM typically has speed ratings of 60 to 80 ns, compared with SRAM specifications which are typically in the 15 to 25 ns range. This added capability makes these SRAM chips much more expensive than DRAM chips. If they cost the same, systems would just use the faster SRAM for their system memory to get better performance.

As mentioned in Chapter 1, the best return on investment appears to be a system cache of 256KB. Many motherboards let you configure the size of the cache; if yours is too small, you may be able to add more cache memory yourself.

@#%$%@!

> You have to begin to lose your memory, if only in bits and pieces, to realize
> that memory is what makes our lives.
>
> Luis Buñuel
> *My Last Sigh,* 1983

Fortunately memory errors are fairly rare. Like most semiconductors, these components tend to be pass/fail—either they work or they don't. However, don't place too much stock in what your system may tell you about its memory. Sometimes it may tell you that the memory is fine when it's not, and at other times it may tell you that there's a memory problem when in fact something else is the cause.

As described earlier in this chapter, some memory failures are caught by the parity system in a computer. This can result in a DOS message such as "parity error—system halted" or similar messages in Windows.

Most computers test their memory every time you turn them on; you can confidently watch the little numbers tick by in the corner of your screen, pleased that you're letting the check run its course without skipping it by pressing Escape the way many systems allow. But it turns out that this self-test is little more than counting fingers and toes; it doesn't exercise the memory in any way. Instead it is simply polling the addresses to make sure that something is out there.

Identifying Memory Problems

If you suspect that you have a memory problem, the first step is to go through the same procedures as covered in the first chapter. Remember *George's First Rule of Hardware Troubleshooting*. If the failure occurs before the computer has warmed up, it is likely a mechanical problem, like a loose connection. If it fails after the computer has been running for a while, it is a chip problem. **Round up the usual suspects**

For mechanical problems, make sure that the memory is firmly seated. For DIP chips, this means pushing on them firmly to make certain that they are all the way in their sockets. For SIMMs, the best bet is to actually remove them and reinsert them. There are small tabs at each end that lock them in place; push the tab aside, and tilt the SIMM forward in its slot. (See Figure 2.4.) It should then lift out. The notch in one corner of the SIMM acts as a key to prevent you from inserting it in its slot backwards. When you reinsert the SIMM, make certain that it is all the way in the bottom of the slot before you start to tilt it up into place. Tilt it until the tabs lock in place—make sure that both tabs lock in the SIMM's holes—and then press down on the edge of the SIMM to make sure it makes good contact with the bottom edge conductors in the slot.

Figure 2.4   SIMMs fit in slots on the motherboard and are held in place by tabs at each end.

For heat problems, go through the same heat prevention and reduction tips described in Chapter 1, including checking the ventilation and removing any dust that may have accumulated.

To do exactly as your neighbors do is the only sensible rule.

Emily Post
Etiquette, 1922

Mismatched specs   If the straightforward solutions don't resolve the problem, you need to do some more digging. The next cause to consider (because it is relatively easy to check) is whether or not your memory matches the motherboard specifications.

Memory too slow   One common mismatching problem is the use of memory that is slower than specified by the motherboard manufacturer. If the memory is too slow, it will not be able to respond as quickly as the CPU requires. If the CPU doesn't get an answer when it needs and expects it, your computer may decide that something is wrong with the memory and either give an error message or crash. The memory may be fine, but it's just not able to keep up. Your system documentation should list the recommended memory speeds for your computer.

Memory speeds are probably one of the most misunderstood factors in a computer system. Many people seem to think that if an 80 ns memory chip works well, you can get more than a 10 percent performance increase by using 70 ns chips instead because they are 10 ns faster. It doesn't work that way. The rating is determined by how fast the memory can respond, but the actual timing of

memory accesses is controlled by the system clock. It's like putting higher octane gasoline than required in a car; you won't get any more power from the engine, but it won't do any harm either.

Oddly enough, you can also have problems if you use chips that are rated much faster than what your system requires. A rate 10 ns faster than specified shouldn't cause any problems, but much more of a difference can lead to problems. These faster chips often require faster refreshing as well, but in a system designed for slower memory, the refresh signals may not come frequently enough to maintain accurate storage in the memory. **Memory too fast**

The third problem you can run into with mismatched memory is the use of three-chip 30-pin SIMMs in a system designed for nine-chip SIMMs. From a memory address perspective, these two designs look identical to a CPU. The different designs can require slightly different refresh signals, however, and although most systems can handle either type, some older systems cannot. Check your documentation for any mention of three-chip SIMMs. If not, play it safe and spend the few extra bucks for the nine-chip versions. **Three-chip SIMMs**

Fixing Memory Problems

> Hasten slowly.
>
> Augustus Caesar

If you've reached this point, it could be that you do indeed have a bad memory chip. It costs too much to simply replace all your memory—especially when it's likely that only one chip or SIMM has gone bad—so the next step is to identify the failed component.

One approach requires the use of a utility program. Many are on the market, including WinSleuth (Figure 2.5) and System Sleuth from Dariana Software, QA Plus from DiagSoft, and CheckIt Pro from TouchStone Software. (See Appendix A for details on these companies.) These programs read and write data to all portions of memory in turn, checking the results carefully. Most programs let you set them up to run for hours, or even overnight, to catch the pesky intermittent errors that are hard to find. Most of these programs then report where the error is, and some even show a diagram of your motherboard, indicating where the bad chip or SIMM is located. **Using a utility program**

You don't need a special program, however, to find a bad memory component; all you need is time and patience. It's easier if you have an extra chip or SIMM around, but you can often make do without, if necessary. **Testing by hand**

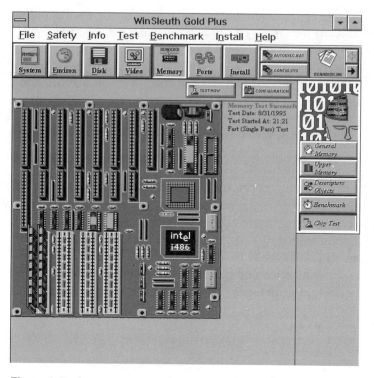

Figure 2.5 A memory test utility such as this one from Dariana Software's WinSleuth program lets you exercise memory to find failed chips.

George's A/B Testing Technique: **This is one of the most fundamental troubleshooting procedures, and you'll find that I recommend it throughout the book. Its name comes from the fact that you take two identical components, of which at least one is suspect—A and B—and swap them. If the problem stays in the same place in spite of the swap, neither component is at fault. If the problem follows one of the components to its new location, you've got your culprit . . . well, at least you have one of them; there is always a chance that there's a second one to be found! This technique is the same as you may have used when fixing Christmas tree lights that were wired in series: taking a bulb that is known to work, and swapping it with each bulb in a burned-out string until you find the one that is broken and the string lights up.**

Many memory error messages include an address. You can sometimes figure out which chip or SIMM is at fault by deciphering the hexadecimal address, but you may be able to solve the problem with the A/B technique.

If you have a known-good SIMM of similar specifications, swap it with one of the suspect SIMMs in your system. Repeat the actions that resulted in the memory error in the first place; if it passes, you may have found the bad SIMM on the first try. (But don't throw that one out just yet—the problem may not crop up right away.) If the problem recurs, replace the old SIMM in its original location, and swap the known-good SIMM with the next SIMM in your system.

If you don't have an extra SIMM available, you may be able to remove half of the memory from your system and use one of the removed SIMMs as your swap SIMM. If you have four SIMMs installed and can remove two and still run your system, check first to see if the system runs without error. If not, then one of the two remaining SIMMs is probably the culprit. Use one of the removed SIMMs as the swap unit, and use the A/B technique until you identify which of the two SIMMs is at fault. If the two SIMMs work fine, however, use one of the removed SIMMs and then the other as the swap unit, and try to find which of them is the failed unit.

If you don't have enough memory in your system to remove half of it, try trading positions of the existing SIMMs or chips. The addresses in the memory error messages should change, and if you can find the position where the error is in the lowest possible address, you should be able to replace the first SIMM with a new one and have a high level of confidence that you have changed the bad unit.

Memory test equipment

This chip and SIMM swapping is time consuming and not completely reliable if your problem is intermittent. You may be able to find a local computer repair facility that has a memory tester. These units are too expensive for the average individual to purchase, but they save so much time that repair services often use them. You should be able to get your memory tested for a small fee. If your local area has no repair service, there are services that will do it by mail order if you can wait while your memory travels back and forth.

Problems with cache memory

If your best efforts to find a bad chip or SIMM fail, or if the addresses cited by the error messages jump all over the place without any apparent correlation to any swapping experiments you may be running, there's a sneaky cause that may be at the root of your frustration: the cache memory.

The L2 cache memory is used to speed up access to the system memory. As the CPU grabs program instructions and data from different parts of the memory, this cache memory ends up pointing to locations all over the memory map. As far as the CPU can tell, information stored in the L2 cache appears to be stored in the actual system memory (which it is, and the cache simply holds a copy of that information). So if the CPU encounters a problem with that data, it assumes that the problem occurred out in the system memory, when in fact it might be the fault of the cache memory.

If you have a memory error problem that seems to defy identification, go into your CMOS configuration program and disable the L2 system memory cache for your system. This will certainly slow down performance, but it will give you a chance to see if the error occurs when the cache is disabled. If it does, the cache can be removed from the suspect list, and you can renew your efforts to find another cause. If the problem does not recur, however, it may be that you have one or more bad SRAM chips in your cache. (Some SRAM chips are soldered to the motherboard, but others are socketed; remember to give them a firm push to make sure that they are securely in their sockets if you suspect a problem with the cache.)

Special Windows Issues

Extensive use   When Windows became popular, memory problems seemed to occur more frequently. Some reasons for this are good, and some are not so good. One of the main reasons why memory problems show up with Windows applications and not with DOS programs is that Windows uses more memory and uses it harder.

For the most part, DOS only uses the first megabyte of memory in your computer. Even if you're using a version of DOS that loads into upper memory or lets you put drivers in upper memory, it is still only using the first megabyte. And if your program uses expanded memory, although it can use memory above the first megabyte, that memory is only for data, not for program code that is accessed repeatedly and frequently.

So, think about it; if your computer has 8MB of memory installed and a memory chip goes bad, the odds are only one in eight that it will occur in the part of memory that DOS and its applications use heavily. That's just a 12.5 percent chance.

On the other hand, Windows runs in protected mode and creates lots of little virtual DOS computers inside your system, each one thinking that it has (at least) one megabyte of memory of its own to work with. This really hammers the extended memory in your system, especially once you start switching between applications. (If you aren't using the Alt-Tab shortcut to switch between open applications in Windows, you're not getting your money's worth from your system.)

 **Some popular programs can also expose flaws in extended memory. Games including Doom and Descent have special memory managers that use extended memory, and the 3D graphics can exercise memory at least as hard as Windows. That's why you are also more likely to encounter memory errors with these games than with typical DOS applications.**

So in today's typical configuration, the chances are that memory flaws will occur in extended memory, and Windows makes extended use of this memory, making it likely that such flaws will create a problem of some sort.

False Alarms

> Falsehood is so easy, truth is so difficult.

> George Eliot

Unfortunately Windows 3.x is not always a credible reporter when it comes to memory errors. In two instances, the messages displayed have little or nothing to do with the real problem that Windows has encountered. These are the "parity error" and "out of memory" messages.

Windows often reports a parity error when in fact the memory is operating correctly. There are a couple of possible causes for this, but the leading candidate is a Windows device driver problem, especially graphics adapter drivers. These drivers often cause data to be written to upper memory, which may overwrite data already there. When Windows goes to make a call to the original data (often a DOS driver or other code that was loaded in AUTOEXEC.BAT or CONFIG.SYS) and finds the data doesn't make sense, it decides that something must be wrong with the memory and gives up. The parity error message must be the closest one at hand for Windows because that's what it throws up on your screen.

The "parity error" red herring

If you suspect that this might be the problem, start by getting the latest drivers for your graphics adapter. First try the standard Windows VGA driver (assuming that your graphics card is VGA-compatible) and see if that eliminates the error messages. If it does, you should get the latest version of the drivers for your adapter. Try contacting the manufacturer of your graphics adapter; they may have a computerized bulletin board system (BBS) of their own where you can download the files, or they may have a section on CompuServe or another online service where the files are available for downloading. If you cannot locate the manufacturer, check the Microsoft Software Library, which is available on Microsoft's own BBS, through Internet FTP, and on CompuServe, America Online, and GEnie. (See Appendix A for more information on these locations.)

Older expansion cards are another, but less likely, source of the false parity error messages in Windows. Some cards generate something called a **non-maskable interrupt,** or **NMI.** For example, some older EGA (Enhanced Graphic Adapter) cards generate an NMI when switching display modes (such as from text to graphics).

If you suspect that this might be the problem, try to replace the questionable component with something more current, and see if the problem goes away. SuperVGA graphics adapters can be found for less than $50, so there's little reason to hold onto a relic that is crashing your system.

Another maddening trick played by Windows happens when you need to open another program. You double-click on the icon, your hard disk thrashes a moment, and then you are greeted by the Windows equivalent of the Bronx Cheer:

The "out of memory" ruse

```
Insufficient memory to run this application. Quit one or
more Windows applications and then try again.
```

The cruelest part of the hoax happens next; you open the Help command in Program Manager, and then About Program Manager (Figure 2.6), and see that the Memory line at the bottom of the window shows that you have many megabytes of free memory. What's up with that?

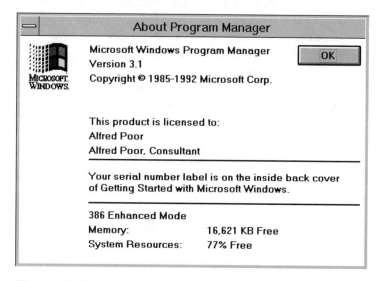

Figure 2.6   The About Program Manager window reports on free memory and free system resources.

The answer lies in a relatively obscure aspect of Windows 3.x; there are three components that govern the running of Windows applications:

- KERNEL, which does most of the heavy lifting, including running the applications and managing the memory.
- USER, which handles the I/O operations, including keyboard, mouse, sound, and communication ports.
- GDI (graphics device interface), which handles the graphics and printing.

The problem is that USER and GDI have scratchpad areas that they use to keep track of items. GDI has one 64KB area, and USER has two 64KB areas. When you look at the About Program Manager window, the Free System Resources line shows a percentage of free resources; this reflects either the GDI or USER space, whichever is lower. If you are low on system resources, you can get an out of memory error.

It's not just running applications that use up these scratchpad spaces. USER needs space to track every window—and *every icon*—that you have created. If you have installed tons of programs and created many separate Program Manager groups for them, you may be using up memory needlessly. It pays to be tidy and periodically clean up your system by deleting any programs and icons that you don't need.

Fortunately there are solutions to out-of-memory problems. A new class of Windows utility has appeared on the market, known as memory doublers or memory expanders. These can do a number of useful tricks, including increasing the amount of memory available for system resources. These programs can also use data compression on memory, which can decrease the number of calls to the disk-based virtual memory swap file, which in turn can result in better performance. Some of the products on the market in this category are Ram Doubler from Connectix, MagnaRAM from Landmark, and Hurricane from Helix. (See Appendix A for more information on these products.)

Unfortunately Windows also uses memory in another way that isn't even reported. Each time a Windows application sets up a place in memory where it has stored data (referred to as an **object**), it requires the use of a "selector". Windows 3.1 has 8196 selectors when running in 386Enhanced mode, but if you are running a bunch of applications that create large numbers of small data objects, you can run out of selectors, which will also trigger an out of memory message. Sadly there is not much you can do in this case but close some files or applications to free up more selectors.

UPGRADING

> Nothing succeeds like excess.
>
> Oscar Wilde
> *A Woman of No Importance,* 1893

As the saying goes, you can never be too thin, too rich, or have too much memory in your computer. No matter how much you have, you could probably use more. For now, it appears that the "sweet spot" for system memory is 16MB, especially for Windows. Upgrading from 4MB to 8MB produces a huge jump in performance, and going from 8MB to 16MB results in about the same amount of improvement again. While you do get some gains when you move up to 32MB, most people find that 16MB is sufficient.

Adding Memory

In the dark ages of PCs, you had to set switches on the motherboard to tell the computer how much memory was installed. Modern micros are more self-aware and can figure this out for themselves.

Before you upgrade your system memory, you have to consult your computer's documentation. Before you can start, you must have three essential pieces of information:

1. The maximum memory you can install.
2. The memory component size and speed specifications supported.
3. The combinations of memory components supported.

Maximum memory   You have to start with the maximum memory limit. If your computer already has as much memory as it can take, you need not bother with adding more. Turn back to Chapter 1 and look into a motherboard replacement.

Most motherboards today can accept 64MB or more memory. The total depends on the number of SIMM slots, their size, and the capacity SIMMs that the motherboard will support. If your system currently uses SIMMs that are smaller than the largest capacity components your motherboard supports, you will have to replace the existing SIMMs in order to reach the maximum capacity.

Specifications   SIMMs come in different capacities and are rated for different speeds. Your motherboard documentation should tell you which capacities and speeds you can use. Most motherboards can use 32MB SIMMs, though some are limited to 16MB SIMMs.

Most computers require memory rated at 60 to 80 ns. Some 486 systems can use the slower end of this range. Some Pentiums may require the fastest.

As mentioned earlier in this chapter, most PC motherboards use SIMMs that support a parity bit for each byte. Some motherboards can be configured to use parity or not, giving you an option. And there are now motherboards on the market that do not use parity at all; even though you can use SIMMs with parity bits in these computers, they will not take advantage of this feature.

So check the supported specifications carefully before ordering memory. You may get memory that might not work reliably, if at all, and you may be paying more for SIMMs that support parity checking when your computer doesn't even use that feature.

There's a new type of DRAM memory that some systems can use. It is called EDO (extended data out) DRAM. Essentially it is a design refinement over the "regular" DRAM that lets the CPU start to access the memory before the last access has been completed. In practice, this doesn't seem to add much to system performance—about a few percentage points. On the other hand, the refinement shouldn't cost much more to manufacture than traditional DRAM

designs. So if you can get EDO memory for the same price as standard DRAM, go for it. Otherwise, the performance difference probably won't be noticeable enough to justify spending more.

In general, you must add 30-pin SIMMs in pairs, using the same specification SIMMs in both slots. Usually 72-pin SIMMs can be installed one at a time, and you often can have different capacity SIMMs in different slots. There are no hard-and-fast rules about memory configuration, however; some motherboards require that 30-pin SIMMs be installed in sets of four, and some motherboards require 72-pin SIMMs to be installed in pairs. You have to check your motherboard documentation to know the limitations.

Combinations

Trading in Memory

When you buy a new system, you should get it configured with the largest capacity SIMMs possible to achieve the desired memory configuration. Why? Because this means that you will have the largest number of empty SIMM slots possible. If your system comes with lower capacity SIMMs, they will fill more slots, giving you the problem of what to do with them when you want to upgrade your memory.

For example, let's assume that your motherboard has four 72-pin SIMM slots, and your system is configured with 8MB of memory. If your system came with a single 8MB SIMM installed when you bought it (or two 4MB SIMMs), you could upgrade to 16MB now by adding a single 8MB SIMM (or two more 4MB SIMMs) because the motherboard has open SIMM slots.

On the other hand, if the system vendor was saving a few bucks by buying lower capacity SIMMs when you bought it, your 8MB could consist of four 2MB SIMMs, filling all the slots. To go to 16MB, you have to open up slots.

As mentioned in Chapter 1, when moving 30-pin SIMMs to a 72-pin SIMM motherboard, you have three options on what to do with your old memory. There are services that will unsolder your memory chips and put them on new SIMM boards. There are also many sources of SIMM adapters that let you plug your existing SIMMs into a SIMM "extension board" so that they fit in a single slot.

Wring out the old

These solutions have one major shortcoming, however. They result in memory modules that stick up far above the motherboard. Depending on where your SIMM slots are located, this can obstruct the space used by expansion cards, or in some cases, conflict with space used by disk drive bays.

When you figure in the cost of the conversion service or expansion device, it may well be cheaper to simply sell your existing memory and buy new chips. There is a thriving and competitive market for used memory, and although you won't get full price for your old SIMMs, you can often recover a large enough portion to make this a competitive approach to the expanders and conversion services. In fact, many memory vendors routinely offer a trade-in service, so you can complete the buy and sell in a single transaction.

When buying new SIMMs, remember that you may want to pay a little extra to buy a single larger capacity unit than a pair of smaller ones. You may want to add memory again in the future, and an empty SIMM slot now could save you cost and aggravation later.

Adding L2 Cache

As mentioned in Chapter 1, the "sweet spot" for L2 system cache appears to be 256KB. If your system does not have this much (or any L2 cache at all), you can get a significant performance boost—especially under Windows—by bringing your system up to this level.

Unfortunately L2 cache memory can be configured in many, many different ways. Some use special single SRAM SIMMs. Others use discrete DIP chips. Some need separate chips for tag RAM, depending on the architecture of the cache. (L2 caches can be designed in different ways, and although some people have strong opinions about which designs are best, most people don't notice the difference when running equivalently configured systems.)

Also, motherboards have different ways for you to tell them how much L2 cache is installed. Some use switches, some use jumpers, and some use special resistor pack strips. And almost all require you to make changes in the CMOS settings as well.

The bottom line is this: You must get detailed specification information about your motherboard in order to upgrade your memory.

I'm going to give away a trade secret here. I'm going to tell you about one of my favorite references that I use to answer all sorts of hardware questions. If you have a system that you purchased from a vendor that has since shuffled off the mortal coil that we call the "mail order computer market," you may not have all the technical details you need to upgrade your memory and not have the foggiest where to go to find it. Many mail order systems use motherboards from suppliers in Taiwan and other Pacific Rim sources, so even if you knew who manufactured the board, you might have a difficult time picking up the phone and giving them a call.

Fortunately there is a company called Micro House, which has spent years compiling tons of technical details about motherboards. They publish this on their Technical Library on CD-ROM, which also includes similar information about hard disks, disk controllers, network interface cards, and even multi-I/O cards. (See Figure 2.7.)

Figure 2.7   The Technical Library on CD-ROM from Micro House is a treasure trove of technical details on motherboards (among other vital computer components).

The CD-ROM with all the topics currently costs $595, which is a bit steep for the average user, but it is invaluable for anyone who has to support more than a couple of computers. For information on Micro House, see Appendix A.

3 Storage

If you would be wealthy, think of saving as well as of getting.

Benjamin Franklin (1706–1790)

My first personal computer (aside from some slide rules, which we *used* to call "computers") was an Apple][I borrowed (then bought) from my younger brother. For some reason that escapes me at the moment (perhaps I don't want to remember trashing the floppy disk controller by sticking it in a slot while the power was still on), there was a period of time at the start when I had to store and load everything on cassette tapes. As the saying goes, it may have been slow, but at least it was unreliable.

Then I got the floppy drives working. It was as if heaven's gates had swung open. Programs saved and loaded in the blink of an eye. (Okay, you had to blink slowly, but who cared?) And there was no end to the available space. I saved program after program, revision after revision, and there was still room for more! I didn't even *know* what the total capacity was, nor did I care, because it seemed to go on forever. Who could ever fill up one of those cavernous 113KB floppy disks, anyway? Needless to say, I found out that *I* could, and sooner than I thought possible.

Since then, disk storage has grown like Topsy (see Figure 3.1), and our expectations manage to rapidly catch up to and exceed the data storage that we can afford to buy for our systems. Even now that hard disks cost less than 30 cents per megabyte—under $350 for a 1.2-gigabyte hard disk drive—people still seem to be running out of space. (But not me! I've got *two* gigabytes, and that's plenty! . . . at least for the moment . . . .)

Figure 3.1   The recordable CD-ROM on the right can hold roughly 3000 times as much data as the floppy disk on the left.

Not to mention the problems we have with backing up all that data. (So don't mention it!) Perfectly sane people who would never drive without wearing their seat belts or bet the mortgage money on a roll of the dice find it easy to simply ignore the fact that all their data and work is unprotected and that it could all be lost in the (fairly unlikely) event that their hard disk turned to iron filings. I wonder what Ben Franklin would have to say about an attitude like *that?*

NEED TO KNOW

To understand what goes wrong with computer storage and how to fix it or upgrade it, you need to understand a bit about how it works.

I realize that by now, you've probably read the same story a bazillion times—the first digital storage was punched holes in heavy paper used to control French looms. (Peter McWilliams says in *The Personal Computer Book* that the French weaving machines actually got the technology from a sixteenth-century automated musical organ and reports that he learned it from James Burke's *Connections* series on PBS.) So I won't rehash that or why hard disks are called Winchester drives (besides, there are conflicting versions of that one) or describe all the different formats used with 8-inch floppy disks because IBM PC-compatible computers (almost) never used them anyway. You don't really need to know that stuff anyhow.

What you *do* need to know, however, is what makes hard drives different. Open a copy of *Computer Shopper* or some other magazine with ads from companies that sell hard disks by mail order, and you'll see a bewildering array of choices (Figure 3.2). What do all these choices mean, and should you worry about them? And once you've sorted through the information about hard disks, you're faced with a similar task when considering ways to back up your data.

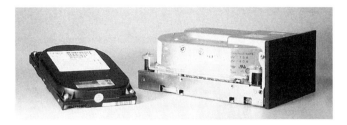

Figure 3.2 Hard disks come in a range of sizes, but physical size has little correlation with capacity or other specifications.

Hard Disks

Our treasure lies in the beehive of our knowledge. We are perpetually on the way thither, being by nature winged insects and honey gatherers of the mind.

> Friedrich Nietzsche
> *The Genealogy of Morals,* 1887

The basic principle of a magnetic storage disk is simple. Coat a disk with a thin layer of rust, and you can apply a magnetic charge to portions of the rust layer that can then be detected by very sensitive electrical circuits. (Okay, so some disk engineers may take offense at the term "rust," but that's the common term for the "iron oxide" that some engineers might prefer. And it's also true that other compounds beside iron oxide are used for the magnetic media layers on disks, so I guess it isn't always rust.)

For floppy disks, the disk is a thin sheet of plastic. For hard disks, the disk is a thin, rigid platter that is usually made of metal—often aluminum for its light weight—but other materials are also used, including glass.

The same basic principle is at work with both floppy and hard disks. The fundamental difference is that the read/write head comes into contact with the surface of a floppy disk (the same way that an audio cassette tape is pressed against the heads of a cassette deck), but the head of a hard disk "flies" an insanely small distance above the surface of the platter. (Most hard disk drives have more than one platter, with read/write heads on both sides of each one.) Because the clearance is so tiny, a piece of dust or particle of smoke could get caught between the head and the platter causing irreparable damage. As a result, hard disk drives are sealed tight, which means that you can't take out the platters and put new ones in as you can with a floppy disk drive. That's why some people call hard disk drives "fixed disk drives"—which makes some sense because floppy disks may be flexible, but they're not soft, right?

Hard Disk Interfaces

> Madam, I have been looking for a person who disliked gravy all my life; let
> us swear eternal friendship.
>
> Sydney Smith
> *Lady Holland's Memoir,* 1855

Before your computer can do anything with a hard disk, it has to be able to exchange data with it. And in order for this alliance to work, there must be an interface. Different kinds of hard disks need different kinds of controllers.

**ST-506 and
MFM/RLL**

IBM chose to use an ST-506 interface developed by Shugart Technology when they built the XT. This interface had firmware (programs stored in ROM—Read-Only Memory—chips) on the interface board that was configured to work with certain hard disk drives, and you could hook up one or two hard disks to a single controller card.

The original XT hard disk used MFM (Modified Frequency Modulation) data encoding. This used 17 sectors per track (we'll get to sectors and tracks in a minute), but you don't need to know that. Just be aware that this was a fairly conservative technology used to create disks that we now consider low in capacity and slow in performance.

The other reason to know about MFM is to be able to contrast it with the other encoding technique used with ST-506 interface hard disks: RLL (Run Length Limited). This is essentially an early form of data compression that allowed a disk with the same physical attributes to be formatted with more sectors per track and to have roughly 50 percent more data capacity. Thus an MFM disk design with a 20MB capacity could be reengineered to create an RLL model with a 30MB capacity. You needed a different controller card for RLL drives than you needed for MFM drives.

Just as some people "push" their processors to run faster than their specifications (see Chapter 1, CPUs and Motherboards), people also used to try to cut corners on their hard disk storage. MFM drives were cheaper than RLL drives, but some brave people discovered that you could often use an MFM drive with an RLL controller, and it would format successfully with the higher RLL capacity. It was like getting 50 percent more storage free.

Well, I believe in the principle of TANSTAAFL (There Ain't No Such Thing As A Free Lunch) and it seems to apply in this case. It has been the rallying cry for groups from environmental activists to economists. It also applies to more aspects of computer technology than most of us would care to admit. Many people who tried this experiment discovered that drives rated for MFM service were not always reliable when formatted with an RLL controller (in much the same way that people get unreliable results when formatting double-

density-rated floppy disks as high density), and they sometimes lost some or all of their data. I like a bargain as much as the next guy—maybe even more— but my time and my data are worth more than the difference in price between the MFM and RLL drives, even back in the XT and AT days. So if you're using an ST-506 interface on some aging system, be sure to match the encoding of your disk to that used by your controller, either MFM or RLL.

When IBM brought out the AT (Figure 3.3), the engineers decided that putting the support for different hard disk types on the controller card was too limiting, so they came up with a new approach. A **drive table** was added to the BIOS, and you had to pick an entry that matched your disk drive. If your drive didn't match an entry in the table, you either had to use one that had similar specifications (which usually meant that you gave up access to a portion of your disk's capacity) or you had to load a special driver (which took up valuable system memory). The BIOSs in most modern computers now have a provision for user-definable entries, so this is no longer a problem with new systems.

Figure 3.3 The original IBM AT disk controller could handle up to two hard disk and two floppy disk drives.

The next popular hard disk interface was ESDI (Enhanced Small Device Interface). The main impetus behind its development was that the 5Mb/sec transfer rate of the ST-506 interface was becoming a serious performance bottleneck for the new, faster processors. ESDI doubled that, with an effective transfer rate of about 10Mb/sec. (Theoretically it can move up to 24 Mb/sec, but the lower number is closer to the actual maximum performance for most ESDI drives.) Like the ST-506 interface, ESDI controllers could have up to two hard disks installed at a time.

In addition to being faster, ESDI drives tended to have larger capacities than ST-506 models. These drives were especially popular in the early days of the 386 systems but can be hard to find now.

> There is no "there" there.
>
> Gertrude Stein

IDE and EIDE

IDE (Integrated Drive Electronics) is not really an interface at all. It refers to a design that places the interface right on the hard disk, so the card to which you connect the drive is often little more than a pass-through connector to your computer's expansion bus. That's why many IDE "interface" cards are so small and simple looking; many people often call them **paddle cards** (or sometimes **pass-through cards**) because they are hardly more than a printed circuit board and a mounting bracket (see Figure 3.4). The interface is really called an **ATA** (**AT Attachment**), but you probably won't ever need to know that because it's seldom used.

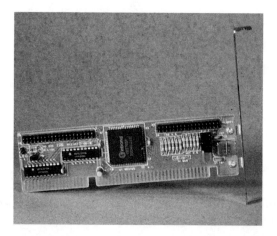

Figure 3.4   Some computer systems use an expansion card to make the connection with an IDE hard disk drive, such as this simple paddle card.

IDE connections can be on a separate expansion card, or they are incorporated right into the motherboard (as is often the case). They can support up to two drives. Because the controller circuitry is on the drives themselves, however, there has to be agreement about which disk is in charge. As then-Secretary of State Alexander Haig discovered during the crisis after the attempted assassination of President Reagan, simply asserting that you are in charge is not sufficient.

As a result, IDE hard disks have two—and sometimes three—different configuration options. The drive can be configured either as the Master or the Slave.

If it is the Slave, it defers control to the circuitry on the other drive. If the drive is the Master, there may be a choice of settings: Master without a Slave drive present, and Master with a Slave drive present. These settings are typically controlled by jumpers on the hard disk.

IDE drives were an overnight success, but the two-drive limitation soon became a shoe that pinched. The result is EIDE (Enhanced IDE) which has two channels—primary and secondary—each of which can handle two drives—one Master and one Slave. EIDE also has the advantage of improving performance, increasing the performance over IDE drives. To take advantage of this, however, you need both an interface and a disk drive that support EIDE.

The extra channel supported by EIDE is important, now that other peripheral devices besides hard disks are using this interface. CD-ROM and tape backup drives with EIDE support are gaining popularity.

Perhaps the oldest hard disk drive interface of all is SCSI (Small Computer **SCSI** Systems Interface). It is actually more like a computer expansion bus than simply being a data port like the others.

Like IDE drives, the intelligence and control resides largely out on the hard disk or other device. Each device is its own logical unit and communicates with the computer through an interface card. You can have up to seven devices on a SCSI bus (plus the interface card, for a total of eight devices), and each is assigned a unique ID number, usually through jumper or switch settings.

The SCSI bus also requires termination at each end. This means adding resistors at the end of the cable to prevent the electrical signals from "echoing" along the bus. Some cards and devices have physical terminators that you have to install or remove, depending on the device's position on the bus. Others have internal terminators that you can activate or deactivate through the use of jumpers or switches. The best devices now have automatic termination features; they can identify their own position on the bus, and if they are at the end of the line, they automatically activate their own internal termination.

SCSI is more flexible than most interfaces, so it is also used for other types of peripherals, including CD-ROM drives, tape drives, and even scanners.

The original SCSI was an 8-bit wide interface that had a data transfer rate of about 5Mb/sec, about the same as the ST-506 interface. The current implementation of SCSI, known as SCSI-2, is backward compatible with the original SCSI (that is, older SCSI devices work with it) and comes in Fast or Fast+Wide versions. Fast SCSI-2 has a transfer rate of about 10Mb/sec, and Fast+Wide adds a 16-bit wide interface to achieve 20Mb/sec transfer rates.

SCSI has earned a reputation of being difficult to configure and temperamental to operate. Although this may well have been true a decade ago, it is certainly not the case now. In fact, you can often install two SCSI interfaces in a single computer system with no problems at all. As a result, SCSI has become the preferred interface for many users; I have it installed in both of the computers that I use for most of my work and testing.

> 'When I use a word,' Humpty Dumpty said in rather a scornful tone, 'it means just what I choose it to mean—neither more nor less.'
>
> Lewis Carroll
> *Through the Looking-Glass,* 1872

Capacities

The world of computer users seems to be divided into two groups: those who have decided that their current hard disk storage is too small, and those who have not yet come to that inevitable conclusion.

The IBM XT came with a 10MB hard disk, and this was boosted to 20MB and then to 40MB on the IBM AT. Today, even low-cost desktop systems come with at least 200MB hard disks, and 500MB to 1GB capacities are affordable and widely used.

There is widespread confusion, however, on just how hard disk capacity is calculated. One reason is that there are two fundamental specifications: unformatted and formatted capacities. Another reason for the confusion is that people measure megabytes with different sized buckets.

We'll get to formatting in a moment, but a disk needs to have its vast wasteland organized somehow before you can plant data on it. Just as fences, irrigation ditches, and windbreaks reduce the amount of tillable land on a farm, so formatting takes up space on your disk. Add the space allocated to the file management system (analogous, I suppose, to building a barn for your tractor and other farm implements), and you lose some more. As a result, a disk has a formatted capacity that is smaller than its unformatted capacity; how much smaller it is depends on the number of partitions you use.

You encounter larger discrepancies, however, when you try to determine just what the formatted capacity of your hard disk is. When I run CHKDSK on my C drive, I get a screen that tells me that I have 276,091,968 bytes on the disk; round that off and you might say I have a 276-megabyte drive. (See Figure 3.5.) But the File Manager in Windows reports that I have 260,832KB of space on the hard disk—which sounds more like 261 megabytes. Thus I've lost 15MB without doing anything. If I then check the capacity of the drive using FDISK (you can type FDISK /STATUS at a DOS prompt and it reports the size and status of your hard disk partitions), the program tells me that I only have 255MB on the disk. There goes another 5MB! And it's all still the same drive; I haven't done anything but have three different programs report its capacity.

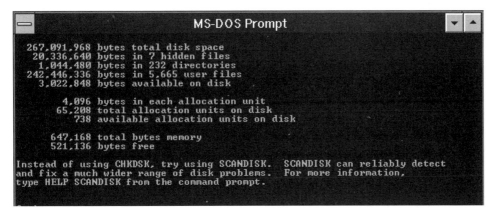

```
                      MS-DOS Prompt

  267,091,968 bytes total disk space
   20,336,640 bytes in 7 hidden files
    1,044,480 bytes in 232 directories
  242,446,336 bytes in 5,665 user files
    3,022,848 bytes available on disk

        4,096 bytes in each allocation unit
       65,208 total allocation units on disk
          738 available allocation units on disk

      647,168 total bytes memory
      521,136 bytes free

Instead of using CHKDSK, try using SCANDISK.  SCANDISK can reliably detect
and fix a much wider range of disk problems.  For more information,
type HELP SCANDISK from the command prompt.
```

Figure 3.5 This is what the DOS CHKDSK utility reports about my hard disk Drive C. But what's the real capacity of this disk drive?

The answer to this problem is one of how you define "megabyte." As we saw in Chapter 2, a megabyte should be thought of as 2 to the 20th power, or 1,048,576. If you divide the total number of bytes on my hard disk—276,091,968—by this number, you get 254.7, which rounds up to the 255MB reported by FDISK.

If you look closely at the bottom status line in Windows File Manager, the number is reported in KB, which is 2 to the 10th, or 1024 bytes. Divide 276,091,968 by 1,024 and you get the 260,832KB that File Manager accurately reports. The mistake was made in defining a megabyte as 1000KB, which it isn't.

Finally, CHKDSK was correct with the count of bytes on the disk, and the error was made by defining a megabyte as a million bytes. Here's the rub, however: Most disk manufacturers don't use the 2^{20} bytes definition for megabyte, but instead simply divide by a million. All manufacturers seem to follow this practice, but it can lead to a shock and puzzlement when users discover that they have nearly 10 percent less disk space than they thought they were buying. So long as you remember that hard disks are really sold in capacities of millions of bytes when the vendor claims megabytes, you can avoid this surprise.

File Storage

> Poor fellow, he suffers from files.
>
> Aneurin Bevan, quoted by Michael Foot
> *Aneurin Bevan,* 1962

Data is stored on disks using magnetic fields. True, but how? You can bore down into this topic to incredibly deep, technical levels that get into the coercivity (how sensitive the recording medium is to magnetic fields), data encoding patterns, and other engineering kinds of topics. Most users won't ever need to know this level of detail. Instead, I will try to pick a middle level that explains what is going on, without providing all the nitty-gritty details that only a propeller-head could love.

Low-level formatting

Think back to first grade and learning to write. If your teacher was like mine, you weren't given a totally blank sheet of paper. Instead, it had horizontal lines printed on it. (I remember a dashed line between two solid lines, too.) And the lines were pretty far apart to give you a fighting chance of fitting your letters between them. (And that was no easy task, given that we had to use those telephone-pole–sized pencils!)

Well, the average first grader is probably smarter about being able to read and write than your typical hard disk drive, so we need to "draw lines" on a disk so that it can write its data between them.

We call this line-drawing process **formatting,** and instead of drawing a physical line on the disk, it is done with magnetism. Small patches of data are put down on the disk's surface at specific intervals to mark divisions. These are organized in concentric circles; the circles are usually referred to as **tracks,** but sometimes you'll see or hear the term **cylinders** which is a throwback to ancient data storage techniques used on old mainframe computers. Each track is divided into sectors, each of which can hold 512 bytes. In general, sectors are arranged as pie-shaped wedges that radiate out from the center of the disk, so that each track has the same number of sectors as shown in Figure 3.6.

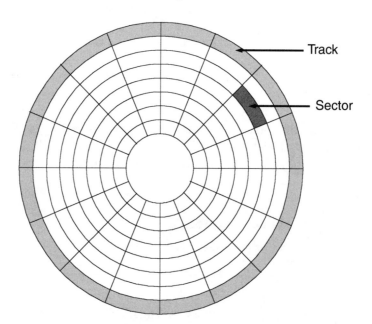

Figure 3.6   Most magnetic disk drives are organized as a series of concentric rings (tracks or cylinders) divided into equal numbers of sections (sectors).

In some newer disk designs, the number of sectors per track changes, increasing as you move toward the edge of the disk. Because these disks have clever electronics that make it seem as if they have a constant number of sectors per track, you really don't need to know about this to make your disks work.

You can figure out the unformatted capacity of a hard disk by multiplying the number of tracks (or cylinders) times the number of sectors per track, times 512 bytes per sector.

Actually the track and sector formatting is just the first step; as a result, we call it a **low-level format,** and all disks must be low-level formatted before you can use them.

Note that IDE and EIDE drives are given a low-level format at the factory, and in general, you should *never* have to give them a low-level format yourself. There are some utilities on the market that will let you low-level format an IDE drive, but don't do this unless you're absolutely sure that you know what you're doing (and you have all your data backed up first). It is possible to make an IDE unusable through an attempt to low-level format it.

> Resistance to the organized mass can be effected only by the man who is as well organized in his individuality as the mass itself.
>
> Carl Jung
> *The Undiscovered Self,* 1957

If there is a low-level format, it would seem that there is a higher level format, too. And there is. This step (or steps) prepares the disk to receive data for a specific operating system. Different operating systems store their data in different ways, and they format disks in different ways. We'll focus on how DOS formats disks.

Disk organization

To prepare a hard disk for use, you need to use two DOS utilities: FDISK and FORMAT. Floppy disks are simpler, and the FORMAT command does everything in one step.

You use FDISK to set up one or more partitions on your hard disk. Partitions can be prepared for DOS or for other operating systems. If you want to be able to boot from the disk, you need to create a Primary DOS partition. You can also create an Extended DOS partition, which can be set up as one or more logical disk drives.

FDISK

Why would you partition your hard disk? Why not leave it all as one big drive? The answer lies in how DOS stores files. It uses a feature known as the **File Allocation Table,** or **FAT,** which is a data table. Each entry in the table has a reference to a file and a location on the disk (Figure 3.7). The locations on the disk are called **clusters,** which are made up of one or more sectors. The FAT has a fixed

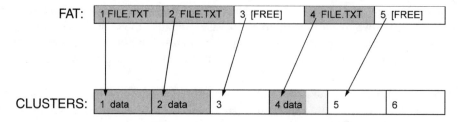

Figure 3.7   DOS uses FAT entries to keep track of where a file is stored on the disk.

number of table entries, which means that the cluster size is determined by dividing the total size of the disk by the number of FAT entries, and then rounding up to the nearest whole sector size.

Floppy disks and hard disks 15MB and smaller have fewer FAT entries than larger hard disks, which explains why the cluster size for the smallest hard disks is larger than the next group of hard disks. Table 3.1 lists the number of bytes per cluster for disk drives of different sizes.

Note that DOS 6.x doesn't refer to clusters. If you run CHKDSK (as shown earlier in Figure 3.5), DOS 6.x reports the size of the "allocation units" for the disk partition; this is just another name for cluster.

Table 3.1   The cluster size varies with the size of the disk partition.

Disk Size	Sectors per Cluster	Bytes per Cluster
Floppy Disks		
360 KB	2	1 KB
720 KB	2	1 KB
1.2 MB	1	512 bytes
1.44 MB	1	512 bytes
Hard Disks		
0–15 MB	8	4 KB
16–127 MB	4	2 KB
128–255 MB	8	4 KB
256–511 MB	16	8 KB
512–1023 MB	32	16 KB
1024–2048 MB	64	32 KB

Cluster size has important implications for how you set up your hard disk. Because a FAT entry can only refer one file to a given cluster, the minimum amount of space that a file can take up is one cluster. This means that a tiny 10-byte batch file takes up a lot more space than you might think. On a 1.44MB floppy disk, it takes up 512 bytes, or about 50 times its size. On a 255MB hard disk, it takes up 4KB of space—more than 400 times its size!

If you tend to have lots of small files, it can pay to configure your hard disk partitions so that you reduce this waste of storage space. A 1GB hard disk set up as one partition uses 32KB clusters. Divide that same drive into partitions that are 255MB or smaller, and the clusters will be only 8KB. Thus small files take up only one-fourth as much space, which means that you will be using your hard disk space far more efficiently.

The DOS FDISK utility sets up something called the Master Boot Record on your hard disk, as well as the partition table, which describes how your hard disk is divided.

After you set up the partitions, you need to use the DOS FORMAT utility to prepare the disk for data. FORMAT sets up the FAT and the root directory for a partition; repeat the command for each partition on your hard disk and you'll be ready to use the hard disk.

FORMAT

Windows 95 uses the same FAT disk structure as DOS and Windows 3.x, but it adds useful extensions to the directory system. DOS files are limited to the "eight dot three" (or 8.3) naming limitation; filenames can have one to eight characters, followed by a dot, and then up to three letters of an extension. Windows 95 uses bits in the directory entries that had been reserved under DOS for operating system use, and allows you to give files names of up to 255 characters, including spaces.

This means that instead of a cryptic 954QWS.XLS name, you can call your worksheet "1995 4th Quarter Western Sales Summary." The directory still tracks an 8.3 filename, which is what would show in a directory listing if you moved the file to a computer that is not running Windows 95, so you don't have to worry about incompatibility due to the long filenames. (The shortened 8.3 names can be more cryptic than what you would have come up with, however, so if you are going to be moving files back and forth a lot between DOS (or Windows 3.x) and Windows 95 machines, you might want to stick with the 8.3 naming convention.)

It turns out that under some circumstances, you can actually *lose* files if you use files with the Windows 95 long filename feature under DOS or Windows 3.x, unless you are very careful. Win95 evidently does not check too carefully to make certain that its abbreviated 8.3 equivalent of a long filename does not conflict with an existing name—and under some circumstances Win 95 can

overwrite an existing file without warning. Microsoft's advice is to always make certain that the *start* of any long filename is unique, but this limits the appeal of this feature.

Fragmentation

> We live in the mind, in ideas, in fragments.
>
> Henry Miller
> *Black Spring,* 1936

There's one more concept about how data is stored on your disks that you need to know. When your computer wants to save something to disk, it looks in the FAT to find out which cluster is available. It then writes the file's data to that cluster. If the file is larger than that cluster, the computer looks in the FAT again to find out the next available cluster. As files are erased, copied, and edited, clusters are made available at different points throughout the FAT. As a result, a new, large file written to the disk may be spread out among discontiguous clusters all over the disk.

This effect is called **fragmentation,** and it can have an impact on your system's performance. Instead of being able to read a whole series of sequential clusters, the disk drive's head has to jump back and forth all over the disk to collect all the pieces. Running a utility like the DOS DEFRAG program (included in DOS 6.x) collects all the pieces of each file and rewrites them to the disk in sequence. The process is like sorting through the jumbled mess on the floor of your closet and pairing up all your shoes; it takes some time at first, but it makes finding a matching pair much easier the next time. (And if your shoes are already neatly arranged in the bottom of your closet, I don't want to hear about it!)

Windows 95 not only includes a new defragmentation utility, but you can also set it up to run automatically. You can configure your machine to defrag its hard disk overnight when you're asleep, which is a convenient feature. To get this automation, you need to use the System Agent feature that is part of the optional Microsoft Plus! package, but it's well worth the investment.

Backup

> They who have nothing have little to fear,
> Nothing to lose or to gain.
>
> Madison Cawein
> *The Bellman*

If the typical double-spaced typewritten page holds 2000 characters, and each character requires one byte to store, then a 500 MB hard disk can store about 250,000 pages of text. That's 500 reams of paper. That's 50 cases of paper. That's about 2500 pounds of paper—okay, only 1250 if you print on both sides, but even then it would still be a stack about seven and a half feet high.

How long would it take you to type 250,000 pages?

Now, think about your hard disk, and how big it is, and how full it is . . . Now think about a 7.5-foot stack of paper disappearing in an instant. Do I have your attention now?

Actually, I'm really not an alarmist when it comes to backups. I freely admit that I don't backup my complete system on a regular basis, but that's a conscious decision on my part and not simply an inaction achieved by default.

The fact is that 90 percent of the data on my computers consists of programs and reference files and drivers and other items that I have on disk or CD-ROM that I could restore fairly easily. Of the remainder, there are lots of files for writing assignments that have been turned in and published long ago, and old electronic mail messages, and other items that I have finished with but hang onto in case I need to refer to them again someday. There's little critical information—mainly bookkeeping data and this manuscript—that would cause me anguish if I were to lose it, so I do keep those files backed up. Carefully. Faithfully. Honest. But I don't worry much about the rest.

Let's also be frank about *why* people don't back up—it's a pain. It takes time, it doesn't really do anything useful for you, you have to have backup media on hand, and you have to be organized about how and when you do it.

Backing up is hard to do.

People who work on networks in big offices have it easy; somebody else has the job of backing up everything on a regular basis. (And if your office has a network and you *don't* have a system of regular backups in place, I'd recommend that you fix that, pronto!) But nobody really pays us to back up our own machines. Backups are a bit like life insurance; we all know that we should have it, but we hope we never need it, and it's a drag paying for it. Or they're like seat belts; car manufacturers are always trying to find ways to make it easier for people to put on their seat belts (or harder or more uncomfortable for them *not* to put on their seat belts), yet some people still insist on not wearing them. It's not easy getting people to do things that are good for them.

As a result, your choice of a backup system is important because if you don't use it, you might as well have not purchased it in the first place. So pick something that matches your needs and that you will use.

Floppy Disks

Don't laugh. Sure, if you were to try to back up a 500MB drive with 1.44MB floppies, you'd have to make a career out of the project (and take a long vacation when you finish), but there is something to be said in favor of floppies (Figure 3.8). If you're like me and most of your critical data is in the form of relatively small files that you save often, stick a floppy in your computer's disk drive and

Figure 3.8   Floppy disks have been around nearly since the first microcomputers, but they still are one of the most convenient forms of data storage.

every time you save to the hard disk, save to the floppy as well. It takes a moment, and you have current backups all the time.

And the floppy approach is affordable. As long as America Online continues its saturation bombing of computer-user mailboxes with their free trial disks, no computer owner in this country should ever have to buy another floppy disk again.

There have been recent attempts to create even higher capacity floppy disks, of 2.88MB capacity and larger. So far, these have not yet appeared to take hold with computer users or manufacturers and are not much of a factor at this time.

Tape

The most popular backup medium is tape. Tape drives use small cartridges that typically hold from 170MB to more than a gigabyte of data. They come in different models that plug into your floppy disk controller, a proprietary interface, or a SCSI controller. For portable convenience and use with more than one computer, you can also get models that plug into a computer's parallel port.

One of the big advantages of tape is the cost; drives start at under $150, and the tape cartridges cost about $12 to $50—only pennies per megabyte.

There are disadvantages, however. Tape is relatively slow, compared with other media. Transfer rates typically range from 150 to 300KB/sec data transfer rates, which is slower than most CD-ROM drives. Also, tape is a sequential storage device. Like an ancient Roman scroll, you have to wind all the way through the tape to get to the section where a specific file is stored, which can be slow and inconvenient. As a result, you cannot use tape backups as "live" data that you can access directly with your computer; you have to restore the data first.

Finally, most tape drives use data compression, and the advertised capacity is usually estimated based on how much typical data can be compressed. Some data compresses more than others—for example, files archived with PKZIP do not compress as much as a straight text file—so you can't count on getting that much data on a single tape. The uncompressed capacity is about half the advertised size, so you may want to check the specifications carefully before you buy.

Removable Media

Another popular form of backup is a removable magnetic disk. These are more expensive than tape, but they have the advantages of being about as fast as a hard disk and allowing you to access data on them in the same way that you can with your hard disk.

One of the leaders in the market is Syquest, and their removable hard disk drives are used a lot by graphics artists and print shops when large files have to be transferred from one computer to another. The 270MB drives come in IDE, SCSI, and parallel port versions, and they sell for about $350 to $700, with the $65 cartridges working out to about 25 cents per megabyte.

Iomega has made Bernoulli Boxes based on a floppy-disk cartridge for years, but have recently come out with a new Zip drive that looks as though it could be a huge success. It comes in SCSI or parallel port versions and sells for about $200. The 100MB cartridges sell for just $20 apiece, making the nickel-per-megabyte cost much more attractive than other removable hard disk options. With data transfer rates of 1MB/sec, the Zip drive is certainly fast enough, but the question is whether or not the 100MB capacity is sufficient these days.

Optical Disks

Then there are the optical disk technologies. CD-ROM is no good for backups because you can't write to one (the ROM stands for Read-Only Memory, after all). There is CD-R, or recordable CD, which lets you "burn" your own CD-ROM disks, and each $12 blank can hold more than 600MB of data (Figure 3.9). In general, however, you can only write once to a CD-R disk, and the transfer rates are slow—about the same speed as tape—for both writes and reads. And although the cost of CD recorders has dropped recently, they still cost $1000 and up.

Magneto-Optical (MO) drives are another form of optical disk technology that uses a combination of lasers and magnetism to record and read data on a special disk. Unlike CD-R, you can erase and rewrite data on the same disk. The latest versions use small, 3.5-inch disks that can hold up to 230MB of data. Fujitsu is the leader, with SCSI interface drives that sell for between $500 and $600, and the cartridges cost about $35 for a per-megabyte cost of about 15 cents.

As I write this, there's a new technology from Panasonic on the market—the PD/CD drive—that uses phase change technology to record on plastic disks (similar to CD-ROM disks), and the same drive can also be used as a quad-speed drive for standard CD-ROMs. This means that you can have a single drive for both CDs

Figure 3.9   You can tell a recordable CD-R disk by its green and gold coloring, compared with the silver coloring of a regular CD-ROM disk.

and backup, and the 650MB PD/CD media can be erased and rewritten like a magnetic disk. Data transfer rates are around a megabyte per second for the PD/CD disks (compared with 600KB/sec for the quad-speed CD-ROM drive features), making it practical for use with live data. The prices for the drives are falling quickly, and they now list for less than $500—about twice as much as a quad-speed CD-ROM drive. The PD/CD disks cost about $60 apiece now, for a 10-cent-per-megabyte cost, but those prices can be expected to drop if this technology catches on.

So pick one, already!   One of these technologies should meet your budget and your temperament, whether you want to just back up little parts or everything at once. But pick one, get it, and use it. Dealing with problems such as those covered in the next section will be a lot more pleasant to face if you know that your critical data is already safely stored someplace else.

@#%$%@!

> Caution is the eldest child to wisdom.
>
> Victor Hugo

The world is divided into two kinds of people: those who divide the people in the world into two categories, and those who don't. I'm from the first group. Therefore . . . in the world of computer users, there are two kinds of people: those who have already experienced their first hard disk disaster, and those who will.

To dispel any myths about the infallibility of experts, I admit that I have had my share of hard disk problems—and some of them were self-inflicted. For example, early versions of DOS didn't ask for confirmation when you typed FORMAT C:, even though this would erase all the data on your disk. (And this was *before* the days of UNFORMAT and other bacon-saver utilities.) It wasn't a mistake that I made more than once . . . well, no more than two or three times.

The point is that bad things happen to good disks, and there's little you can do to prevent it, so the best you can do is be prepared. So here are a very few of the things that can go wrong with hard disks and storage devices, and some of the ways you may be able to get out of the jam.

Floppy Disks

You might be surprised, but data stored on floppy disks should be retrievable nearly indefinitely. It's more likely that you will get rid of the computer that has a drive that can read the disk before the disk loses its hold on the data.

Still, the magnetic fields on the disk's surface can lose some strength over time, and if you have critical data, you might want to make fresh copies of the disks every few years. (This also gives you the opportunity to decide whether or not you really *need* to keep that data around after all this time—if you do, you might want to consider something even more durable, like burning it into a recordable CD or something similar.)

Still, there may be times when you go to read a floppy disk and the computer balks. You may get sector not found errors, or even the dreaded "General failure reading drive A; Abort, Retry, Fail?" message. After the initial moments of panic and fury have passed, read on.

> ***George's First Rule of Delinquent Disks:*** **Try to read the disk in another computer. There are variations in alignments and rotation speeds of floppy disk drives, or for just about any drive with removable media for that matter. If the floppy disk is out of spec in one direction and your drive is out of spec in the other direction, you may not be able to read the disk, but there is a good chance that you can find a different computer with a disk drive that might work with the floppy. If you can find another computer that can read the disk, what then?**

1. Take a fresh disk, and go to the first computer.
2. Format the floppy. (If there is already data on the disk, use the FORMAT /U command to skip saving the unformat data.)
3. Take this newly formatted disk to the computer that can successfully read the problem disk.
4. Copy the data from the problem disk to a temporary directory on that computer's hard disk, and then copy it back to the newly formatted disk.
5. Take the copy back to the original computer, and you should be able to read the data without a problem.

This technique works because the second computer can read and write to both the problem floppy and the floppy formatted by the original computer. If you cannot find a computer that can read the problem floppy, that disk may have an unrecoverable error. If you cannot read the newly formatted floppy, there might be a problem with your computer's floppy disk drive. We'll cover these possibilities in a moment.

What if you have a floppy that's the wrong size for your computer, or your computer's floppy is broken? This was the problem when I needed to install software that came on 3.5-inch disks, and the 3.5-inch drive in my system was broken. I had a laptop with a 3.5-inch drive, but my test system only had a working 5.25-inch drive.

Interlink

The answer is Interlink, which is a file exchange program that is included with DOS 6.2. You can also use LapLink or some other commercial program, but chances are that you already have Interlink on your system, so you may as well use that.

To use Interlink, you need a cable to connect the two computers. You can either use a "null modem" cable to connect the machines using serial ports, or you can use a special parallel file exchange cable for use with parallel ports. Both types of cables are often sold as "LapLink" cables, and you should be able to find a serial or parallel version at most computer stores. (The DOS Help system also has the pinout information you need to create your own cables if you want. For more details, type "HELP INTERLNK—Notes" without the quotes at the DOS prompt.)

To run Interlink, you must first connect the two computers. One will be the *server;* it shares its disk drives with the other computer, which will be the *client.* On the server, run the DOS command INTERSVR. This runs a program that makes it ready to share its drives. Then load the Interlink device driver to the client computer by adding

```
DEVICE=C:\DOS\INTERLNK.EXE
```

to its CONFIG.SYS file.

Reboot the client, and the server's disks should now be available on the client as drives with letters after the client's own disks. You can now access the server's floppy disk to install software on the client, or use the client's floppy disk to install software on the server.

Unfortunately you cannot access a CD-ROM using Interlink, but it works great with floppies.

Windows 95 does not include Interlink. Instead it has a feature called Direct Cable Connection. As with Interlink, you can use either a parallel or serial connection to exchange files between two computers. If you are connecting a laptop and a desktop computer, you might want to check into Windows 95's Briefcase feature (see Chapter 8, Portable Stuff), which is designed to help you synchronize files between two different computers.

If you suspect that something is seriously wrong with the floppy disk itself, you can try to resurrect its data. There are a number of data recovery programs that may be able to help, including Norton Disk Doctor (part of the Norton Utilities collection) or the PC Tools DiskFix. (See Appendix A for more information on these products.)

Fouled-up floppy

These programs can repair damaged data in the "housekeeping" portions of the floppy such as boot sector and the FAT. They also can sometimes read data that has a weak signal and rewrite it so that DOS can read it. These utilities can't work miracles, but they can often rescue data that might otherwise seem hopelessly lost.

If you think it is your floppy disk drive that is ailing, however, try running a diagnostic program such as QAPlus, CheckIt Pro, or System Sleuth. (See Appendix A for details.) These programs can exercise the floppy drive with a series of reads and writes to verify that it is performing correctly.

Failed floppy drive

Hard Disks

> Chance never helps those who do not help themselves.
>
> Sophocles

More is at stake with hard disks. There's more data, and you typically rely on it to boot up your computer every day, so if it skips a beat, your heart is likely to have a sympathetic response, causing *it* to skip at least a beat.

There are some excellent and thick books about disk storage problems and data recovery, and I won't pretend to cover all the possibilities here. I will go over all the most likely problems that you'll encounter and show you how to get out of the trouble in most cases.

To save space, let me just say this once: If you suspect that something may be wrong with your hard disk, back up any critical data first. If you can access the data, be prepared for the possibility that you might never see it again, so if you want to be sure you have it, make a backup. You don't have to back up everything (though that may be more convenient in some circumstances), but be sure to grab everything that you can't do without. It's cheaper in the long run; it takes far less time to make some unnecessary backups than it is to reconstruct even a few months of checkbook entries, let alone a year or two.

When in doubt, back up!

Boot Problems

The most common problem is when you turn on your computer, and you get an error message that refers to a "nonbootable" disk or no disk found or something similar. There are a number of possible causes, but here are the most common ones.

DOS boot files   In order for DOS to load, you need at least three files in the root directory of the boot drive (whether it is a floppy or hard disk). COMMAND.COM is the best known, but there are two hidden files that you must also have. The names of these files have changed over the years with different versions of DOS from different sources, but in MS-DOS 6.x, they are MSDOS.SYS and IO.SYS. When you format a disk using the FORMAT /S command or use the DOS SYS command to make a disk bootable, these are the files that are copied as a result.

The DOS file system supports a number of different file attributes, including Hidden, Read-Only, and System file. You can view a file's attributes using the DOS ATTRIB command, but the problem is that you have to know that a hidden file is there before you can go look for it. There's a much easier way to view—and change—a file's attributes. File Manager in Windows 3.x has a View menu option, and if you select By File Type command, you'll see the By File Type windows as shown above in Figure 3.10. If you check the bottom box, Show Hidden/System files, each file's attributes will be listed to the right of the file's date and time stamp information. You can also view and edit a file's attributes by selecting the file in the file list, and then using the File Properties command or pressing Alt-Enter to open the Properties window as shown in Figure 3.11.

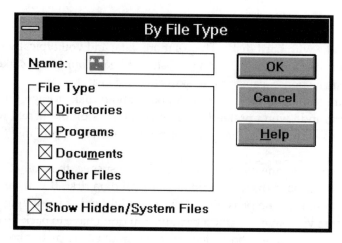

Figure 3.10   The Windows File Manager program lets you view a file's attributes.

```
┌──────────────────────────────────────────────────────────────────┐
│ ▭                    Properties for IO.SYS                         │
├──────────────────────────────────────────────────────────────────┤
│                                                                    │
│  File Name:      IO.SYS                    ┌──────────────────┐   │
│  Size:           40,774 bytes              │       OK         │   │
│  Last Change:    5/31/94  6:22:00AM        └──────────────────┘   │
│  Path:           C:\                       ┌──────────────────┐   │
│                                            │     Cancel       │   │
│  ┌─Attributes──────────────────────┐      └──────────────────┘   │
│  │                                  │      ┌──────────────────┐   │
│  │  ☒ Read Only    ☒ Hidden         │      │      Help        │   │
│  │  ☐ Archive      ☒ System         │      └──────────────────┘   │
│  └──────────────────────────────────┘                            │
│                                                                    │
└──────────────────────────────────────────────────────────────────┘
```

Figure 3.11   The file Properties window from Windows File Manager.

Do not change a file's attributes unless you are sure that you want to do so. Also keep in mind that although the Read-Only and Hidden attributes can be used to prevent other users from altering or finding certain files, it is also easy to circumvent these precautions using Windows File Manager, so don't rely on them for critical or confidential applications and files. Other more robust forms of security such as encryption provide better security.

The boot files have changed a bit for Windows 95. Many people have the wrong impression that because Windows 95 replaces both DOS and Windows 3.x, DOS is dead and we're not going to use it anymore. In fact, DOS has simply gone into hiding. Instead of the two hidden files—IO.SYS and MSDOS.SYS—there is now just a single system IO.SYS file. And although your computer no longer needs CONFIG.SYS and AUTOEXEC.BAT files under Windows 95, they are "preserved for backward compatibility with certain applications and drivers," as Microsoft states in the *Windows 95 Resource Kit.* What this really means is that Windows 95 doesn't know how to use a lot of the hardware that's out there, and that some DOS and Windows programs rely on certain DOS functions and features, so DOS is really alive and well and living under an assumed name under Windows 95.

So one reason that your disk may not boot is that the system files may have been lost or corrupted. The first step to try is to boot using a floppy disk—your Emergency Floppy Disk that I'll describe later on would be a good choice—and see if you can access your hard disk at all. If you can, use the DOS SYS command to refresh the boot files, and try to reboot.

Partitions and the Master Boot Record

If you can't access the hard disk at all after booting from a floppy, you will want to verify that the partition information is intact. Use the FDISK /STATUS command for a readout of the current partition information. This shows what logical drives are defined.

Some people have been told never to run FDISK because it can cause you to lose all your data if you mess up the partition information, and this is generally good advice. But what most people don't know is that with the /STATUS parameter, the program only *reads* the partition information and thus there is no way that it can *alter* the data.

If the correct drives are listed, run FDISK (without the /STATUS parameter) and choose 4, Display Partition Information, on the menu (Figure 3.12). Make sure that you have a partition marked PRI DOS (for Primary DOS) and that it has an A in the Status column to indicate that it is active.

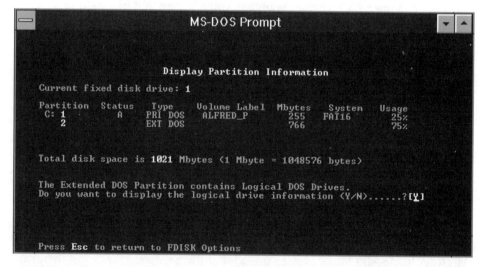

Figure 3.12 The FDISK Display Partition Information option shows more detail about the status of your disk's partitions.

If all this is okay, try refreshing the Master Boot Record. Use the FDISK /MBR command at the DOS prompt. Disk repair utilities such as Norton Disk Doctor can fix problems under these circumstances.

Configuration problems

If you have not been able to access the hard disk at all and FDISK cannot find it, it may be that your computer CMOS configuration has been corrupted. Use your computer's configuration utility (it may be a program in the ROM BIOS that you access with a keystroke during the boot-up process or after it is complete, or by executing a separate program.)

If you don't have the documentation explaining how to do this and you can't get the information from the manufacturer, you can use a commercial program (such as DiagSoft as listed in Appendix A), or a shareware or public domain CMOS editing utility. Lots are available on bulletin boards and services such as CompuServe and ZD Net (which are also listed in Appendix A).

Check to make sure that your hard disk is configured correctly in the CMOS settings. SCSI drives typically are set up as "Not Installed" because the controller takes care of communicating with the drive, but most other types—including IDE drives—need to have a drive type entry in the CMOS settings. Some use a predefined entry; others need to have user-defined settings where you enter the drive's track and sector information. It helps if you have written these down ahead of time. If you haven't, you may be able to find the information in your documentation or by calling the manufacturer. Some new motherboards actually can interrogate the hard disk and find out what the correct entry should be.

If you don't have the specifications on your hard disk, you can take your case apart and find out the model number of the drive, and then find out the specifications from a reference or the manufacturer. Or you can accomplish essentially the same thing without taking the case apart. SpinRite 3.1 from Gibson Research (see Appendix A) has the ability to interrogate your hard disk drive and determine its configuration. This is the information you need to make a user-defined entry in your CMOS configuration.

Physical Problems

Now we're getting to serious trouble: You can't access your hard disk, yet the CMOS configuration is set correctly. It's time to take off the computer case cover.

Turn on the power to the computer; do you hear or feel (put your fingers on it lightly) the hard disk spinning up to speed? Don't be distracted by the sounds of cooling fans.

A stethoscope would be handy here, but a simple drinking straw does an adequate job of giving you a fine, directional listening device—the thick, plastic ones found in sports drinking bottles are especially effective.

If the drive is not spinning, check the power connection carefully. Try a different power connector. If it still isn't powering up, it may be dead. Check the Disaster Recovery section later in this chapter.

If there's power to the drive, check the data cable connections. With the power off, reseat the cables, and even reseat the controller card in its slot. If possible, try the drive with a different controller, or a different drive with the controller. Run any diagnostic program you might have that can test the controller and make sure that it is working correctly. If none of this reveals the source of the trouble, it's time for professional help.

Format Problems

Perhaps your hard disk boots, but when trying to load or save a file you get a message such as "data error reading drive C:", or "sector not found reading drive C:". These messages are also preceded by what may sound like a grinding noise from the disk drive. The noise is the result of the hard drive doing the technological equivalent of the old comedy routine triple-take. It expects to be able to read (or write) the file data at a certain location, but the operation fails. It goes back to the FAT entry to make sure it has the right location, and tries again. After trying a number of times, it gives up.

The most likely cause is a relatively isolated problem on a portion of the disk's surface. Back up the files that you need (or everything) and then run a disk diagnostic program. The DOS SCANDISK is good, or you can use any of the commercial utilities that I've mentioned so far. These programs can locate bad sectors and generally can move the data to fresh portions of the disk that are not damaged.

In the worst of cases, you may have to reformat the hard disk (or a partition of it) either to refresh the format information or to lock out larger areas of bad sectors. Some programs, such as SpinRite, can do this without erasing your data, but don't rely on this feature as justification for not backing up your critical data first. Something still can go terribly wrong (like a loss of power), and you can lose some or all of your data.

File Problems

Finally, you can have file problems. Sometimes DOS or application programs get confused. They may write to a cluster that is already occupied by a different file. They use clusters and then fail to make an appropriate entry in the disk directory, or fail to mark the clusters as available when they delete a file. You can get crosslinked files, lost clusters, and all sorts of other problems with the file storage system.

DOS SCANDISK, Norton Disk Doctor, and the other disk repair utilities all can do an excellent job of recovering from these types of errors. The easiest thing to do is simply start them and let them repair what they can. In the case of a crosslinked file, you almost invariably lose some of one or both files involved, but you typically can recover some of the data.

Deleted by accident   If you should delete a file by accident, don't open or save any other files! Run an undelete utility (DOS 6.x comes with one) right away because if another file overwrites the cluster entries in the FAT, your data will be lost forever. (When DOS deletes a file, it doesn't actually *erase* the data; it simply marks the clusters where it is stored as "unused." When a new file needs to be saved, DOS then uses those clusters, overwriting the original data that was part of the deleted file.)

Here's a trick that's related to files but not in the way that you would expect. It has to do with files that *should* be deleted but aren't. If you are working in Windows, many large applications create temporary files while working with large amounts of data. Word for Windows does this, for example. The files may be stored in the directory assigned as TEMP in your DOS environment—type SET at the DOS prompt to see what the current setting is—or they may be stored in a working directory. Most of these files have names that begin with a tilde (~), and most end with the .TMP extension.

When you close an application and Windows normally, these files are erased as part of the housekeeping routines. If Windows or the application should crash, however, these files do *not* get erased. This is handy to know so that you can go and erase all of them and recover lots of hard disk space, but it can also serve another purpose. If the program crashed *before* you had a chance to save your work, you may be able to open the temporary file and recover it. Word for Windows temporary files, for example, have lots of the most recently typed text. You can open these files with Windows Write, and cut and paste the data to a new file or right into a Word document.

Even if you can't find your work in a temporary file, you may be able to find it in the Windows permanent swap file. This is a hidden file in the root directory of your hard disk and is called 386SPART.PAR. It will be huge, but you can open it with Windows Write and use the Find command to search for a relevant word. If you have been running lots of applications and Windows has had to use the virtual memory of the swap file, you may be able to find some useful fragments.

These two tricks have saved *my* bacon more than once.

The Emergency Disk

> I don't try to describe the future. I try to prevent it.
>
> Ray Bradbury
> Quoted by Arthur C. Clarke in the *Independent*, July 16, 1992

Speaking of saving bacon, here's a simple step you can take to buy yourself a lot of insurance against future disk problems: Create an Emergency Disk. This disk should allow you to boot your system and get as much of it running as possible in the event of a hard disk problem.

At the very least, this is a bootable floppy that you can use to start your computer using the *exact same version* of DOS that you have on your hard disk. This version requirement may seem silly, but you can't mix the system files of different versions and have them work correctly. So whenever you change the version of DOS on your hard disk, update your Emergency Disk as well.

You should also keep current copies of your CONFIG.SYS and AUTOEXEC.BAT files, plus copies of any programs or drivers called by those two files. And you should add the following DOS programs: FDISK.EXE, FOR-MAT.COM, SYS.COM, SCANDISK.EXE, and SCANDISK.INI. If you're running Windows 3.x, it is a good idea to copy all your .INI and .GRP files from your Windows directory as well because you'll need them to recover any customized settings. (If you don't have room for all those files, SYSTEM.INI and WIN.INI are the two most important ones to save.)

You can also create an Emergency Disk using some of the commercial utilities, but make sure that the end result has these listed items at the very least. The commercial programs may also back up your CMOS configuration settings, which can be an easy way to restore them if they should become corrupted. You can also get shareware CMOS store and reload utilities that perform a similar function if you don't want to spring for the commercial packages.

Once you have created this disk, keep it handy. Some people tape it to the bottom or inside of their computer case so it stays with it. You can also take a plastic storage bag with a locking edge and tape that to the case, and in addition to your Emergency Disk, add copies of essential documentation, CMOS settings, tech support phone numbers, and any other essential information that you won't want to have to go digging for when things go wrong.

Also, remember to keep your Emergency Disk up to date. When you add a new CD-ROM drive, change sound cards, or upgrade your version of DOS, make sure you update the disk as well. Having an out-of-date Emergency Disk can be only slightly better than not having one at all.

Backup Problems

> Trust everybody, but cut the cards.
>
> Finley Peter Dunne
> *Mr. Dooley's Philosophy*, 1900

We make backups and hope that we never use them. They're a lot like fire alarms and parachutes (unless, of course, you're a skydiver)—how can you be certain that they will work when you need them?

The answer is to verify the backups before you need them. If you are using a "live" storage medium like an optical disk, you can read the data right on your computer and even use a utility to compare the contents of two files to verify that they match.

Tape is a bit more difficult because you generally can't access the data right off the tape (and it would be so slow that you wouldn't want to, anyway). You typically have to restore a file to a disk before you can compare it. Still, I recommend that you do this with your backups to make sure that the files can be restored reliably.

If you have a backup device from which you are trying to restore and something goes awry, you may be able to read the backup on another device or on another computer. If this fails, contact your backup drive's manufacturer; many offer data recovery services and they may be able to get your data back . . . for a fee.

Trust, but verify.

Disaster Recovery

> Never confuse movement with action.
>
> Ernest Hemingway, quoted by A. E. Hotchner
> *Papa Hemingway,* 1966

A disaster on your hard disk may be recoverable, too, though you'll need to go to a third-party service for this. Even if you hear a terrible grinding and the drive stops spinning and when you take the drive out of the computer and can hear little bits rattling about inside, don't give up. Even if one of the platters in your hard disk is hopelessly trashed, the chances are good that the other surfaces are undamaged.

Recovery services can take your disk apart in a "clean room" environment, reassemble it with new components, and read whatever data that can be salvaged from the surviving surfaces. This is not an inexpensive service, as you might imagine, and you won't have your data back the same day, which makes it far more expensive and inconvenient than a good backup system. But if you don't have a backup system, it's much better than nothing, especially if the data has strategic or financial importance for your business, and it would cost more to re-create the data from scratch than it would to recover whatever you can. I don't have a specific service to recommend. You can find ads for them in major magazines, especially *PC Week* and *InfoWorld,* and I would recommend that you call a few to find out what their fees and terms are.

One important point: Although these outfits can work wonders with drives that have been erased and even reformatted, don't push your luck. The instant that you think you might have a serious problem that needs this type of service, turn off your computer and take out the drive. If you go reinstalling DOS and Windows and mucking about with the files, you stand a good chance of overwriting—and thus obliterating—the very data that you want to save.

When in doubt, *don't!*

UPGRADING

Next to questions about CPUs and motherboards, I get more questions about storage upgrades than anything else. Just as a house can never have enough closet space or kitchen cabinets, so it is with room to stuff our data and our programs.

I suspect that if we were tidier and less inclined to hang onto that old version of the software and all of last year's memos, we might not face the perennial shortage of disk space. (Watch what happens when someone suffers a catastrophic hard disk failure, and see how little of that "old stuff" gets reinstalled.)

The only saving grace of the situation is that the prices for storage have dropped steadily over the years like an out-going tide that never comes back in. So no matter what you have, it seems as though it's always a good time to think about upgrading your storage.

Hard Disks

> Animals can be driven crazy by placing too many in too small a pen. Homo sapiens is the only animal that voluntarily does this to himself.
>
> Robert Heinlein
> *The Notebooks of Lazarus Long*, 1973

The important question about adding a hard disk is: How big? The important answer is: How much can you spend? The key is to figure a budget and then shop. If you look at the per-megabyte price of hard disks, you'll find a dip where the unit price hits bottom and then starts to rise again. The closer you can get to buying at that optimal point, the more bytes you'll get for your dollar.

It really doesn't make sense to buy anything much smaller than 500MB these days, and with 1GB drives selling for under $350, the cost increment to reach that level probably is not a budget-buster for most users.

Here's another dark secret. I don't buy new hard disks for my own use. I buy used, refurbished drives.

Now, this is definitely not for everyone. These drives have only a 90-day warranty (which is plenty for me but may not be enough for you) and come with virtually no support. And I don't know where these drives have been or if anything is wrong with them. Some of them may even be new and are just surplus stock that have made it into the remainder market. The reason I do it is the same reason why someone will buy a late model used car; somebody else has paid the bulk of the depreciation that comes from driving a new car off the dealer's lot, and you get a nearly new ride for much less than the new purchase price. (Yes, I'm cheap.)

You also have to know what you're doing. Many times a used drive will be offered at a price that is close to the new price—used equipment dealers get squeezed badly by the falling prices of new hard disks. But the bargains are there if you want to look for them. Three good sources for used, refurbished, and surplus equipment are *Processor, Computer Hot Line*, and *Compu-Mart*. (See Appendix A for details.)

After you decide how much hard disk you want to buy, you have to decide about the interface. If you have an older interface, such as MFM or ESDI, I strongly recommend that you consider changing to IDE or SCSI. The premium you would pay for a new drive for the older interface is often more than it would cost to buy a new interface with a less expensive drive. If you already have SCSI or IDE, I would recommend that you stick with whatever you have.

Picking the interface

If you are going to make a change, I would recommend going with IDE if you are just going to have one or two hard disks. If you are going to add a CD-ROM drive, I recommend EIDE with two channels. If you are going to add CD-ROM and a backup device (other than one that plugs into a parallel port) or a scanner or any other device that comes in a SCSI version, I would recommend the SCSI interface because it is more powerful and flexible than the EIDE interface.

Adding an IDE or EIDE Drive

If you're adding an IDE drive, the first question is whether or not you have a connector available for it. As described earlier in this chapter, IDE is a single-channel interface, and it can support up to two devices: one Master, and one Slave. If you already have two IDE devices installed in your system, you cannot use a regular IDE interface for the third. Instead, you will need to use an EIDE adapter to add a second IDE channel.

There are two ways you can go to add the second IDE channel. The first way is to simply add an interface card that provides just the second channel. This approach makes good sense if you have an available expansion slot and you are happy with the existing IDE interface. The other way to go, however, is to add an EIDE controller with both channels, and scrap your existing IDE interface. If your existing IDE interface is on an expansion card, this approach has the additional advantage of not requiring any more expansion slots.

Adding EIDE

The new EIDE interface has one more advantage that may outweigh all other factors, because it may make it easier to add a drive larger than 528MB.

Block party

One of DOS's limitations is that it cannot address a storage device that has more than 1024 cylinders, 16 heads, 63 sectors per track, and 512 bytes per sector. If you multiply 1024 times 16 times 63 times 512, you get 528,482,304 bytes, which is 528MB the way that disk manufacturers measure it. (Divide this by 1,048,576 to get "true" megabytes, and you get 504MB, which explains why you will see this listed sometimes as the upper limit for DOS.)

There are four ways to get around this limitation. The best is if your computer motherboard's BIOS includes support for a feature called **logical block addressing, or LBA.** Second, if your motherboard does not have LBA, you may be able to upgrade the BIOS to add support for this feature.

Another way to get around the limitation is to use a special software driver, which is often provided by vendors with their large hard disk drives. I don't particularly like this solution as much as the others because the driver must be loaded as part of your CONFIG.SYS file and this consumes precious system memory.

If your motherboard does not support LBA and a BIOS upgrade isn't feasible or you're planning to buy a new interface card anyway, I recommend that you purchase an EIDE card that has an on-board BIOS that supports LBA. In fact, this is a good idea even if you're not adding a drive larger than 500MB because the extra cost is small and it will make future expansion or upgrades easier.

Assigning roles   Okay, so now you've got an IDE disk that you want to add to your system, and you have an IDE connection available. What next?

First, there's the question of which connection to use. If you have an IDE CD-ROM (also sometimes referred to as an ATAPI drive), place it on the *secondary* EIDE channel; for best performance, only use the primary channel for hard disks.

Next, make sure your jumper settings are correct on your drives. Your existing drive may need to have its jumpers changed from "Master" to "Master with Slave Present," so you'll need to check the documentation or with the drive manufacturer to make sure. Set up your new drive as "Slave" and connect it to your IDE interface.

The next step is to partition and format your drive, which I'll get to after I cover how to install a SCSI drive.

Adding a SCSI Drive

SCSI drives are easier to configure than IDE drives in some ways because the intelligence in the SCSI controller eliminates the problem of the DOS 528MB hard disk size limit. On the other hand, when you add a SCSI drive, you need to check two settings: ID number and termination.

Each device on a SCSI chain has to have a unique ID number, from 0 through 7. Many SCSI adapters come with software that will poll your existing SCSI devices and report which IDs are already in use by which devices. If you have one of these utilities, I recommend that you use it before setting the ID on your new SCSI drive. The alternative is to check each device (including the interface card) individually, which can be time consuming.

It's easiest to set the termination if you install your new device in the middle of the SCSI chain rather than at the end. The reason is that you know your existing installation is working correctly, so all you should have to do is remove the termination from the new device. If you were to install the new device at the end of the chain, however, you would have to make sure that the new device is terminated correctly *and* remove the termination from the device that had been at the end of the chain.

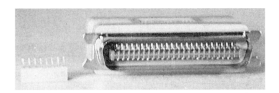

Figure 3.13 Internal SCSI devices use different kinds of terminators, including resistor strips like the one on the left; whereas external SCSI devices often use a terminating plug like the one on the right.

If you have an internal device, it may set its termination automatically, or you may need to set a jumper, or you may have to install or remove a resistor strip as shown in Figure 3.13. If the SCSI device is external, you may need to use a terminating plug like the one in the picture.

Before you can use a SCSI hard disk, you need to low-level format it. You probably have a low-level format utility that came either with your hard disk or with your SCSI interface. If not, contact the SCSI interface manufacturer and see if one is available.

Partitioning Your New Drive

Your next step is to run FDISK to partition the new disk; make sure that you don't inadvertently alter the partitions for your existing disk.

People sometimes get a bit baffled by how DOS assigns disk drive letters to partitions. Here's the sequence:

1. The first two letters are assigned to your floppy disk drive(s). If you don't have two drives, the second one is assigned as a logical drive using the first drive.

2. The next letter, C:, is assigned to the Primary DOS partition on the first physical hard disk drive.

3. The next letter (or letters) are assigned to the Primary DOS partitions on subsequent physical hard disk drives.

4. The next letter (or letters) are assigned to the logical drives that have been set up in the Extended DOS partition in the first physical drive.

5. The next letter (or letters) are assigned to the logical drives that have been set up in the Extended DOS partitions of subsequent physical drives.

6. Finally, letters are assigned to any drives that are established through DOS drivers, such as CD-ROM drives.

This is easier to understand with a concrete example. Let's say you have a typical installation with a hard disk and a CD-ROM. You have partitioned the hard disk so that it has a Primary DOS partition (so you can boot from it) and then you have divided the Extended DOS partition into two logical drives (because you want to keep the cluster size small). You also have a CD-ROM drive. Drive C: will be assigned to your Primary DOS partition on the hard disk. Drives D: and E: will be the two logical drives in the Extended Partition, and the CD-ROM drive will be Drive F:.

Now, let's install another hard disk of the same size and with the same partition arrangement. The Drive C: assignment will be unchanged, but Drive D: will now be assigned to the Primary DOS partition on the second hard disk. Drives E: and F: will be assigned to the logical drives in the first drive's Extended DOS partition, and Drives G: and H: will be assigned to the two logical drives in the Extended DOS partition on the second hard drive. And bringing up the end of the line will be the CD-ROM, now assigned as Drive I:.

There's no avoiding the fact that you may have to change the configuration of some programs after adding a new hard disk because the drive assignments will change. You can avoid this "ping-pong" effect between drives, however, where the drive letters are not assigned to the physical drives in sequence.

In our same example, if you do not configure a Primary DOS partition on the new hard disk, but instead make three logical drives in an Extended DOS partition, the drive assignments may seem more sensible and have less impact on your software configuration. In this case, the partitions on the original disk will remain C:, D:, and E:, and the new drive's partitions will be assigned letters F:, G:, and H:. The CD-ROM will still end up being Drive I:, and that's unavoidable.

The only downside with this approach is that you will not be able to make the second drive bootable because it won't have a Primary DOS partition. For most people, however, this won't be a hardship, and you may find that the more "logical" assignment of the drive letters is more important.

Now all you have to do is use FORMAT to format the new logical drives on your hard disk, and you're ready to run.

Backups

As described earlier in this chapter, the type of backup device you choose is not nearly as important as the fact that you have a backup system at all. But since you do have some choices, here are some guidelines.

Pick a medium that provides a low per-megabyte cost, yet that also has fairly fast performance. You're not likely to use a backup system that requires lots of time.

Make sure that the medium can hold a sufficient amount of data. In general, this is the maximum capacity of your largest logical disk. In my particular case, I have a gigabyte drive in my main computer, but I really only need a backup device with 255MB capacity because I have partitioned my drive into four logical drives. I can always use a larger capacity device by making separate sections for the different drives, but I don't *need* that much space.

As I have already indicated, I have a strong preference for "live" data storage because I can get more use out of my backup device. Not only can I use it to store copies of my day-to-day work, but I can also store rarely used data on it and use that data directly in my applications when I want it—without having to restore it to my hard disk first. For example, I have a huge collection of clip art files that I have consolidated from all the smaller collections that have come bundled with many of my application programs. I don't use my collection very often, but when I do, I want to have access to all the files. I'm willing to put up with slower access for these files than I'd get from my big hard disk, in return for the convenience of being able to use them when I need them. For me, the answer is removable disk media, not tape. But as the saying goes, your mileage may vary.

Choosing the medium

Once you have decided what type of storage device you want to use, you have to figure out how to hook it up to your computer. Many tape drives attach either to your floppy disk controller or to a separate, proprietary interface. This can be convenient and easy, though it does not always give the fastest performance.

Choosing the interface

If you have more than one computer, an external device that plugs into a parallel port can be handy because you can then move it from machine to machine. On the other hand, if you have a local network or a file exchange hook-up (like Interlink or LapLink) between your machines, you may be able to use a device that is installed in a single machine to back up the others.

My preference—for performance and cost reasons—is for a device that connects with my existing storage controller, either EIDE or SCSI. My reasoning is that this simplifies installation and configuration, reduces the chances of conflicts within my computer's hardware, and will most likely give me the fastest backup and restore performance (as well as the fastest access to archived data when I want to use it as live data, like my clip art).

As I discovered when I got my first Bernoulli Box, you can never have too many backup cartridges (or disks, or tapes, or whatever your device uses). I find that it is a good idea to have a rotating set for complete backups because you sometimes don't discover that you have a problem in your system until after you've gone through one or two backup cycles. If you have more than one generation of backups, you may still have a good copy of the files in question.

Never too much

If you're using the backup system to access archived data, you may find that you need lots of cartridges for this purpose, especially when you discover how well it works for those rarely used applications that eat up so much space on your hard disk.

Whatever you decide to do—from saving individual files on floppies to doing complete system backups—make a plan and stick to it. It's cheaper and easier to spend some time backing up your data now than it is to reconstruct it all after it's been lost.

4 Displays

Lead, kindly Light, amid the encircling gloom

John Henry Newman

I vaguely remember our first television set. My father was always interested in electronics, and I guess we were close enough to one of the early broadcast sources, but all I can recall is a large cabinet with a small glass window on which small moving images would appear. It was magic.

The same technology that made those early pictures possible now sits on millions and millions of desks around the world, an essential part of the microcomputer revolution. If we were still bound by the slow and noisy output of a Teletype machine to find out what goes on inside our computers, most of us would still be working with pencil and paper. The display is our best window on the world of information that lies inside our computers.

Fortunately the huge market for television sets has made the production of computer displays relatively inexpensive, and the units themselves are incredibly reliable; I have had only one computer monitor fail, and that breakdown was most likely caused by trying to work in a small office in the middle of a mid-Atlantic summer heat wave without air conditioning.

Unfortunately the whole area of displays and adapters is probably one of the most misunderstood in all of personal computerdom, which leaves people more puzzled than usual when it comes to troubleshooting or purchasing a new display.

NEED TO KNOW

We are all hungry and thirsty for concrete images.

Salvador Dalí
Diary of a Genius, 1966

Several different technologies are now used to display information from a personal computer, including liquid crystals and other exotic designs. I'll cover flat panel displays in Chapter 8, Portable Stuff, but for this chapter I'll simply focus on the traditional computer monitor and the graphics adapters that provide the images that they display.

CRT Specifications

There are some different TLAs that people use for desktop monitors: VDT is a *video display terminal* and CRT is a *cathode ray tube*. The first is a functional description, but the second is a more technical term that describes how it works, which is why I prefer to use CRT. The parts of the term CRT are as follows:

- "Cathode" refers to an electrode within the tube that emits the electron ray.

- "Ray" refers to an electronic ray or beam. It sounds like something out of Flash Gordon, but a stream of electrons (or three streams, in most cases) is responsible for creating the image you see on your screen.

- "Tube" refers to the vacuum tube that the screen uses. One reason that screens are heavy is that it takes a lot of glass to withstand the pressures caused by the vacuum inside the screen.

If you have picked up a computer magazine or walked into a computer store lately, you may have noticed that lots of different monitors are available. One of the best ways to understand how a CRT works is to understand the differences in monitor features.

Screen Size

> No city should be too large for a man to walk out of in a morning.
>
> Cyril Connolly
> *The Unquiet Grave*, 1944

Monitor size is specified by the diagonal measure of the front of the CRT. This is not the same as the size of the image on the screen because the image cannot reach all the way out to the corners of the tube. The size of the screen does have something to do with how much information you can put on the screen at once, but it's only part of the story. The image resolution also plays a part; two monitors with the same resolution will show the same amount of information, even if one is twice the size of the other.

Geometric growth
Another important fact to keep in mind is that as the diagonal size increases, so do other important dimensions. The typical computer monitor has a case that is about as deep as the diagonal measure of the screen, so if you get a 17-inch monitor (which seems to be a popular size these days), remember that it needs

about a foot and a half of clear space behind the point where you want the front of the screen to be. That's more than most desktops can accommodate if the desk is pushed up against a wall, as is often the case.

The best I can manage here in the Electronic Cottage is room for 15-inch displays, but I can get two of them side by side on my desk so that I can use two computers at one time. I know that sounds sick, but when I'm testing products or experimenting with different solutions to hardware problems, it helps to have a separate testbench system in addition to the one that I write on, and I like to have the two keyboards and monitors next to each other so I don't have to move.

Dot Pitch and Its Relationship to Resolution

Now we come to the part that gets people confused. I'll start with the punchline: There is no correlation between dot pitch and resolution or the size of the pixels on your screen. The first part is a physical characteristic of your monitor; the rest exists only as a logical concept and a signal created by your graphics adapter. Now to explain what all that means to you, and why you should care.

How does a computer monitor create an image? The stream of electrons inside the tube travels from the electrode and smacks into the inside surface of the screen. That surface is coated with special chemicals called **phosphors** that glow when excited by an electrical current. By turning the stream of electrons on and off and by directing the narrow stream across the inside of the screen, back and forth, in horizontal lines, an image of glowing phosphors can be painted on the screen.

That healthy chemical glow

In the early days of the IBM PC, we often used monochrome monitors. They had phosphors that glowed either green or yellow, which created text in those colors on a black background. When desktop publishing took off later, users wanted monitors that looked like paper, so the "paper-white" monitors were developed. These use phosphors that glow white, and so you get black and white monochrome displays.

Phosphor placement is easy on a monochrome monitor; simply paint the whole inside of the front face of the tube with the chemicals, and when electrons hit the surface, that part glows.

The problem with color monitors is considerably more complicated, however. Color monitors, like your home color television set, have three different types of phosphors, which glow red, green, or blue, depending on their chemical composition. (Combine red, green, and blue light and you get white light. I won't go into the details here, but if you want to know more about color, check out M. David Stone's *The Underground Guide to Color Printers,* which explains this and a lot more.)

But you can't simply "paint" a surface with all three types of phosphors; you need to place them precisely so that they can be hit with electrons. Monitors have to have the phosphor coatings made in small dots with precise placement.

Taking aim with electrons

Color monitors have three separate electron guns, one for each color phosphor. The electron streams from these guns pass through a screen or mask, so that the electrons from one gun will only hit the phosphors of one color.

Figure 4.1 shows a little experiment that demonstrates how the electron masks in a monitor work. Take a white Post-it or a sheet of white paper, make two quarter-inch dots of different colors about a half inch apart, and stick it on a wall. Punch a hole in the edge of a card or sheet of paper with a hole punch (or use some three-hole notebook paper). Hold this card (or sheet) out about arm's length, so that it is about six to nine inches from the Post-it (or paper) with the dots on the wall. Close (or cover) your left eye, and move the paper so that you can see the left dot. Now close (or cover) your right eye and look with the left eye, and you should see the right dot. One hole can restrict the view of two eyes so that they each can just see one dot.

The screen in the monitor works the same way, except it's like you have a third eye in the middle of your forehead; it would see a dot in a third position, below and between the other two.

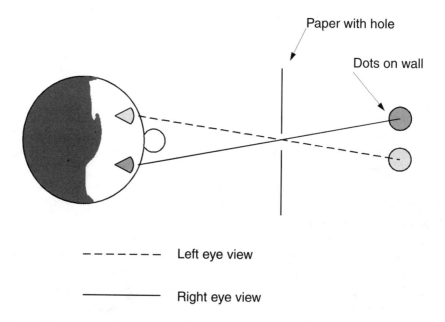

Figure 4.1   You can perform a simple experiment that demonstrates how a dot mask works.

A typical monitor uses a dot mask to screen the electrons, with the holes evenly spaced to form a pattern that looks triangular or hexagonal (depending on your point of view). The phosphors are then arranged in sets of three—or **triads**—to line up precisely with each of these holes. Figure 4.2 shows the layout of the phosphors in a typical screen.

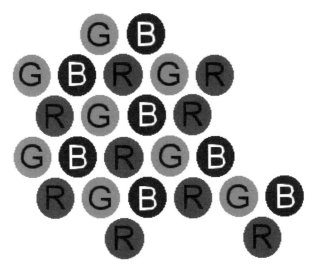

Figure 4.2   Phosphors in a typical monitor are arranged in triangular groups of three (R = red, G = green, B = blue).

Okay, now here is where dot pitch enters the story. The spacing between the dots is known as the **pitch** (in the same way that pitch refers to the spacing of letters on a typewriters). (You *do* remember typewriters, don't you?) The **dot pitch** is the distance from the center of one phosphor dot of a given color to the center of the next nearest dot of the same color. (Except at the edges, there should be three other closest dots of the same color that are all the same distance, as shown in Figure 4.2.) Consider these two points:

1. Dot pitch is a physical characteristic; it does not change when you change the resolution of your software.

2. The dot pitch of the monitor must be small enough to display the resolution image you are trying to paint on it. Just as it's nearly impossible to endorse a check when all you have to write with is a 3-inch wide paintbrush, you cannot display a white pixel on a monitor's screen unless the beams for that pixel hit at least one of each of the three different color phosphor dots. That is, the phosphor dots must be sufficiently small to be able to represent a pixel. If they are too large—like drawing with a fat paintbrush—they can't depict the image.

> It is not, truly speaking, the labour that is divided; but the men: divided into mere segments of men—broken into small fragments and crumbs of life, so that all the little piece of intelligence that is left in a man is not enough to make a pin, or a nail, but exhausts itself in making the point of a pin or the head of a nail.
>
> John Ruskin
> *The Stones of Venice*, 1851–1853

Dots enough!   So how do you decide what dot pitch is sufficiently small?

You can start by figuring out how big your pixels are. Take the width of the image on your screen, and divide by the horizontal resolution. On a typical 14-inch diagonal monitor, the image area is about 265 mm wide. At VGA resolution, there are 640 dots in that horizontal space, making each one about .41 mm wide.

For a good quality image, you want to make sure that there is *at least* one phosphor triad for every pixel; one and a third triads is a good rule of thumb. If you look at Figure 4.2 again, you'll see that the horizontal distance between adjacent phosphors of the same color is actually a bit less than the dot pitch spacing. As a result, you can display adjacent white pixels at something less than the dot pitch. Factor in the extra one-third triad, mix with some trigonometry, and you come up with the following formula for recommended maximum dot pitch:

```
max. dot pitch = 0.87 × image width / number of horizontal
pixels
```

Be sure to measure the image width in millimeters. Since dot pitch is reported using metric measurements, I stuck with them for this calculation. If you pick a monitor with a dot pitch that is larger than the recommended size, you run the risk of the images looking coarse or grainy. To avoid this, either pick a monitor with a finer dot pitch or run the larger dot pitch monitor at a lower resolution. The formula can be applied to any monitor size and display resolution. The calculations for a number of popular values are listed in Table 4.1.

Table 4.1   Recommended maximum dot pitch measurements for various monitor sizes and display resolutions.

Monitor Size	Image Width	Resolution: horizontal × vertical			
(Diagonal)	(Horizontal)	640 × 480	800 × 600	1024 × 768	1280 × 1024
14 inches	265mm	0.36mm	0.29mm	0.23mm	0.18mm
15	284	0.39	0.31	0.24	0.19
17	322	0.44	0.35	0.27	0.22
20	379	0.52	0.41	0.32	0.26

We're almost out of the woods on this one, but we have to consider another type of monitor.

Stripe Pitch

Some monitors use a stripe mask instead of a dot mask. These monitors use CRTs based on Sony Trinitron or similar designs, in which the three electron guns are side by side. To let each one see just one color phosphor, the mask has fine, vertical slits instead of a series of holes. The phosphors themselves are also arranged in vertical stripes, as shown in Figure 4.3. These screens do not have a dot pitch measurement, but instead have a stripe pitch measurement, which is the distance from the center of a phosphor stripe of a given color to the center of the next phosphor stripe of that same color. Assuming everything else is equal, you need a smaller stripe pitch than you need dot pitch on the same size monitors running at the same resolution.

Slot mask monitors

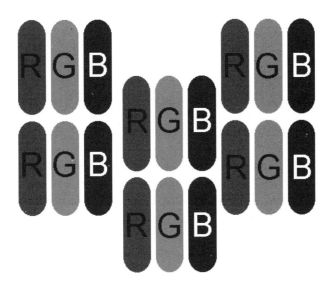

Figure 4.3 Sony Trinitron and other CRT designs use in-line electron guns, so the phosphors are arranged in vertical stripes (R = red, G = green, B = blue).

A stripe mask monitor cannot produce a white pixel that is narrower than the stripe pitch. If all three phosphors are not illuminated, you can't get a white pixel. Apply the same one-and-a-third rule of thumb for stripe masks and you get the maximum recommended stripe pitches listed in Table 4.2.

Table 4.2 Recommended maximum stripe pitch measurements for various monitor sizes and display resolutions.

Monitor Size	Image Width	Resolution: horizontal × vertical			
(Diagonal)	(Horizontal)	640 × 480	800 × 600	1024 × 768	1280 × 1024
14 inches	265mm	0.32mm	0.25mm	0.20mm	0.16mm
15	284	0.34	0.27	0.21	0.17
17	322	0.39	0.31	0.24	0.19
20	379	0.46	0.36	0.28	0.23

In practice, many other factors affect image quality, and these can offset the advantages of finer phosphor spacing. If the electron beams are not aligned accurately, or the monitor's electronics cannot produce an image with sufficient fidelity, you can lose picture quality. The best bet is to look at monitors and compare the same image side by side before you buy.

Refresh Rates

> To sit in the shade on a fine day, and look upon verdure is the most perfect refreshment.
>
> Jane Austen
> *Mansfield Park,* 1814

Okay, the next misunderstood monitor topic is **refresh rate.** One reason for the confusion is that we also use the term **scan rate,** which sometimes means the same thing as refresh rate. Another reason is that there are actually two scan rates at any given time.

The refresh rate is the same as the vertical scan rate, and it refers to how many times a second the electron beam (or beams) start over again at the top of the screen to paint the image on the phosphors. This rate is measured in Hertz (Hz), which simply means "times per second." (Hertz actually means "cycles per second," which does not mean that you have to count passing Schwinns or Canondales; instead it is a way that engineers count waves, and you can think of the way that electrons paint the image as a wave.) The refresh rate used on your monitor depends entirely on the signals sent to it from your graphics controller card, but the monitor must also be able to process that signal and produce the image.

Flicker-free   Most signals are sent with a 60 to 72 Hz vertical scan or refresh rate. Speeds of 70 Hz and higher help avoid annoying flicker. Your eyes are more susceptible to flicker toward the periphery of your field of vision. (Why? It has to do with rods and cones on the retina of your eye, and the fact that human eyes are designed to detect motion in peripheral vision as an adaptation either to improve hunting skills or to decrease the chances of becoming some carnivore's dinner.) So people tend to notice flicker more with larger screens because more of the screen image is in your peripheral vision.

The slower 60 Hz refresh rate is also a problem in places with fluorescent lighting. These lights also have a 60 Hz refresh rate, and the interference between these and your monitor can accentuate the flicker problem.

So, in general, you'll want to run your monitor in as high a refresh rate as the monitor and graphics card can manage together.

The other scan rate is the horizontal scan rate, which is measured in thousands of times per second, or KHz. It is the number of times per second that the electron beams start over at the left edge of the screen, ready to paint the next scan line. The horizontal scan rate must be a bit faster than the vertical scan rate times the vertical resolution. In general, however, you won't need to be concerned with this. The key issues for a monitor are the maximum vertical scan rates that it can handle at various resolutions.

You do need to be concerned about the difference between **interlaced** and **noninterlaced** display modes, however. Fortunately few of the newer graphics cards and monitors run in interlaced mode, but they are still out there so you must beware. An interlaced image is painted on the screen in two parts; first the even scan lines are painted, then the odd lines. Therefore it takes two passes to get the complete image. Home televisions use interlaced images, but for a number of reasons—including the fact that television phosphors glow for a while after they're hit with electrons—we tend not to notice the flicker much.

Interlaced images

On a computer screen, however, which has "fast decay" phosphors (they fade quickly after being hit with electrons), the flicker caused by an interlaced image is much more noticeable. Computer monitors resort to interlaced images because this lets them produce the image using less information per second. Thus the electronics do not need to be as powerful or sophisticated as they would need to be to produce a noninterlaced image at the same resolution.

> **It's the slow decay rate of the phosphors that makes some old monochrome monitors poorly suited for graphics and games. The phosphors had such a slow decay rate that moving a mouse pointer around the screen would leave a glowing trail like the wake of a boat at night in a tropical ocean. (The boat's wake glows because millions of tiny sea creatures are bioluminescent—they make light—when disturbed. It even happens in the Chesapeake Bay at certain times of the year.) These old monitors worked great for straight text, but they can be pretty annoying to use for more modern applications.**

If your monitor is running in an interlaced mode, and you cannot get it to work successfully in noninterlaced mode at that resolution, you may need to drop down to a lower resolution to be able to run noninterlaced and thus eliminate the flicker.

Controls

> Television's perfect. You turn a few knobs, a few of those mechanical adjustments at which the higher apes are so proficient, and lean back and drain your mind of all thought.
>
> Raymond Chandler
> *Raymond Chandler Speaking,* 1962

Monitors also differ in the type of controls they use. Almost all monitors rely on analog controls for brightness and contrast, and the less-expensive models also use analog controls for image size and position (Figure 4.4). An analog control is one that uses a variable resistor or similar device, and you can generally identify an analog control because it uses a knob or roller for its adjustments. Analog controls are less expensive to build, but they can only adjust the image for one resolution at a time, and you may have to adjust the image size or position when changing resolutions.

Figure 4.4   Less expensive monitors use analog controls.

More expensive monitors use digital controls, which you usually find as buttons (Figure 4.5). Monitors with digital controls often have the advantage of being able to store settings for multiple resolutions, so that you do not have to make adjustments to the image when changing resolutions.

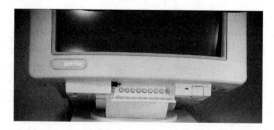

Figure 4.5   More expensive monitors generally use digital controls.

Some monitors with digital controls now offer on-screen menus. They only have a few buttons, and you change their function by following prompts that appear right on your screen. This is much easier than poking around under the edge of the monitor, trying to read the tiny writing on the various controls. A few monitors include little LCD message windows. These can be helpful diagnostic tools, especially when they can report the resolution and scan frequencies in use by the current image.

The best monitors also have controls that let you adjust their screen geometry. This includes straightening the edges of the image if they are curved (**pincushioning** and **barrel distortion**) and making sure that the three electron beams overlap precisely when trying to create a white line (**convergence**).

What About Electromagnetic Emissions?

> If it can't be expressed in figures, it is not science; it is opinion.
>
> Robert Heinlein
> *The Notebooks of Lazarus Long,* 1973

If your mind is already made up about electromagnetic emissions from monitors, go ahead and turn the page. I won't be offended, and there's no need for you to read this next part.

Let me start with an obvious statement: You would be foolish to want a computer monitor that had zero electromagnetic radiation emissions. (If you do want one, let me know because I've got plenty here that I'd be happy to sell to you.) Why do I state this with such confidence? Because visible light is a form of electromagnetic radiation, and I'm fairly certain that you'd not be pleased with a monitor that could not produce an image.

The concern with monitors is about certain kinds of electromagnetic emissions. Let me point out right here that we are *not* talking about **ionizing radiation,** which most everyone accepts as being a potential hazard. Ionizing radiation is the sort that you get from radioactive materials, and it gets its name from the fact that it can strip atomic particles from individual atoms, which can be a bad thing.

But the concern over monitors is not about ionizing radiation, it is simply about electromagnetic radiation—the same stuff as radio waves and light. The waves in question come at the lower range of the electromagnetic spectrum (sort of the opposite of microwaves) and are referred to by their TLAs of VLF (Very Low Frequency) and ELF (Extremely Low Frequency).

These waves are present in the typical environment. They are produced by most electrical motors, by electric blankets, by electric stoves, by computers, and yes, by cathode ray tubes such as computer monitors.

May I take your order?

Swedish standards

Currently three standards for computer monitors want to qualify for low emissions ratings. MPR and MPR II were established in Sweden and for years were the benchmark for low emissions. More recently, the TCO standard was established by the Swedish Confederation of Professional Employees. It sets more stringent limits on the amount and kinds of emissions permitted.

As far as I am aware, these Swedish standards were not based on any scientific studies that demonstrated what levels of emissions are safe or dangerous. Instead, they are based on numbers that were apparently pulled out of the air.

I know firsthand how difficult it can be to measure the emissions from a monitor reliably. Everything from what is displayed on the screen to how you position the measuring device affects the results. And there is also the problem of background levels—emissions that already occur in your environment. These emissions must be eliminated before you can get an accurate reading of a monitor's emissions.

So we are faced with a difficult measurement used to certify that a monitor emits less than a certain amount of electromagnetic radiation, and we don't even know what the safe level is. So if you want to be conservative, go ahead and insist on a TCO-compliant monitor, but do so knowing that you may still have a dangerous monitor, or that you have paid more for a monitor that may be no more or less dangerous than one without any emissions rating.

In my opinion, the health risks from monitor emissions are negligible. There are plenty of occupations where workers are bathed in much, much higher concentrations of VLF and ELF radiation, and yet there appears to be no epidemiological evidence that this is a health risk. There have been some scares in years past about pregnant women and CRT exposure, and the city of San Francisco even passed some stringent laws limiting exposure (a move that received lots of national press exposure). Additional studies, however, have failed to prove a link between emissions and the health problems, and even San Francisco has rescinded the restrictive laws (a move that received somewhat less exposure in the national press).

Fix the bigger problems first.

In my opinion, sitting in any chair for eight or more hours a day is a greater health risk than being near a computer screen for that amount of time. That Twinkie or donut that may be sitting on the corner of your desk is more of a health risk than your monitor. There is strong scientific evidence that poor diet, obesity, lack of exercise, stress, and the use of tobacco products pose significant risks to your health—risk factors many, many times greater than that suggested by even the most ardent supporter of the theory that monitor VLF and ELF emissions are dangerous.

So buy a low emissions monitor if you want, but keep in mind that there are many, many other things that you can probably do in terms of diet and exercise that will have a far greater impact on your health than the simple act of choosing a monitor for your computer. If you're already doing something about those other risk factors, that's terrific and I commend you. If you're not, I respectfully suggest that you pay attention to those before you spend much time worrying about your monitor's emissions.

Display Adapter Specifications

> There is never finality in the display terminal's screen, but an irresponsible whimsicality, as words, sentences, and paragraphs are negated at the touch of a key.
>
> Alexander Cockburn
> *Corruptions of Empire,* 1988

So far, we've only covered the first half of the display equation: the monitor. But how does the computer tell the monitor what to display?

The missing link is the graphics adapter. I used to call these things **video adapters** along with everyone else in the industry, but now that we have special hardware for displaying and recording full-motion video from broadcast television stations and video cameras, it's confusing to use this term so most of us in the industry have switched over to calling them **graphics adapters.** The switch over is confusing too, no doubt, but in the long run, it should help clarify the situation.

Of course, not all display adapters for PCs can display graphic images. The Monochrome Display Adapter (MDA) for the original IBM PC was a text-only display. It is unlikely that you'll run across a text-only adapter these days, however, so we'll focus on the graphics cards.

I'm also going to limit this to a discussion of VGA (Video Graphics Array) or SVGA (Super VGA) adapters. These boards put out an analog signal, which means that the wires carry electrical current that is in the form of waves. I'm leaving out older cards such as the EGA (Enhanced Graphics Adapter), CGA (Color Graphics Adapter), and MGA (Monochrome Graphics Adapter, which is sometimes called a Hercules monochrome adapter), which used digital signals; the electrical signals were either on or off. Digital signals were replaced by analog signals because it would take too many wires to create an image with more than a handful of colors, but just six wires can carry analog signals for an image with more colors than you can distinguish.

Resolution

> Men who wish to know about the world must learn about it in its particular details.
>
> Heraclitus, translated by Guy Davenport
> *Herakleitos and Diogenes,* 1976

Nearly all of a graphics adapter's specifications are interrelated—the limits of one almost surely affect the limits of another. However, let's start with resolution because this is the specification that people seem to be the most interested in when buying.

VGA resolution is actually a number of different resolutions, depending on which mode is in use, but we tend to refer to it by its highest graphics resolution: 640 by 480 pixels. The next popular resolution is 800 by 600, which people often call **Super VGA,** or **SVGA.** The one after that is 1024 by 768, which is sometimes called **XGA** (for the IBM Extended Graphics Array that has this resolution).

VESA to the rescue   In fact, all three of these display resolutions can be rightly called SVGA, or Super VGA. All are covered by specifications developed by the Video and Electronics Standards Association. More commonly known as VESA, this industry organization includes most major manufacturers of displays, adapters, and computers among its membership.

Before the VESA specifications for SVGA, there was little agreement on the signal characteristics for resolutions higher than 640 by 480. (The VESA specification also covers 640 by 480 resolutions for color depths of 256 and higher, which are not part of the original IBM VGA specification.) The specifications include details such as vertical refresh rate, but they also cover more technical timing minutiae that make it possible for the monitor to synchronize correctly with the display adapter's signal.

It's nearly impossible to find a VGA-only card on the market these days. It is also hard to find a card that can only produce a 1024 by 768 image with an interlaced signal (as opposed to the lower-flicker, noninterlaced mode). You will find differences based on resolutions, with some cards going up to 1600 by 1200 or higher. Keep in mind that you need a monitor with an extremely small dot pitch to be able to use these higher resolutions.

Also, although two cards may support the same range of noninterlaced resolutions, one may be able to do so at a higher vertical scan rate than the other. Providing your monitor can handle the higher refresh rates, you will get less flicker from the faster image. The faster card will also likely cost more than the slower one.

Color Depth

There is no blue without yellow and without orange.

Vincent Van Gogh, in a letter, June 1888
The Complete Letters of Vincent Van Gogh, 1958

Another difference between cards is the maximum color depth supported at various resolutions. It takes memory to hold the information that makes up the image. Increasing resolution increases the memory requirements some, but increasing the number of levels of color shades in the image can increase the memory that much faster.

Table 4.3 shows the different color depths in terms of bits per pixel and the number of simultaneous colors supported by that mode.

Table 4.3 Bits per pixel and number of colors.

Bits per pixel	Maximum colors	Use
4	16	Text or very simple graphics.
8	256	Average use—not great for photographs.
16	65,536	Low-end graphics arts—okay for photographs.
24	16,777,216	Excellent for photographic editing.
32	4,294,967,296	You won't be able to see the differences.

A typical system uses a graphics driver for 8-bit color, which provides 256 different colors at a time. (By using an indexed palette, many cards can actually draw on a much larger number of colors, but only display 256 of them at one time.) For most graphics art work such as editing scanned photographic images, 16-bit color is adequate. Since it is moving twice as much data per pixel than an 8-bit mode, there is a performance hit. And 24-bit color—which Carl Sagan might refer to as "millions and millions of colors"—triples the amount of data compared with 256 colors and should only be used on high-power systems that are designed to handle the strains of professional graphic arts tasks.

Most inexpensive cards offer a trade-off between resolution and color. You can have lower resolution with more colors, or you can have higher resolution with not as many colors. Also, the graphics adapter must have sufficient memory on board in order to create an image; more colors and higher resolutions require more memory.

High-res on
small screens

**Some say that you need at least a 17-inch monitor in order to use a higher res-
olution such as 1024 by 768. They complain that the icons and text are too
small on a 14-inch screen at that resolution. They have a good point, but I disagree with them. I find 1024 by 768 with 256 colors to be the ideal combination
for my 14-inch screen.**

When you increase the resolution of display of a given size, you are putting
more information on the screen. There are two ways that you can allocate this increased information, however. In the case of text, for example, you can use the
same number of pixels per character and put more characters on the screen, which
will give you smaller characters but more of them. Or you can put the same number of characters on the screen and use more pixels to make each one, which will
give you the same size and number of characters as before, but they will look
smoother. This second choice is like going from a 150-dot-per-inch printer to a
300- or 600-dpi printer (Figure 4.6).

```
VGA screen    1024 by 768
Sample text   Sample text
```

Figure 4.6   These are enlarged views of text from different resolution displays.
Though both appear to be the same size on the same size monitor, the text in
VGA resolution (on the left) is not as smooth as the text from a 1024 by 768
resolution image (on the right).

As you might imagine, most of my time on the computer is spent dealing
with text. I use Word for Windows, which has a Zoom feature that lets me make
the text any size I want. By viewing it at 100 percent size on a 14-inch screen at
1024 by 768 resolution, I don't see any more letters than I would at VGA resolution, but the letters are much smoother and easier to read. I don't know for sure,
but perhaps this is part of the reason that I'm still not wearing glasses at an age
when most of my colleagues are. In any case, I find this resolution much more
pleasing for text.

And yes, the icons are small, but they're in color and they have pictures and I
can recognize them quite easily. In fact, they take up less screen space this way,
which I view as an advantage.

This whole issue is clearly a matter of taste, but all I ask is that you not accept
the conventional wisdom at face value, but consider trying a higher resolution on
your screen even if you have a small display, like mine.

Expansion Bus

The type of bus your display adapter uses has little to do with resolution and color depth, but everything to do with performance.

As described back in Chapter 1, CPUs and Motherboards, local bus expansion slots were developed to increase the amount of data that can be moved around in a computer in a given amount of time. The 16-bit ISA bus operating at just 8 MHz only moves a fraction of the data handled by a 32-bit VL-Bus operating at 33 MHz.

Along with your hard disk, your graphics adapter is a device that requires huge amounts of data in a short period of time. For example, consider how much data there is in a single 256-color VGA image; 640 times 480 pixels times 1 byte per pixel (8 bits to the byte) comes out to 300 KB. Now consider a 1024 by 768 image with 65,536 colors: 1024 times 768 times 2 bytes (16 bits) is 1536KB, or one and a half megabytes—and that's just for each image. Any time you change the image (like move the cursor or type a letter), that same amount of data has to be sent again.

Local bus is best

As a result, you will get much better performance out of a local bus graphics adapter than you will from an ISA model (Figure 4.7), assuming that the two cards are otherwise the same. For many applications where graphics performance is important (from games to high-end image editing), this difference in performance can be enough to make it worth getting a new motherboard simply in order to be able to use a local bus graphics adapter.

Figure 4.7 These three different graphics adapters are for different expansion buses: (from the top) ISA, VL-Bus, and PCI.

Accelerator Chips

> Speed, it seems to me, provides the one genuinely modern pleasure.
>
> Aldous Huxley
> *Music at Night and Other Essays*

The final difference in graphics adapters is the kind of chip it has. The original VGA chip was simply a "dumb" buffer, which meant that it could accept data from the computer's CPU, store it in memory on the graphics card, and then send it to the monitor (via a DAC, which stands for Digital-to-Analog Converter and is the piece that changes the digital data into a wave signal that can be used by an analog monitor). This design meant that the CPU had to calculate the content for every pixel on the screen and send this information to the graphics card.

Engineers got the idea that they could build a chip that would interpret commands and create the pixel information on its own. This has two advantages. First, it gives the CPU less work to do in preparing the display information, so it can get back to doing other calculations sooner. The other advantage is that instead of sending a stream of data that said "make a white dot, make a white dot, make a white dot, . . ." and so on, the CPU could simply send a command that said "make a line of white dots from here to there." This requires much less information, and thus the image data can be transferred much more quickly to the graphics card. Both of these effects can result in huge improvements in graphics performance.

Few dumb VGA cards are around today; most have some form of acceleration. Some use relatively little acceleration and are found on the least expensive boards. Others, like the chips from S3 and ATI, are quite sophisticated in the functions that they accelerate and can have a performance advantage—especially in programs like Windows and drafting programs. The fastest chips use a 64-bit connection to their memory for best performance.

There are now cards that boast 128-bit design. These use three separate 64-bit accelerators, one each for the red, green, and blue information. Unless you are working with 24-bit images at resolutions of 1200 by 1024 or higher, less expensive cards will probably give you nearly the same performance for a much lower cost. You'll only need a 128-bit card if you do high-end graphic arts work.

In general, if you need maximum DOS speed, a simple local bus graphics card may give you the best performance. For Windows, a local bus accelerator card is generally better. As for which is the fastest card, that changes almost weekly; check with magazines like *PC Magazine* for comparative performance reviews.

This isn't really a Windows 95 item, but it may turn out to be. There is a whole new breed of graphics accelerators poised to hit the market, but they have not yet arrived as this book is written. These new accelerators are designed to

speed up the drawing of three-dimensional images. 3D images take lots of calculations, especially when you get into shading curved surfaces and so forth,
and there's a lot that an accelerator can do to take the load off the CPU. Games
like DOOM and Descent have created huge interest in 3D worlds for games,
and it is likely that the game market will drive the development of these new 3D
accelerator cards. The chances are good that many of these new games will
run under Windows 95, so if you're a game fan, watch the development of the
3D graphics adapter market closely in the next year or so.

@#%$%@!

> The dreadful dead of dark midnight.
>
> Shakespeare
> *The Rape of Lucrece,* 1594

Monitors and graphics adapters are incredibly reliable. They almost never fail or
have problems, but when they do, the problems can be incredibly annoying. If
any hardware problem is going to be of the "in your face" variety, it's one that affects your display.

Display Problems

Most of the problems with monitors occur right out of the box. Either something
is wrong with the unit (from manufacturing or shipping damage) or there is a
problem with configuration. And some "problems" are really just the result of a
limitation of the monitor or the graphics adapter.

In the unlikely event that your monitor does expire, it may be cost effective to
repair it—especially if the monitor is of relatively recent vintage, is well matched
to your current display adapter, and you don't have plans to upgrade your computer or display system in the near future. You may be able to find a local repair
service, but if you can't, many services advertise nationally in publications such
as *Computer Hot Line* and *Processor* (see Appendix A).

Convergence

> When you go to buy use your eyes, not your ears.
>
> Czech proverb

One of the most common problems with a monitor's image is improper convergence. To create a white line, the three electron beams must overlap precisely. If
one or more beams are not aligned correctly, they won't overlap and you'll see a
colored halo around an object that should otherwise be white. If the red beam is

off, for example, you may see a red or pink tint to one side of the object and a cyan tint on the other side.

It is not practical to expect a CRT to have perfect convergence at all points on the screen. Most are excellent at the center of the screen, but show some slight signs of misconvergence in the corners. The worst have noticeable problems in the corners or even along the edges of the image.

Few monitors have convergence controls, especially less-expensive models. If your monitor has a serious convergence problem, you may need to send it back to the factory to get it readjusted.

The best way to avoid convergence problems is to not buy them in the first place. It can be a good idea to test drive a monitor before you buy it so that you can see the image quality first. Ideally, you should test it at the same resolution that you intend to use on it.

You can buy commercial programs to test and adjust your monitor for optimal performance, and the best that I have seen is Displaymate from Sonera Technologies (see Appendix A). You may not have this program when you go shopping for a monitor, and besides, computer store staff sometimes get a bit fidgety and defensive if you try to run your own software on their systems.

So here's a quick and simple way to check the convergence of a monitor that you're thinking about buying. It uses Windows Paintbrush, which you'll find in the Accessories group in Program Manager in just about any system that has a version of Windows 3.x installed.

Start Paintbrush program and maximize the program to fill the screen; the drawing color is black by default. Select the Fill tool (the paint roller) and click on the workspace to fill it with black. Now select the vertical scroll bar, and move the slider all the way to the bottom, which will reveal a white area. Fill the white with black. Now move the horizontal scroll bar all the way to the right, to reveal more white, which you also fill with black. Move the vertical slider all the way back to the top, and fill the remaining white block with black.

Move the horizontal and vertical sliders all the way to the left and up, so that you're working with the upper left corner of the image. Change the drawing color to white by clicking on the white square in the palette at the bottom of the screen. Select the smallest line width, which will produce a one-pixel width line. Choose the Rectangle Drawing Tool (in the left column, and not the Filled Rectangle Tool in the right column.) Draw a box that fills the work area (though you do not have to worry about exactly filling to the corners.) Move the scroll bars to the bottom and right positions, and draw another box that fills that space.

Now press Ctrl-P to view the image on the full screen (Figure 4.8). You should see two intersecting white rectangles on a black screen; depending on the Windows driver, you may also see white bands at the top and bottom as well. The two rectangles can tell you much about the monitor.

Figure 4.8   Create this simple image in Windows Paintbrush to test a monitor's convergence.

First, look at the lines closely to see if they are truly white. If the monitor has convergence problems, you will see colored edges along the lines, and in the worst cases, you will see separate lines, such as a red line beside a cyan line. A faint tinge in a few areas is not likely to affect the image quality, but severe alignment problems will make for a blurry image.

These lines will also show you if the image is curved at the sides or top, and whether the horizontal and vertical lines have the same apparent thickness and brightness. Most display resolutions use "square" pixels, so the lines should look the same. On some monitors, however, the verticals are noticeably thinner, which reduces overall image quality.

Tinted image

> The Mediterranean has the color of mackerel, changeable I mean. You don't always know if it is green or violet, you can't even say it's blue, because the next moment the changing reflection has taken on a tint of rose or gray.
>
> Vincent Van Gogh, in a letter, June 1888
> *The Letters of Vincent Van Gogh,* 1927

Another problem can be that the entire image has a tint to it. If the effect is slight—the white Windows background looks a little blue or pink—that may simply be a function of the phosphors used in the screen. If it is a strong color (red or yellow or magenta, for example), you may have a big problem.

This effect is most likely caused by a problem with one of the electron guns in your monitor. For example, if you lose the blue gun's electrons, the image turns yellow (because red and green light combine to make yellow, and it would take the missing blue light to finish off the mix to create the desired white color).

The most likely cause of this problem is a faulty connection between your graphics adapter and your monitor. Check to make sure that the cable is firmly seated in its connectors at both ends. If the problem persists and your monitor is the type that has a separate cable, try using a different cable. If this fails to resolve the problem, try the A/B testing technique. Try the monitor on another computer that is known to work correctly, or try your computer with another monitor that is known to be good. This will help you determine whether the problem lies in the graphics adapter or the monitor.

If there is indeed a problem inside the monitor, you will need to either have the unit serviced or replaced.

Lines in Slot Mask Tubes

> Painting and sculpture are but images,
> Are merely shadows cast by outward things
> On stone or canvas, having in themselves
> No separate existence.
>
>   Henry Wadsworth Longfellow
>   *Michael Angelo*

I've had lots of people write to me asking how to fix a problem they have with certain types of monitors. I had a letter from one person who returned three monitors of the same model because they all had the same flaw. As it turns out, the monitors were not defective—the flaw is simply a product of the monitor's design.

The monitors were all based on the Sony Trinitron tubes—though the new Mitsubishi Diamondtron tubes use a similar design—and the "problem" is a normal part of the slot mask. As described earlier in this chapter, tubes of this sort use a slot mask instead of a dot mask. Because the slot mask is a sheet of thin metal with lots of thin vertical slots running from top to bottom, it is important that the slots be held steady. A wire connects the two edges of the mask (two wires are used on larger monitors) to hold the mask in a slightly bowed shape, similar to the curve of the monitor's front glass. The electrons from the three electron guns hit this tension wire and are absorbed by it. In effect, the tension wire casts a shadow on the phosphors, resulting in a faint gray or black horizontal line on the white screen of a typical Windows application.

The funny thing about this effect is that some people don't even see it; others find it so noticeable that it's distracting. Whether the effect bothers you or not seems to be a matter of taste and perception. Personally, I love the clear, sharp images you get from a slot mask tube—largely a result of the fact that the glass is flat in the vertical dimension—but I'm one of those who notice the thin line and prefer to use a different monitor design without this flaw.

Flicker

> Transport of the mails, transport of the human voice, transport of flickering pictures—in this century as in others our highest accomplishments still have the single aim of bringing men together.
>
> Antoine de Saint-Exupéry
> *Wind, Sand, and Stars,* 1939

As described earlier in this chapter, flicker in your computer display can be annoying and tiresome. The most common cause for flicker is the graphics card's production of either an interlaced image or a noninterlaced image with a slow refresh rate (60 Hz or less).

The solution is to choose a display mode that does not produce an interlaced or slow-refresh noninterlaced image. This is the job of your graphics adapter, and you need to configure the adapter to produce the appropriate signal for your monitor. You typically use a DOS utility program that is provided with the graphics adapter—it may be called INSTALL, SETUP, VGAMODE, VMODE, or something similar—to set the board up for your monitor. Most programs provide a list of monitors from which you can choose; pick your monitor or one that has similar specifications. Some of these configuration utilities give you the choice of entering custom settings if your monitor is not listed; you should be able to find the required information in your monitor's documentation.

If you pick a refresh rate that is faster than your monitor can handle for a particular resolution, the image on the screen will be collapsed, scrambled, or folded over on top of itself. Do not run the monitor any longer than a dozen seconds or so under this condition; it is possible to permanently damage the monitor by sending it a signal that it cannot handle.

Windows 95 has a wonderful ability to change display resolutions and color depths on the fly (Figure 4.9); you have to restart Windows 3.x in most cases to accomplish the same changes. Windows 95 does not do anything about the refresh rate of the signal, however. You will still have to use the graphic adapter's DOS configuration utility to set it to work correctly with your monitor.

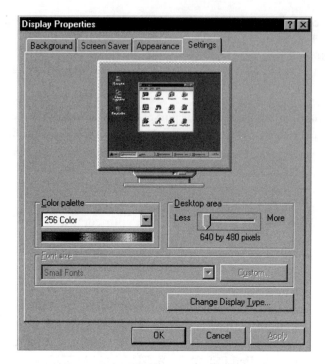

Figure 4.9 Windows 95 lets you change screen resolution and color depth without restarting Windows.

Waving Image

Another problem you may encounter with your display is that the image swims from side to side. This can be a slow motion or a fast jitter. It can be a very small motion, or it can drift over a noticeable distance.

The larger, slower movements are often caused by interference of some sort. A poorly shielded source of radio interference may be adjacent to the monitor, such as a motor, unshielded speaker, or even another monitor. (You may have seen pictures of engineering workstations with two monitors side by side; those monitors are built with special shielding so that they do not interfere with each other.) Try moving your monitor or the other items around it and see if the problem is changed or eliminated.

Power problems   Another source of the problem can be "dirty" power; the interference may be entering through your power line. A power conditioner may be the solution; it may eliminate the problems with the power. You can also try plugging the monitor into a different power circuit somewhere that has a different power source and that may not have the same power problems.

The faster, jittery movements are often simply a function of the monitor's electronics struggling to keep up with the signal it is receiving. Try stepping down to a lower resolution or slower refresh rate and see if the problem is diminished.

These problems can also be the sign that a component within the monitor may be near failure. If you can't reduce or eliminate the problem with these suggestions, you can either send the monitor in to be checked by a technician and repaired if necessary, or you can just live with the problem if it's not too obnoxious and simply wait until the monitor gives out before you get it repaired (or replaced).

Changing Image Size

> Consistency is contrary to nature, contrary to life.
>
> Aldous Huxley
> *Do What You Will,* 1929

There's one more common and disagreeable problem that you may encounter with monitors, but it's another case of there not being a defect, but rather just a limitation of the device. Here's the typical scenario.

Your computer boots up in VGA text mode (as most computers do), and you have to fiddle with the image size and position controls to get the image to fill the screen and be centered. Then you start Windows, which you have configured to run at some other resolution . . . let's say 800 by 600. When the Program Manager screen appears, you have to reach over and twiddle the dials again to get the image the right size and position. And then when you quit Windows (or run a DOS application in full-screen mode), you must make the changes all over again. What a pain!

The image may be too small, or it may be so large that it folds over on itself at the edge. It may be shifted to the left or right. In any case, the image is clearly not optimal and is definitely in need of adjustment. (And in some cases, even with the controls turned all the way in one direction, you *still* cannot get the image the size or position you want.)

The problem here is a combination of factors. The graphics adapter card is sending signals that your monitor cannot automatically synchronize with, so the image size and position are wrong. This is rarely a problem with monitors that have digital controls because they can store different settings for different signals. Once you make the adjustment for a given signal, the monitor should remember those settings for the next time it sees the same signal.

Monitors with analog controls don't have the memory that digital monitors have. These monitors are set at the factory to synchronize with signals that have certain characteristics. You may be able to solve the problem by configuring your graphics adapter to work with a different monitor (or by entering custom settings for your monitor), but if this doesn't solve the problem, your only choices are either a new monitor or resigning yourself to making the adjustments.

Adapter Problems

Graphics adapters are even less prone to problems than monitors. Typically, they simply break down—totally, irrevocably, and in a manner that leaves no doubt. (A couple of times, I've even been rewarded with a sizable puff of blue smoke as the parting gift from a dying adapter.) Unlike a monitor, if your graphics adapter should give up the ghost, don't bother with repairs; replacement is almost certainly your most cost- and time-effective solution.

Related to graphics adapters are a few problems that you may encounter that don't involve repair or replacement.

Black Icons in Program Manager

You've just changed your Windows 3.x configuration to use a higher color depth or higher resolution, and all of a sudden, all your Program Manager icons have turned black! What could have cursed your system so?

This is not a problem with your monitor, nor is it a problem with your graphics adapter. What has happened is that you have run out of memory. When this problem occurs, you'll probably also see an error message that states "Extremely Low On Memory: Not Enough memory to convert all the program icons." You can convert them by hand by selecting an icon and pressing Alt-Enter (to open the Properties window) and then pressing Enter (to choose OK). If you have lots of icons in a single Program Manager Group, you may have to break up the one group into a number of smaller ones with fewer icons to be able to complete the process.

Special S3 Problems

Another problem may occur with graphics adapters that use some graphics accelerator chips from S3 (a graphics chip manufacturer). If you have a serial port configured as COM4 in your system, it may cause a conflict with the graphics adapter because the chip uses the same I/O port address as COM4. The only solution is to disable the serial port or reassign it to COM1, COM2, or COM3. Some of these cards also use IRQ2, which may cause conflicts with other devices.

Crashing Windows

Graphics adapters can also be the source of problems that don't seem to have anything to do with them. One of the prime examples is the infamous parity error message that you can get while running Windows 3.x. In some cases, you may get a GPF (General Protection Fault). In any case, things come to a grinding halt.

The problem may not be memory or anything remotely related to parity; it is quite possible that the problem is caused by your graphics adapter's driver. The first step is to switch to the plain vanilla VGA driver for Windows. If the problem does not recur, the driver is a prime suspect. Try to find a more recent driver for your card and see if that doesn't clear up the problem.

The trick of switching to the Windows VGA driver is a good tip to remember whenever you are having trouble with Windows. By eliminating the graphics adapter driver from the list of possible factors, you can simplify the troubleshooting process. Since conflicts caused by the graphics driver can manifest themselves in so many different ways, this can be a good first step.

Finding the Latest Driver

> If we do not find anything very pleasant, at least we shall find something new.
>
> Voltaire
> *Candide,* 1759

This last item brings up a good point; how do you find the latest Windows driver for your graphics adapter?

You might think that because you sent in the registration card when you bought your computer or graphics adapter or whatever, the company would notify you if something was changed or improved. (Or if something that would crash your copy of Windows was discovered and fixed.) You might think that the company would use this information to keep customers informed, to develop a group of consumers loyal to their brand.

As the late John Belushi would say at this point, ". . . but Noooooooooooo!" The companies don't do this. As far as I can tell, registration cards are sometimes used to validate warranty claims and on rare occasion serve as a screening device for access to technical support. In fact, the prime purpose of registration cards is to build a marketing database, both for the company's own products and as a list that can be sold to other computer equipment marketers. And these companies wonder why they have such a hard time getting customers to send in their registration cards!

So, the company isn't going to send you a new driver when it has been developed. And they won't call you up or send you a letter to say "Hello, we have a new driver. Would you like a copy?" You'll have to do it yourself, and you'll need a modem.

The first place to look is the online service to which you belong. Many major companies now have sections on CompuServe, Prodigy, and America Online where you can download the latest drivers and utilities for their products. If you

Dialing for drivers

can't find your company on your online service, the chances are good that they have a bulletin board service that you can dial into and download drivers. Failing that, you can check the Microsoft Software Library, which contains drivers for many different products (such as printers as well as graphics adapters). Information on how to access the Microsoft files is listed in Appendix A.

If you don't have a modem, find someone who does. If all else fails, try calling the tech support number for the company that made your graphics adapter; you may be able to talk them into sending you a copy on disk.

UPGRADING

If the time has come to change your outlook on your world of computing, changing your display system is a relatively easy task. You need to consider several factors.

Matching Monitor and Adapter

> I love her too, but our neuroses just don't match.
>
> Arthur Miller
> *The Ride Down Mount Morgan*, 1991

First and foremost, you need to make sure that the monitor and graphics adapter are well suited for each other. It makes little sense to get a display adapter that creates very high resolution images if your monitor does not have a phosphor dot pitch small enough to adequately create those images. Similarly it doesn't matter if your monitor can handle fast refresh rates to eliminate flicker if the graphics adapter can't produce the images that quickly.

As a result, it makes the most sense to upgrade both the adapter and the monitor at the same time. Because budget and hardware configuration issues may create the most constraints on the adapter side of the decision (there is a wide range of prices for adapters), you may want to pick the adapter first and then find a monitor that makes a good match.

Among the hardware constraints is the question of the expansion bus. If performance is important to you, remember that a local bus card is going to be much, much faster than an ISA bus card. In fact, the difference is so dramatic and the cost differential so small that I don't recommend that you buy a new ISA card for any reason if display speed is important. Instead, it often is worth buying a replacement motherboard with local bus slots (even if you simply buy a bare board and reuse your existing CPU, memory, and other components) in order to get the performance gain from a local bus graphics adapter.

Once you install the adapter and hook up the monitor, be sure to follow all the instructions for the card configuration. As I described earlier in this chapter, you will need to set up the card so it uses the correct refresh rates for the different resolutions that the monitor can handle.

You also need to reconfigure Windows 3.x by installing the correct driver for the new graphics adapter. Some adapters use a different driver for each different resolution and color depth (which you can change using the Windows Setup program, as shown in Figure 4.10; others come with a Windows utility that lets you reconfigure the driver for different resolutions and color depths such as the ATI utility shown in Figure 4.11.

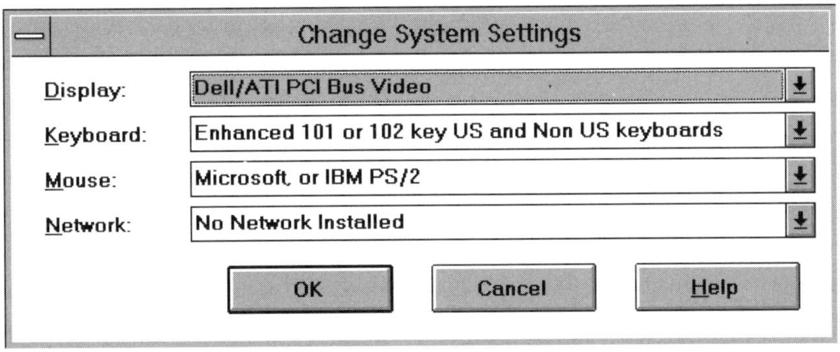

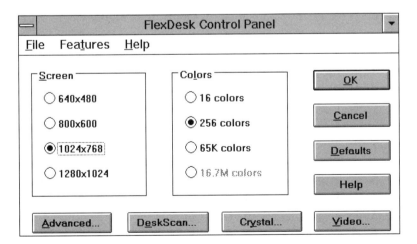

Figure 4.10 You can either run the Windows SETUP program from the DOS prompt or use the Windows Setup utility within Windows to change your graphics adapter driver.

Figure 4.11 Some graphics adapters have utilities, such as this one from ATI, that let you change the Windows driver's resolution and color depth, among other settings.

DOS vs. Windows Performance

As mentioned earlier in this chapter, an accelerator chip can greatly improve performance for Windows and CAD programs. The gains are a result of a smaller data stream from the CPU to the graphics card, and the fact that the accelerator chip takes over some of the computing tasks from the CPU.

The flip side of this is that cards with accelerator chips are sometimes slower for DOS applications than a relatively "dumb" card that simply pipes data right through from the CPU. One reason for this is that most DOS applications do not have custom drivers that can take advantage of the graphics accelerator functions. If you need optimum DOS application performance, you may not want an advanced accelerator chip.

Two of the best comparative measures of performance are the Graphics Winmark for Windows and the PC Bench DOS Video for DOS, part of the *PC Magazine* benchmark suites. These are available on request from the magazine; see Appendix A for information on how to get free copies of these programs.

Picking a Monitor

Chances are good that you'll find a range of monitors that will work well with your chosen graphics adapter. How can you narrow the field?

A good place to start is size. In general, my advice is to get a monitor that is as big as you need, but no bigger. The rapid increase in size, weight, and cost is a major deterrent to buying huge monitors, so unless your budget and your workspace knows no bounds, you'll probably settle for a 15- or 17-inch screen. (You don't save enough to make a 14-inch screen worth it, so the only reason to get one would be if you really don't have the room for a 15-inch one.)

Seeing Is Believing

> If you can't believe a little in what you see on the screen, it's not worth wasting your time on cinema.
>
> Serge Daney
> *Sight and Sound,* July 1992

If you're just buying a monitor, I recommend that you consider getting it from a store and not by mail order. In general, I'm very comfortable buying by mail, but I have seen enough variation between individual monitors of the same make and model that I prefer to try them out in the store before I buy one.

If you go this route, try out the floor model first, and then be sure to explain to the sales representative that you want to test the monitor you're purchasing before accepting it. The store staff may not always go for this approach (it can be harder for them to sell a box that has been opened than one that is still factory sealed), so it's best to make sure that you've reached an understanding before you start. This strategy has served me well in the past; when I tested a major brand monitor in the store before buying it, the image turned out to be tinted red (sort of like the view in Doom right after you inadvertently deploy a rocket into the door in front of you, when instead you meant to open it) and was clearly defective. My quick check saved me miles and hours of driving, plus the possible aggravation of trying to return the unit.

As for the dot mask versus slot mask design, that's a matter of taste. As I mentioned earlier, I love the smooth, vertical flat dimension of the Trinitron-style monitor, as it seems to give an image more depth, but the vertical phosphor stripes cannot produce as thin a vertical white line as a phosphor dot design of the same pitch, and I'm one of those who notices the shadow cast by the mask tension wire. So this is another reason to make your purchase in a store; you can try out the different technologies and see for yourself.

Years ago Zenith came out with a flat screen monitor. Dot mask monitors have curved faces; the surface is rounded as if it were cut out of a sphere. "Flat square" tubes are neither flat nor square, but the radius of the curved face is larger—so it appears flatter—than a traditional CRT. Slot mask monitors are only curved in the horizontal dimension; they are shaped as if they were cut from a cylinder instead of a sphere. Somehow, Zenith engineers were able to create a dot mask monitor that was truly flat in both dimensions. Even though the monitor was only capable of VGA resolution, many users preferred it because the image was so crisp and seemed to have more depth than other designs. Unfortunately the Zenith monitor was a dead-end; the company was never able to bring a higher resolution version to market.

Well, you soon may be able to buy a new monitor with a flat face—maybe even by the time this book reaches your hands. I have heard that Matsushita (parent corporation for Panasonic and a major manufacturer of CRTs) has developed a new tube with a flat screen. I have not yet seen one of these tubes, and as far as I know, no monitor manufacturer has yet announced a product that uses it, but it would be worth making a few inquiries when you buy because these could turn out to be outstanding monitors.

Two Monitors in One System

Some people want to have two monitors in one system, which is a trick that Macintosh computers have been able to manage for a long time. There are some expensive high-end professional cards that have this capability, but most consumer market SVGA cards don't take kindly to a competing card's presence.

It's not quite the same thing, but you can have a monochrome text and an SVGA monitor installed and active in the same system. They are not exactly active at the same time because one will display DOS text screens and the other will handle all the graphics displays. To switch back and forth between the two screens at the DOS prompt, simply type MODE MONO to select the monochrome display and MODE CO80 to switch to the color display. Within Windows, you can open a full-screen DOS session. Then type MODE MONO to activate the monochrome adapter. You can then work with your character-based application on this screen. To go back to the Windows graphics screen, simply press Alt-Tab; the contents of the monochrome screen will remain unchanged when you switch. And to make your monochrome application active again, just switch back with the Alt-Tab shortcut again.

This is a handy trick when you want to be able to refer to a DOS application while working in a Windows application (or vice versa).

Late-Breaking Inside Information

Windows-based systems may soon get affordable, true dual-monitor support. Appian Graphics (a division of ETMA Corporation) has recently announced a new SVGA accelerator card that has not one but two SVGA connectors on the card, so you can connect two monitors to the one card. It will have drivers for Windows 95 that will let you "stitch" the two images together, so your Windows desktop will spread from one to the other. I haven't seen the card in action yet, but if this is a feature that is important to you, it looks like the market will be supporting this feature in the near future.

Windows 95: Plug and Play Saves the Day

Not all graphics adapters and monitors will be able to take full advantage of Plug and Play features, but over time, I expect that you will see more and more devices that support this feature. The bottom line is that you should not have to be concerned about drivers or configuring your adapter or monitor if they are Plug and Play compatible. Simply turn off your computer, insert the card or attach the monitor, and power up. Your Windows 95 installation should identify the new hardware, adjust any drivers as necessary, and then configure the equipment so it is ready to run.

Plug and Play monitors should be able to tell the graphics adapter what resolutions it can handle, so that Windows 95 will only give you choices of supported modes. All this should greatly simplify display configuration problems.

To a certain extent, Windows 95 will also be able to configure graphics adapters that are not Plug and Play compatible. Such products are referred to as **legacy** devices, and Windows 95 can do a fair job of automatically identifying them even without Plug and Play support. Only if this automatic process fails will you have to resort to a manual configuration, similar to that used by Windows 3.x, using the Add New Hardware Wizard (Figure 4.12).

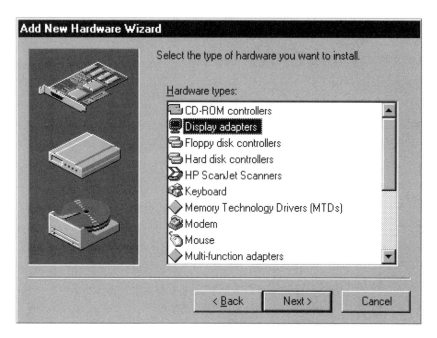

Figure 4.12 The Add New Hardware Wizard in Windows 95 makes it relatively easy to configure your system for a display adapter that does not support Plug and Play.

5 | Printers

A very great part of the mischiefs that vex this world arises from words.

Edmund Burke (1729–1797)

As much as words may cause mischief, it seems that the task of putting words onto paper presents some vexations of its own. If you have never mumbled a clouded epithet at your laser printer, if you have never been frustrated by smeared text or a wrinkled letter or a self-sticking label that decided it wanted to take up permanent residence in the heart of your printer's paper path, then just turn this page and proceed directly to Chapter 6, Multimedia Stuff.

But before you do, take a break and stroll down to the corner store and buy me a lottery ticket—with the charmed life you lead, some of that impossible luck is bound to rub off! And remember, this chapter will always be here waiting for that inevitable day when your lucky streak ends.

Okay. They've gone on to Chapter 6, and we can grouse about our printer problems in private. Even if you love your printer, there are almost certainly times when it lets you down with a paper jam or garbled output or some other mishap. The trick is to prevent as many of these events as possible and to be able to recover with good grace and low blood pressure when they do happen.

NEED TO KNOW

The most important service rendered by the press and the magazines is that of educating people to approach printed matter with distrust.

Samuel Butler
Samuel Butler's Notebooks, 1951

The first step is to understand just how printers work. With typewriters, it was fairly easy—a piece of metal banged against an inky ribbon and transferred its imprint onto the page. It was a relatively simple, mechanical process.

It's more difficult now, as we harness boiling bubbles of ink and high-powered light beams and other bits of magical technology that would seem to be of little use in making marks on paper. So here's an overview of how they work.

Major Technologies

A dozen years ago, there were two main printer technologies: daisywheels and dot matrix. Daisywheels used elements that had fully formed characters—just like the typewriters on which many of them were based—and dot matrix printers used an arrangement of fine pins. Daisies were slow, loud, and made good-looking output, in contrast with dot matrix printers, which were fast, loud, and made generally legible output.

The market has changed a bit in a dozen years. Laser printers have taken over the high-quality output segment, and ink jet printers have taken over just about all the rest.

Laser

> The thing to do is to supply light and not heat.
>
> Woodrow Wilson
> Speech, January 29, 1916, Pittsburgh

The first affordable desktop laser was the Hewlett-Packard LaserJet. Lasers are fast, quiet, and capable of producing output so clear that it can be used as camera-ready originals for print shops. You can pick between a wide range of prices and features, from personal printers designed for light duty that cost less than $400, to high-powered dynamos that churn out more than 20 pages per minute, can print on both sides of the page, and hold thousands of sheets of paper at a time.

The term **laser printer** is really a misnomer because some printers in this group don't even use a laser. For years, I lobbied for the term **page printers** but it never really caught on, which turns out to be just as well because we now have ink jets and other technologies that also would qualify to be called page printers. So let's start with the true laser printer, and then we'll get to the exceptions.

The key to a laser printer is that it works much like a standard photocopier, and Figure 5.1 shows a generalized diagram of the main components. Light is used to expose a photosensitive drum, which then picks up charged particles of toner, which are then transferred to the paper, which then carries it through a fusing roller where a combination of heat and pressure melt the toner so that it sticks to the paper.

In a typical photocopier, the image is created using light bounced off your original document, and this light is transported to the drum by a series of lenses. In a laser printer, the light comes from a diode laser, and a spinning, multifaceted mirror reflects the light so that it scans across the face of the drum.

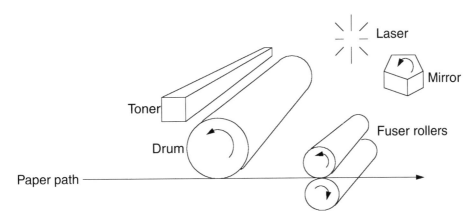

Figure 5.1   This schematic diagram shows the basic parts of a laser printer.

Where the light hits the drum, the electrical charge of the drum changes. In some printers, toner is picked up wherever the light strikes the drum, and this design is called a **write black** system because the light writes with black toner. Other printers use a **write white** approach, where the toner sticks to the drum everywhere but where the light strikes. There are pros and cons to each design, but in general, you don't need to be concerned with which one a printer uses. Be more concerned with how the resulting print quality looks to you.

The toner is made up of tiny particles that can carry an electrical charge. Here is a list of the ingredients for a typical toner:

- Ferrite
- Carbon black
- Iron oxide
- Styrene acrylic polymer
- Pigment

To put it a bit more plainly, toner is made of plastic (styrene acrylic polymer) with rust (ferrite and ferric oxide) and soot (carbon black) mixed into it, with a little additional pigment to adjust the coloring. It is made by heating the plastic, mixing in the additives until they are evenly distributed, and then cooling the mixture to form a brick. The brick is then ground to a fine powder, and screens are used to separate the particles of the correct size.

As with any dust, you should avoid breathing toner. Early photocopiers and laser printers did not do a great job of containing the toner that didn't make it onto the paper, but current models do a much better job of controlling this problem.

Different toners have different compositions, however. This is why you cannot use photocopier toner in a laser printer, or even use toner designed for one printer engine with another. The size of the particles and their electrical properties can be very different. Using the wrong toner can have an adverse effect on image quality. Even more important, the melting points of the plastic components can be different, which can cause some nasty problems indeed, as we'll get to in the middle part of this chapter.

Consumable packaging

One of the main differences between different laser printers is how the consumables are packaged. Hewlett-Packard LaserJet printers have always used a one-piece design. A single cartridge contains the photosensitive drum and the toner supply, and when the toner runs out, you replace the entire cartridge. Other printers are designed with a long-lasting drum, and you add toner separately because the toner will run out long before the drum needs replacing.

There are advantages to each approach, but I must admit that I am partial to the one-piece design. It is easier to handle; separate drums are frequently designed in such a way that it is too easy to scratch or otherwise damage one when installing it, and drums are the most expensive consumable component in the printer. With a cartridge, you get a fresh drum with each cartridge, so you should get like-new image quality every time you change the cartridge. And it turns out that on a per-page cost basis, the cartridge approach costs no more than the separate component designs.

Some folks are concerned about millions of printer cartridges filling up landfills, which is understandable. Some folks have a problem with throwing out a perfectly good photosensitive drum just because a cartridge ran out of toner, and as a long-standing cheapskate myself, I can certainly relate. But I don't recommend refilling one-piece cartridges.

There are plenty of arguments for and against recharging, and you probably will be fine if you choose that route—I know lots of people and businesses who have done so without problems. But I prefer to be more conservative and put only factory-fresh cartridges in my printer. (Maybe that's why it's still going strong after more than 8 years and 10 cases of paper. Sometimes I wish that it would finally give out so I can get something a bit more current, but as long as it still works fine, I can't bear to get rid of it.) If you don't want to be part of the landfill problem, but agree that you don't want to participate in the recharging solution, check with your printer manufacturer. Many have a component recycling program in which they'll pay for the shipping. You may also be able to sell your old cartridges to recharging services for cash, even if you don't want to buy recharged cartridges in return.

Other "Lasers"

Two other technologies—LCD and LED—are also called laser printers, even though they don't have any lasers in them. The difference between these designs and the "real" laser printers is the light source, as shown in the diagrams in Figure 5.2.

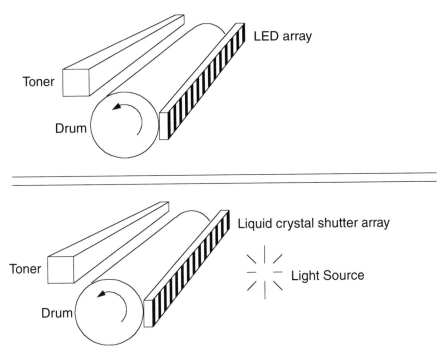

Figure 5.2 LED and LCD printers differ from laser printers in that they use different light sources.

LED printers

Okidata has made the LED printer popular, though there are other manufacturers who also use this approach. Instead of having a single laser as the light source, this type of printer uses a strip of LEDs (light-emitting diodes) mounted just above the surface of the photosensitive drum. A typical printer has an unprintable region of about a quarter inch on each side of a letter-size sheet of paper, which means that the print line is 8 inches long. To get a 300 dpi (dot per inch) resolution, the strip must have 2400 individual LEDs.

The advantage of the LED design is that it eliminates a mechanical component found in the laser design: the whirling mirror. On the other hand, if one of the LEDs (or the electrical connection leading to that light) fails, that dot will never get printed on the page. If your printer is only missing a few of these lights, you probably won't be able to see the difference, but if enough fail—especially in sequence—the effects can be noticeable. Okidata backs their LED print heads with a three-year warranty, which helps increase confidence in the technology.

LCD printers

LCD printers are not common, but you may still run across one. Instead of using lots of lights like an LED, the LCD uses a single one . . . and a bright one at that. The light is piped to an array of liquid crystal cells—similar to those used in a laptop display—which act like tiny shutters. When the cell is on, it lets the light through; when it is off, it blocks the light. LCD printers have the same problem as

LED printers in that if one of the 2400 LCD cells malfunctions, that dot will be permanently affected. LCDs also do not have as quick a response time as LEDs or lasers, and so print speed may be limited.

Making the light choice

In the end, the type of light used in a printer is less important than the other factors. The odds favor a true laser, but you should pick your printer based on print quality, paper handling, speed, features, cost per page, and overall price, and not worry about the light source inside the box.

> An elephant: a mouse built to government specifications.
>
> Robert Heinlein
> *The Notebooks of Lazarus Long*, 1973

The resolution game

One of the specifications that people look at closely when comparing laser printers is resolution. The biggest problem here is that resolution can be measured in lots of different ways, and manufacturers do not all use the same terms to report these measures. It's no wonder that there is a lot of confusion on this topic.

The most credible measure of resolution is the **engine** or **addressable resolution.** This refers to the number of actual dots of toner that the printer can place on a page in a given distance (typically reported as dots per inch). This is the lowest and most conservative specification.

Most printers today also offer some form of enhanced resolution. This improves the print quality by varying the size or placement—or both—of the toner dots on the page.

Figure 5.3 illustrates how Hewlett-Packard Resolution Enhancement Technology works to create smoother angled lines using the same number of dots as a unenhanced output from the same printer. The diagrams show a nearly horizontal line crossing a nearly vertical line. The square grids are just there for reference purpose; they don't actually appear on the printed page.

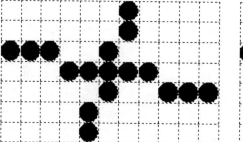 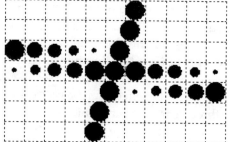

Figure 5.3 A comparison of how Hewlett-Packard Resolution Enhancement Technology on the right smooths lines compared with unenhanced output, shown on the left.

In the left diagram, you can see how the unenhanced line has large jumps when the line shifts from one row or column of dots to the next. This is what causes a stair-step effect called **aliasing,** which is also known by its popular term, **the jaggies.**

The diagram on the right shows how the enhanced resolution uses five different sizes of dots to smooth the nearly horizontal line. The changing dot size lets the printer "feather" the adjacent rows into each other, which eliminates the abrupt transition. These sizes are created by controlling how long the laser light illuminates the drum for a given point, which in turn affects the change in charge and how much toner will be picked up at that point.

For the vertical line, a different approach is used. The dots are the same size but are shifted slightly to the left or right of the normal position. This is accomplished by causing the laser to fire slightly early or late for that position.

These changes are accomplished without changing the speed of rotation for the drum or any other component. The printer still can only print a certain number of dots per inch, but it can be more precise about where it puts them and how large they are.

The question is how you report this resolution. If the print engine is capable of putting down 600 dots per inch, you could call this a 600 dpi printer, but that wouldn't indicate that it produces better output than an unenhanced 600 dpi model. Because the dots can be shifted to three positions horizontally, you might say that it is equivalent to an 1800 dpi printer. And since it uses dots that are one-fifth the normal size, you might even say that it has 3000 dpi resolution. Hewlett-Packard takes a conservative approach to specifications and calls this a 600 dpi printer with enhanced resolution.

Some printer manufacturers take a print engine of one resolution, and then slow down the drum rotation (or speed up the laser scans) so it produces two rows of dots in the space that other printers produce only one row. This is why you sometimes see specifications for printers that have 600 by 1200 or 300 by 600 dpi resolution. One problem with this approach is that if the toner dots are round, they must either be too big for the higher resolution (thus overlapping considerably) or too small for the lower resolution (thus creating gaps).

A slow roll

Finally, there is the question of whether the rest of the printer components are up to the task of creating the claimed resolution. Are the toner particles sufficiently small to create the tiny dots? Does the photosensitive drum have a fine enough sensitivity that it can hold a charge in as fine a resolution as claimed? Can the printer's controller electronics turn the laser on and off fast enough to actually create dots this small?

The bottom line on resolution is that you have to trust your eyes and take the specifications with a grain of salt. Look at actual print samples using the type of paper you intend to use, printing the types of images you intend to print, before you decide to buy. You might want to invest in a small magnifying glass—

especially if you plan to use the output as camera-ready originals for a printing project—to make it easier to see the differences in image quality.

Ink Jets

> Gimme the Plaza, the jet and $150 million, too . . .
>
> Headline in the *New York Post*, February 13, 1990

Ink jet printers started to take over the low end of the printer market when they offered black and white printing that was nearly as good as a laser, faster and quieter than a dot matrix printer, and for the same price as a dot matrix printer.

Then Windows took off, and people started seeing their work in color. Color on dot matrix printers was never really satisfying, but color from an ink jet printer looks great. And now that an ink jet with four-color ink (cyan, magenta, yellow, and black) costs no more than the black-only printers did—you can buy one for less than $400—the ink jet segment of the market has exploded. By some projections, four out of five printers sold in 1999 will be color ink jets.

Early ink jet printers were messy and temperamental. Modern designs practically eliminate the problems of spilled ink and clogged print heads by putting ink and print head in a single, convenient, disposable cartridge. (Yes, you can get refill kits for these cartridges, but for reasons similar to those for laser printers, I don't recommend refilling ink cartridges.)

The print mechanism is fairly simple. A resistor heats a minuscule amount of ink to the boiling point, which expands and ejects a tiny droplet of ink. This drop then hits the paper. Pretty simple. Some designs add other steps, such as the printers that have heaters and fans to dry the ink rapidly so it doesn't stay wet and smear.

The main differences between ink jet printers are speed, print resolution, and the way they print color. In general, I don't recommend a three-color printer. These printers use just cyan, magenta, and yellow inks, and all three are combined to make black. This approach is expensive to print all black text, and for color, the combined black is not as attractive as true black ink. Some printers solve the text problem by letting you remove the color cartridge and replace it with a black-only cartridge, but then you have to switch cartridges back and forth when you want to switch from printing in color to printing just in black.

A better design is to have all four colors present all the time. Because you typically use more black than colors, it is better to have a separate black cartridge from the color cartridge—and separate cartridges for all four colors is best of all, though there is not always room for this in small printers.

You can also get an ink jet printer that only has black output, but these are getting harder and harder to find because there is little savings compared with color models. So if you're looking for an inexpensive yet versatile printer, there's probably an ink jet in your future.

Impact Dot Matrix

> It was said of old Sarah, Duchess of Marlborough, that she never puts dots over her i's, to save ink.
>
> Horace Walpole
> Letter, October 4, 1785.

The daisywheels are gone, and the only printers left from the early days of desktop computing are the dot matrix printers. Although these printers still fill some important roles and I don't expect them to become extinct anytime soon, there is no question that their part on the computer stage is rapidly diminishing.

Here's another name problem: dot matrix. In its literal meaning, the term refers to creating images (such as letters and graphics) using a pattern of dots arranged in rows and columns. In the early days of desktop computers, this was to distinguish these printers from the daisywheels and mainframe line printers that used fully formed characters (and thus were more or less limited to text-only output).

Times have changed, however, and all our printers use patterns of dots. Lasers (and their close relatives) use dots of light to place dots of toner on the paper, and ink jets spit tiny drops of ink. So all these printers could reasonably be called dot matrix printers. When I'm being careful, I often refer to the category as "impact dot matrix" because it uses a physical impact to create the image on the paper; lasers and ink jets do not make an impact. I still often slip into conventional practice and just use "dot matrix" like everybody else.

These printers make their marks on paper by hitting them. The print head has 9 or more needle-fine wires called **pins,** which use a combination of electromagnets to fire the pins and springs to pull them back to their starting position. When the pin fires, it strikes the paper. Between the pin and the paper (if the printer is set up correctly), there is a ribbon. If there's still some ink on the ribbon, the impact of the pin transfers some of the ink to the paper, creating a dot.

Pin the dot on the paper.

The more pins the printer uses, the more dots it can place in a single pass of the print head. The fewest you are likely to find is 9 pins, and some high-quality printers may have as many as 24 pins. The pins may be staggered so that they can overlap when fired over the same point on the page. Some printers have high-quality modes where the paper is advanced only slightly between passes, so that the print head is slightly offset when it covers the same part of the page. This allows the dots to overlap a lot, but it slows down output.

The fact remains, however, that impact dot matrix printers are rarely used for high-quality text output. Instead, it is their "impact" that appeals to many business users; you have to have an impact to make a duplicate copy in one pass, using either an interleaved carbon sheet or special "carbonless" duplication forms. So if you want to print copies of checks or invoices, you probably need to use an impact dot matrix printer.

For years, I have been told that multiple-part paper for laser printers was under development, and that it would be ready for market any day now. I still have not seen any actual samples of such paper, but it does not seem too farfetched an idea that some sort of "carbonless" paper could be created to duplicate the points where toner appeared on the top layer (perhaps using pressure). So I stop short of saying that the *only* way to make copies in one pass is to use an impact printer. Someday, this idea will have to make it out of the paper company laboratories and onto office supply store shelves. It's only a matter of time.

The other advantage of dot matrix printers is that they use fan-fold, tractor-feed paper, instead of the cut-sheet paper used by almost all laser and ink jet printers. (There are some laser and ink jet printers that do use tractor-feed paper, but they are the rare exception.) Fan-fold paper comes in large boxes, which means that you don't have to reload paper very often, compared with a cut-sheet printer that typically is limited to just 1000 sheets or fewer in its input bin. Also, many companies already have a lot of money invested in invoices, checks, and other forms already preprinted on fan-fold paper stock. And tractor-fed forms are handy when you need to place information in precise locations, as when filling out forms.

On the other hand, paper jams, paper that won't tear at the perforations, and the cost of throwing away outdated stocks of preprinted forms are a few of the reasons that people have moved to cut-sheet printers (and their ability to print forms on demand) and away from tractor-feed models.

High-End Color

> The purest and most thoughtful minds are those which love colour the most.
>
> John Ruskin
> *The Stones of Venice*, 1852

The high-end color category of printers includes a range of technologies, including color laser, color ink jet, thermal transfer, dye sublimation, and solid ink printers. The issues surrounding these printers could fill a book. In fact, they *have* filled a book. M. David Stone has written *The Underground Guide to Color Printers*, and if you need one of these printers, you need this book.

Major Languages

> Language serves three functions. The first is to communicate ideas. The
> second is to conceal ideas. The third is to conceal the absence of ideas.

> Otto Jespersen

If you think about it, getting a printer to do what you want is a little tricky. If you want the printer to print the information you send to it, how are you supposed to tell the printer to do something different instead of print those instructions? Why doesn't your printer always just act out Gracie's role in the classic Burns and Allen closing? When George Burns would tell her "Say 'Goodnight,' Gracie," she'd always say "Goodnight, Gracie." But sometimes you want your printer to change fonts or start a new page or print a graphic image instead of just printing the letters and numbers it receives. How does it do that? The answer to this and many more complicated issues is the printer language.

In the beginning, computer printers were pretty dumb. They emulated old teletype machines that couldn't do much but print letters and numbers, advance the paper, and return the print head to the left edge of the page.

Teletypes also could make a bell ring to get the attention of the operator. And your PC still remembers (as do a few printers). At the DOS prompt, type ECHO ^G (where you make the ^G by holding down the Ctrl Key and pressing G), and then press Enter. That beep is a vestigial remainder of the way one operator could wake up a sleeping colleague at the other end of the line.

Since a few codes were left unused by the characters, numbers, punctuation, and control codes for line feed and carriage return, one was assigned as the Escape character. (For those of you who keep track of these things, the Escape character is decimal 27 in ASCII.) When a printer "sees" an Escape character coming down the line, it treats the information that follows it as a command to be executed if possible. As a result, we tend to refer to printer commands as "Escape commands" or "Escape sequences."

When all we had were dot matrix and daisywheel printers, the kinds of things that these printers could do were fairly limited: bold text, underline text, superscript or subscript, and expanded or condensed (dot matrix only). These could be handled easily by one or two characters after the Escape character.

Then came the laser printer. All of a sudden, we could have different fonts, high-resolution graphics mixed in on the same page, letters printed sideways or upside down, and more. As a result, the commands that printers could answer had to become more complex. We now tend to refer to them as **printer languages**—similar to programming languages—because you can program the layout of complex pages using these commands.

Two main printer languages are in use today: PCL and PostScript. Most printers support one or the other or both, and each has its own advantages and disadvantages.

PCL

Hewlett-Packard actually released printers that supported its Printer Control Language (PCL) before the first LaserJet appeared, but it was the LaserJet line that put the language on the map. Originally it was a fairly simple set of commands that let you switch fonts, create some simple graphics, and print bitmap images in different resolutions. The language has grown to become PCL5, which includes scalable fonts (fonts that can print in any point size), and nearly all the commands of the HP pen plotters. There are even variants of the language that support full color printing.

PostScript

In the other corner is Adobe PostScript. PCL is just a printer command set compared to PostScript, which is truly a programming language in its own right. PostScript appeared with the Apple LaserWriter, and this combination of hardware and software more or less established the desktop publishing market. This in turn revolutionized the way paper documents are produced in this country, and saved the Macintosh from following the Lisa and the Apple ///. It supports scalable fonts, a wide variety of graphics commands, and color.

Which Is Better?

There are good reasons to choose either language. PCL is a leaner language—PostScript often takes a dozen characters to print just a few—and so the PCL print stream for a given page tends to be smaller than an equivalent PostScript print job. This means that the page will be sent from the PC to the printer faster and that less interpretation and processing is required at the printer's end. From start to finish, a PCL print job should come out of the printer sooner than a PostScript version of the same page.

PCL has the added advantage that it's cheaper to build. For PostScript, printer manufacturers must either license the language from Adobe or build or license a compatible clone. Hewlett-Packard doesn't license PCL, and since it is a simpler language, it does not take as much time or effort to create a compatible printer. Even though Adobe has slashed the licensing fees in recent years, a PCL printer still costs significantly less than a PostScript printer with similar features.

On the other hand, the big advantage of PostScript is its portability. Everything from personal laser printers to professional typesetting equipment can interpret a PostScript print job and, within limitations, will produce the same page from a given print file. Unless you're a graphic artist, however, this is not as compelling a reason as price might be.

Why Windows Makes Languages Less Important

If you're using Windows, the language your printer uses is not nearly as important as it was in the past. TrueType allows most printers to print scalable fonts, and the Windows printer driver shields you from having to deal directly with the printer's Escape commands. (My first book was about the Hewlett-Packard Laser-Jet, and I wrote lots of examples of how you could enter Escape sequences right in Lotus 1-2-3 or dBASE or other DOS applications, but you don't really need to know any of that type of information anymore.)

If your printer is supported by Windows, it doesn't really matter what language it uses. You will probably be able to take full advantage of the printer's capabilities just by using the font and feature controls in your Windows applications.

GDI Printers

I must mention one more class of printers before leaving Windows; they're known as **GDI printers.** GDI is a Windows term that stands for Graphics Device Interface and refers to the part of Windows that creates images (of text and graphics) that are to be displayed on your computer's screen.

Some designers looked at this and wondered why they were making their printers create a page image when Windows had already done the work. Why not let the computer create the image and then pipe the page over to the printer? This would clearly put an additional strain on the computer's CPU, but with the new processors coming along, there would surely be enough extra cycles that the CPU could handle the extra work.

Well, it's a good idea, but I don't think it works out well in practice. It takes a long time to send the page image across to the printer—longer, it would seem, than just sending a bunch of commands and letting the printer do the imaging work over there—and the fact is that most CPUs do seem to show the strain of the extra load. When a GDI printer is processing a print job, other Windows processes are slowed noticeably.

GDI printers need less sophisticated electronics in their controllers because the CPU handles all the heavy calculations. If this simplification translated into significantly lower costs, that would be one thing, but in general, these printers aren't priced any differently from their more intelligent competitors. As a result, some people end up calling GDI printers "Gosh Darn Ignorant" printers.

Look Ma, no brains!

@#%$%@!

Printers have dozens of creative and challenging ways that they can malfunction. Some are easy to solve; others aren't.

Language Problems

One of the most common problems with printers is a language barrier. If you are using the wrong driver for your printer with Windows or other software, your printer may print out results that are somewhat less intelligible than you desire.

Auto-emulation

> One man's "magic" is another man's engineering.
>
> Robert Heinlein
> *The Notebooks of Lazarus Long*, 1973

Another source of mismatched language problems can arise when your printer can respond correctly to two or more languages, such as PostScript and PCL. Most newer printers with this capability also provide a feature called **automatic emulation switching** or something similar. This means that the printer controller listens for data coming through the interface connection with the printer. It analyzes the first bunch of characters and decides what language is being used for the print job. It then switches to that mode and starts to interpret the data and layout the pages. Compared to the old days when you had to go through all sorts of gyrations to reconfigure a printer to use a different language, this is a magical improvement.

The only problem is that sometimes the analysis is wrong. And you end up with pages and pages that go directly to the recycling bin.

The most common reason for this problem is that the software sending the print job does not use a recognizable set of commands at the start of the print data stream. For PCL jobs, some printers look for an Escape-E sequence (which is the PCL reset command that clears the controller's memory so it's ready for the new print job). For PostScript jobs, the lead-in characters are often %! or %%. If a print job does not start with one of these cues, the controller may well misinterpret the print job and produce "unpredictable" results, as they say in the trade.

Another cause for this problem is that you are sending two different print jobs using different languages, but the second follows so close on the heels of the first that the printer doesn't recognize the break and keeps right on going without changing gears.

Assuming that you cannot get your software to provide a stronger hint, you have two choices. First, you can try using the other printer language from that software; perhaps the printer will do a better job of identifying that stream.

Second, you can simply pick one language or the other and stick with it. Printers with the auto-emulation feature also have a way to configure the printer to expect just one language instead of picking between two. With your software and printer singing from the same sheet music, you'll get more predictable results.

Network Problems When Printing in Windows

I know I said that I wouldn't be covering local area networks in this book, but I have to make a few exceptions to that promise in this chapter. You can sometimes get garbage from a Windows application printed on a network printer that would otherwise print fine on the same printer connected directly to a workstation.

The reason for the problem may be that the TrueType data is getting garbled in transmission. Novell NetWare sends print jobs as either text or bitstream. If set for text, any Tab characters (decimal 9 in ASCII) get expanded to spaces. This can cause problems if you're sending bitmapped graphics as part of the print job, which is exactly what happens when TrueType fonts are used.

The problem arises if one (or more) of the data bytes in the graphics data happens to have a decimal value of 9. If NetWare is handling print jobs in text mode, this one character will be expanded to many space characters, which scrambles the graphics data. Use the PRINTCON utility to change the network's configuration to bitstream print jobs, and the problem should disappear.

Interface Problems

> What we have here is a failure to communicate.
>
> Stuart Rosenberg
> *Cool Hand Luke,* 1967

Before a printer can print anything, the data has to get from the PC to the printer. This is handled by the interface, and although this is a fairly straightforward issue, you have to know about a few "gotchas" and a few interface-related problems that you might encounter.

Parallel Ports

The **parallel connection** is the most popular choice for printers. It is fast, easy, and takes no configuration to speak of because all the settings are well standardized on both the printer and the computer end of the connection.

It gets its name from the fact that the data is sent in parallel lines (Figure 5.4). A full byte of information is sent at one time, using separate wires for each of the eight bits. The specification for the connection is complicated, but in general, you want to use a cable that is no more than 10 feet long so that you are sure to get reliable signals across the connection. There are some high-quality cables that can be used for longer runs, up to 150 feet if necessary, and you can get all sorts of devices to handle even greater distances; check with a supply company such as Black Box (listed in Appendix A). Keep in mind that the 10-foot limit is not an iron-clad guarantee that you have a reliable connection because it is possible for a cheap quality cable of that length or shorter to have problems.

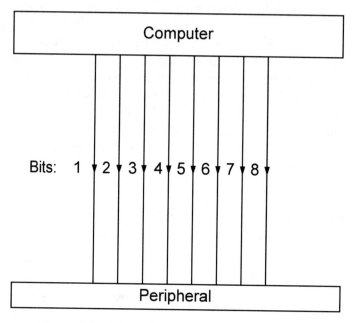

Figure 5.4   Schematic of a parallel data connection

Before the IBM PC, most microcomputers used the same connector at the computer end, but IBM engineers changed that. They decided to use a male 25-pin D-connector on the computer (even though this had traditionally been used for serial port connections), so parallel cables now have a female 25-pin D-connector on one end.

Most printers use a 36-pin Centronics connector at their end of the cable. This is a thick connector with a ridge of contacts running down the middle. Although this is the most common by far, we are just beginning to see printers coming out with a new, more compact connector, which is often called a MDR 36M, a 1284-C, a Centronics-C or a high-density Centronics connector (Figure 5.5). Face it, this connector is too new for the industry to have settled on what to call it. It is also a 36-pin connector, but it is smaller connector with a small ridge down the center—much like the newer, compact SCSI connectors.

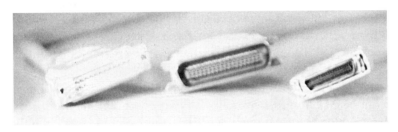

Figure 5.5 These are the three typical connectors used on parallel cables: the 25-pin female connector for the computer, and the Centronics and the new high-density Centronics connectors.

The point about these new connectors is that you can no longer take for granted that a standard parallel cable will work with a new printer. Because printers do not include a parallel cable when you buy them, you have to provide your own. So now, when you buy a new printer and are planning to use a parallel port, be sure to check on which type of connector it uses so you can get the right kind of cable to go with it.

There is also a new kind of parallel port on the computer end of the cable, even though the connection looks the same. The original parallel port is primarily designed for one-way communication—the computer sends over print data, and the printer can signal back whether or not it is ready or has run out of paper, but that's about it. New printers expect to be on a more equal footing with their computers and have a lot more to say. As a result, new bidirectional ports have been designed so that the printers can communicate with the computer, too.

Enhanced parallel ports

> **Don't confuse bidirectional communications with bidirectional printing.** The first refers to the flow of data in both directions between computer and printer. The second term refers to the movement of the print head in a dot matrix or ink jet printer. In bidirectional printing, printing is done on both passes, left to right and right to left. The purpose of this approach is to make printing faster. Not all printers have this feature, and some may have it for some print quality modes but not for others.

Bidirectional communications let the computer ask the printer about how it is configured, which in turn allows you to control the printer from your keyboard and screen instead of using the printer's front panel controls. It also lets the printer provide more meaningful messages, such as telling you not only that it has a paper jam, but where in the printer the paper has become stuck—older printers could only report that there was a problem of some unidentified sort.

As an added benefit, these new parallel ports can also transmit data much faster than the older standard, which is necessary to make the most of today's fast laser printers. You will find references to EPP (Enhanced Parallel Ports), ECP (Microsoft's Enhanced Communication Port standard), and IEEE 1284-compliant ports (an Institute of Electrical and Electronic Engineers standard), but all refer to bidirectional, high-speed parallel ports.

If your computer doesn't have one of these ports, and you think you could benefit from faster data transfer between your computer and your printer, you can easily add such a port. You may need to disable your existing parallel port if you can't remove it from your system, but you can get high-speed parallel ports on an ISA expansion card for less than $40. Many of the newer multi-I/O cards include this feature (along with high-speed serial port support as well). Note that if your computer's BIOS does not support the high-speed bidirectional parallel port, you may need to load a software driver in order to take advantage of this feature.

Parallel problems

In most cases, parallel connections are pass/fail. If you have the correct parallel port selected (LPT1 or LPT2) for your computer, the printer should work. There is an easy way to make sure that your parallel connection is working correctly, simply using DOS. First, hook up the computer and the printer, turn them on, and make sure that your printer is ready and has paper. Then, at the DOS prompt, type:

```
COPY CON LPT1
```

and press the Enter key. Nothing happens except that the cursor drops to the next line, which is blank (no DOS prompt or anything). This command tells the computer to copy whatever comes from the CONsole (the keyboard) directly to the parallel port (LPT1). If your printer is attached to LPT2, change the command accordingly.

If you don't know whether your parallel port is LPT1 or LPT2, you can use the Microsoft Diagnostics utility (MSD.EXE) to report what ports your system has, or you can simply try LPT1 first and if that doesn't work, try LPT2. (And if *neither* of those works, go run MSD and see what it reports.) To run the Microsoft Diagnostics program, simply type MSD at the DOS prompt, and the program should start and present you with a screen similar to the one in Figure 5.6. If the program does not run, look for it on your DOS distribution disks.

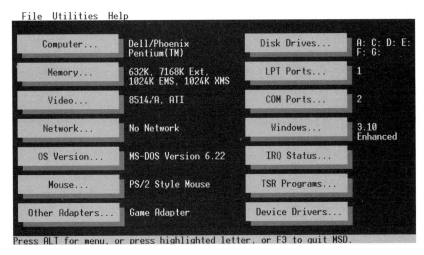

File Utilities Help

Computer...	Dell/Phoenix Pentium(TM)	Disk Drives...	A: C: D: E: F: G:
Memory...	632K, 7168K Ext. 1024K EMS, 1024K XMS	LPT Ports...	1
Video...	8514/A, ATI	COM Ports...	2
Network...	No Network	Windows...	3.10 Enhanced
OS Version...	MS-DOS Version 6.22	IRQ Status...	
Mouse...	PS/2 Style Mouse	TSR Programs...	
Other Adapters...	Game Adapter	Device Drivers...	

Press ALT for menu, or press highlighted letter, or F3 to quit MSD.

Figure 5.6 You can use the DOS utility MSD to examine your system's configuration.

If your printer uses PCL or most dot matrix and ink jet emulations, press Ctrl-L, then Ctrl-Z. This causes the following characters to appear on the blank line:

```
^L^Z
```

Then press Enter. Your screen should report "One file copied" and return to the DOS prompt, and your printer should eject a blank page. This is because the Ctrl-L is the way to send a decimal 11 ASCII character, which is the Form Feed (page eject) control character for most printers. The Ctrl-Z is the End Of File character; it signals to DOS that the input from the CONsole is complete and that the data should be copied to the port. If the printer does not eject a page, you may have a communication problem between your computer and printer.

If your printer is a PostScript printer, the preceding command won't work. Instead, type:

```
showpage
```

Then press Enter and type:

```
^Z
```

Press Enter again. This sends the PostScript page eject command, and your printer should spit out a blank page.

Possessed printer   Aside from a simple lack of communication across a parallel port, I have seen situations when computer and printer communicate inaccurately. The give-away for this problem is that there is a pattern to the errors. For example, when sending just a simple text file to the printer, some letters get consistently substituted for others. In one example I encountered, the alphabet came out as "ACCEEGGI-IKKMMOOQQSSUUWWYY[" and spaces came out as exclamation points.

You might suspect that demons have invaded your printer and are toying with your sanity, but there's a less-than-supernatural explanation.

The root of this problem is in the data received at the printer. The ASCII value for a space is a decimal 32 (10000 in binary), and the exclamation mark is decimal 33 (100001 binary). This means that if the last bit in the connection were stuck at a value of "1" instead of changing between "1" and "0" as it should, spaces would print as exclamation marks. Capital A is decimal 65 (1000001 binary) so it would not be affected by the stuck bit, but B is decimal 66 (1000010 binary) so it would come out as a C, which is decimal 67 (1000011 binary). This carries on all the way to the end of the alphabet, where Z—decimal 90 (1011010 binary)—would come out as an open square bracket, which is decimal 91 (1011011 binary).

This problem could be caused by a serious (and potentially expensive) problem in your computer's controller electronics, or it could be a (less expensive) problem with the parallel port in your computer. Most likely, however, it is the result of a bad connection. The first step is to try again using a good quality printer cable (no longer than 10 feet) and see if that solves the problem. If that does not clear it up, try the printer with another computer or the computer with another printer to see if the A/B test technique can isolate the cause.

Serial Ports

Serial ports are used more often for mice and modems than for printers, but they are used for printers on occasion. They are not as fast as a parallel port, and they can be much more difficult to configure successfully.

Figure 5.7 shows a diagram of how data travels through a serial port connection. Essentially the data must run through a single wire from the computer to the printer (and if the printer wants to talk back, that data flows back through a separate, single wire.) Instead of sending all eight bits of a byte's information at once like a parallel port, a serial port sends each bit down the line, one at a time, in series—hence the name.

In order for two serial devices to communicate correctly, they must agree on how the data is being transmitted. This is why you must carefully configure serial ports in order to establish a successful connection. You need to set the speed (baud rate), how many bits will come at a time (7 or 8), whether the eighth bit will

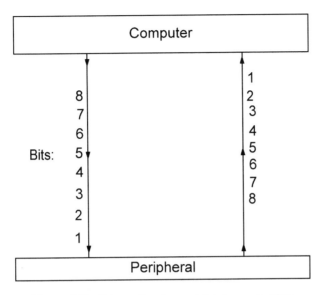

Figure 5.7 Schematic of a serial data connection.

be used for error checking (even or odd parity, or none if using 8 bits), and how many bits will signal the end of a bunch (one or two stop bits). Many communications programs will handle this with your modem automatically, but for printers you typically have to adjust the settings on both the computer (typically through the DOS MODE command or the Windows Ports applet in Control Panel) and on the printer (through the printer's control panel or switch settings).

You also need to make sure that the ports on the computer and the printer can talk and listen to each other. There are some standard signal assignments for the 9- and 25-pin serial connections (Figure 5.8), but different printers expect to have different combinations of the signals connected to the computer in different ways. To be safe, consult with the printer manufacturer about what connections a serial cable should have, and then get a cable with precisely those connections. (I have often been given wrong information from printer companies about serial connections, so be prepared to try more than once.)

Figure 5.8 Most PCs use either a 25-pin or a 9-pin connector for their serial ports.

Testing the connection

You can use the same procedures to test a serial connection as described earlier for parallel connections, but use COM1 instead of LPT1. Remember also that you may have to set the communication parameters using the DOS MODE command first, to match those used by the printer.

COM port conflicts

PC-compatible computers have one major drawback when it comes to serial ports. This is not a problem if you are only using two serial ports (COM1 and COM2), but you can run into troubles if you need three or four serial connections. The problem is that serial ports are assigned a hardware interrupt (IRQ), which is one way that the port and the computer can communicate that there is activity at the port. Table 5.1 lists these assignments.

Table 5.1   Standard IRQ assignments for serial ports in PC computers

Serial Port	IRQ Assignment
COM1	4
COM2	3
COM3	4
COM4	3

If you have three serial devices—such as a mouse, modem, and serial printer—two of the three devices will have to use the same IRQ if your serial ports use the standard configuration. This leads to problems if you try to use both devices at the same time. If you use a printer on COM1 at the same time that you're using a modem on COM3, you are likely to run into this conflict.

You may be able to work around this if your serial ports can be configured to use a different IRQ. You will probably have to change a jumper on the expansion card or your motherboard, and you will also have to change the port's IRQ setting in the Windows Control Panel's Ports applet, using the Advanced settings feature.

Another possible fix is to replace one of your serial peripherals with another that's designed to use a different port. For example, you can get a bus mouse that does not require a serial port or can use a parallel connection for your printer instead.

Sharing Printers

> What makes loneliness an anguish
> Is not that I have no one to share my burden,
> But this:
> I have only my own burden to bear.
>
> Dag Hammarskjöld
> *Night Is Drawing Nigh,* 1964

Printers are often one of the most expensive components in a computer system, and they spend a lot of their time doing nothing. As a result, if you have more than one person working near each other, it makes sense to look for ways to share one printer among all the users. Some problems can arise from this practice, however.

Autoswitching Printers

The easiest way to share a printer is to pick one that has multiple ports, with all the ports simultaneously active. This means that the printer can accept data from more than one port at a time.

At its simplest, this feature means that the printer listens for incoming data on all ports. If it detects a print job coming in on one port, it gives a "busy signal" to computers on the other ports if they try to send a job.

A better implementation includes print job buffering. If the printer is busy printing a job from one port, the data from another port is received but held in a portion of the printer's memory until the first job is finished. Some printers with this feature have a fixed amount of memory available to each port, but better printers allocate the memory on a dynamic basis, changing the amounts assigned to the different ports based on their needs.

You will also often find auto-emulation included with automatic port-switching features. If you do not need the automatic emulation sensing for a given computer, you might want to configure the printer's port for that connection to the printer language that the computer will be using. For example, if the computer attached to the printer's parallel port will only be using a LaserJet-compatible driver, configure the printer's parallel port to assume that the data will be in PCL format. This can improve print speed and eliminate the potential problem of a misidentified print language.

Some port-switching schemes rely on a time-out setting in order to detect when one print job ends so that another can start. In some cases, you can configure the time-out period. Set it too short and one print job may be interrupted by another; set it too long and you may end up waiting longer than you'd like before the printer decides that it's ready for another print job.

If you have an application that pauses as it prints (such as a database program that does a lot of processing before sending the next page of the print job), you can avoid the problem of the printout becoming interleaved with other jobs, and fix it *without* resorting it an inordinately long time-out setting. Instead, print the output to a disk file (Windows as well as most programs makes this easy to accomplish), and then copy the output file to your printer so that it can be sent to the printer without pauses.

Switch Boxes

If your printer does not have simultaneously active ports, you can get the same effect by adding a switch box. These units have a wide range of features and prices, but they can be split into two large categories: manual switches and intelligent switches.

Do it by hand.   A **manual switch** is simply a mechanical switch box (Figure 5.9). Manual switches are frequently called **AB switches** (for sharing one device with two computers) or **X switches** (for sharing two devices with two computers). The switch may be a rotary knob or pushbuttons, but they all function in more or less the same way—you have to physically do something in order to change the connection.

Figure 5.9   A manual switch box is okay for some situations, but should never be used with a laser printer.

A manual switch works fine for some devices, especially dot matrix printers, but never use one for a laser printer. Always get a good-quality unit because cheap models may send a voltage through a connecting wire by accident as you switch from one setting to the other, which could cause permanent damage to your printer's electronics (and that's the *most* expensive part of the machine). Better models use "break before make" switches, which means that each contact is disconnected from the first device *before* it is connected to the second one. Even with this extra design protection, you should not use one with a laser printer or any device with expensive and complex controller circuitry. For example, Hewlett-Packard's LaserJet warranty does not cover damage from mechanical switches. For printers such as these, you're better off spending the extra money for an intelligent switch.

Intelligent switches perform much like the automatic port-switching features that are built into some printers. They can recognize incoming print jobs, and some can even buffer print jobs from more than one computer at the same time. High-end printer sharing devices even have configuration options that include the printing of an identifying page before each print job so that you can tell which computer sent it.

Magic fingers

Network Printers

The problems surrounding network connections could fill an entire chapter—if not an entire book—but there are a few points worth mentioning. First and foremost is the fact that you don't need to get an entire network if all you want to do is share a printer among a group of users. Many printers have built-in sharing features, or you can add them for much less cost and hassle than it takes to install and configure a full local area network.

In the past, sharing a printer across a network meant that you needed to use a computer as a server for a shared printer; you either attached the printer to your file server or a dedicated workstation. This is no longer necessary, as more and more printers—especially those with larger capacities designed for shared use— offer optional network connections. These direct connections to the network are also getting easier and easier to configure. You used to have to enter all sorts of arcane trivia about the printer's network interface and the server and the birth-date of the programmer's eldest aunt from Schenectady, but now the printer and the server seem to sort this stuff out more or less for themselves and you can be up and running much sooner and with less effort.

Finally, not all network connections are the same, especially in terms of speed. For example, standard Ethernet is rated at about 1.25MB per second, which is one-tenth as fast as the newer connections such as Fast Ethernet (also called "100-BaseT"). In the other direction, LocalTalk (also known as AppleTalk) has a data transfer rate of less than 30KB per second—one-fourth the speed of standard Ethernet. So slow performance over a network may be the result of the network's limitations, not any particular problem with the printer itself.

Power Problems

Most computer products have become increasingly stingy about their use of electrical energy over the years, but laser printers still consume a considerable amount of power. If your electrical service is marginal, you may notice that even a personal laser printer is having an adverse effect on other electrical devices.

While printing, it is not unusual for a laser printer to draw from 500 to more than 1000 watts. At standby, they can still draw from 50 to 250 watts of power. Lasers also have to heat their fuser roller, which is done in bursts that only last a matter of milliseconds, but that can create power demands that are three to four times greater than the average amount of power drawn while printing. When you figure that a typical hair dryer draws about 600 to 1000 watts or that an average household lightbulb draws 60 watts, it is easy to see how a laser printer can cause your lights to dim.

There is no easy fix for this problem, but you shouldn't ignore the problem, either. You can try plugging the printer into a different outlet in hopes that it is served by a different power circuit, but that may not help. You may need to run a special electrical circuit with sufficient capacity from your main breaker box. If you don't fix the problem, you can damage other equipment due to low voltage, or you may have to cope with blown fuses or tripped circuit breakers.

Paper Problems

> Do not on any account attempt to write on both sides of the paper at once.
>
> W. C. Sellar
> *1066 and All That,* 1930

The most common problems with printers center around paper. It jams, it wrinkles, or the print smears on it. Since the output on paper is the tangible result that you want from a printer in the first place, these are the problems that can be most vexing.

Why Paper Curls

One of the most common complaints I have heard is that people are unhappy with the performance of one laser printer or another because the paper comes out curled or with ridges running down the middle. The chances are excellent that their problems aren't really caused by the printer, but instead are a function of the paper.

Right off the bat, let me say that you should not skimp on paper quality. Being a cheapskate, I used to buy the least expensive photocopier paper I could find and use it in my laser printer. Paper is paper, right? Wrong! I noticed after finishing off a case or two that there were many little tufts of paper dust floating around inside the printer—much like the dust balls I find behind our piano. This stuff does not do anything good for the mechanical parts of the printer, and

when it accumulates so that it feeds through with a sheet of paper, it can get between the toner and the paper and you don't get a clean image. You don't have to buy the best paper in the world, but I do recommend that you stick to a name brand of decent quality.

Most people know enough to buy paper by its specified weight; most laser printers are rated to handle 15- to 28-pound paper stock, and 20-pound stock is the weight most frequently used for lasers and photocopiers.

Some people know that papers of the same weight can vary in terms of thickness and stiffness, which are attributes that are rarely specified in printer manuals. If you want to use paper that is stiffer or thicker than normal (or thinner or flimsier, for that matter), get a small sample first to see if it feeds reliably before you buy a case of it.

Even fewer people seem to be aware of an essential factor for paper, perhaps because it also is rarely specified anywhere: its moisture content. Paper that is too moist *or* too dry will not feed correctly, nor will it take a good image. Reams of paper are sealed in paper packages at the paper mill to keep them at the right moisture level, but this starts to change the moment that you break the seal. (Since people tend to use fewer sheets at a time of expensive desktop publishing papers, these papers are often bundled in stacks of 100 or 200 sheets, instead of a full 500-sheet ream.)

How dry I am.

Too much moisture can cause paper to curl excessively when run through a laser printer. You can reduce this effect by making sure that you are printing on the correct side of the sheet; the label on the ream of paper should indicate which side of the sheet you should print on first. So only open as much paper as you need at a time, and keep your open packages in a closed space where the humidity is not likely to change the paper's moisture content by a great deal.

Poor Toner Adhesion

As described earlier, toner is a plastic powder that gets placed on the paper by static electricity and then is melted into place by a combination of pressure and heat. The toner actually sticks to the fibers at the paper's surface. Or at least it tries to stick to them . . . .

One problem can occur when you use a heavily textured paper, such as some classic laid bond papers. I have seen some of these papers that have almost a pinstripe pattern of ridges on the paper's surface. This is visually attractive and makes the paper interesting to the touch, but it is lousy for laser printing. The toner on the top of the ridges adheres just fine to the page, but the toner down in the "valleys" often does not get sufficient heat and pressure to stick to the paper. The toner can be easily rubbed off when you handle the printed sheet, which can make a mess on your hands and clothes and can make the information printed on the page more difficult to understand.

The opposite case also occurs—paper can be too flat. Ink jet printers often produce their best output on coated paper because the smooth top provides a uniform surface for the ink so that it does not wick and spread into the paper's fibers. Using similar coated paper in a laser printer does not work well at all. The toner has little that it can grab onto when it melts, and so it forms little plates of plastic on top of the page. These can actually flake off when handled—especially on a crease where the paper is folded—which is not as messy as the powdered toner, but it still can turn your printed document into a mystery to be deciphered.

Twice-Printed Paper

You also have to be careful about where your paper has been. I once received a letter from a reader who complained that he had fed a preprinted form into his laser printer so he could print his responses in the blanks, and he kept getting ghost images of the original form on subsequent pages from the printer.

The problem came about because the preprinted form had not been printed on his printer; it most likely had been created on a photocopier. As described earlier, the different melting points and other characteristics of the photocopier toner (as compared with the reader's laser toner) meant that it reacted differently to the temperature of the fuser roller in the laser printer. It became too melted, and some of the photocopier toner was transferred onto the fuser roller itself, where it was slowly applied to subsequent pages as if it were an offset printing press. The only solution to that problem is a careful cleaning of the fuser rollers, or possibly even their replacement (which can be an expensive repair).

Now, I have lousy handwriting, so I understand the desire to fill out forms with a computer, but there are a number of ways that this particular problem can be avoided. One way is to use a scanner or a fax machine to create an image of the form. A number of personal scanners and some fax software packages include a utility to find the blanks on a scanned form so that you can fill them in.

If you don't have a scanner or fax, you can still get the job done with a photocopier. Make a photocopy of the original form on a transparency. Then create your computer document that has the information to go in the blanks. Hold the transparency up to your printout to make sure that the answers line up with the blanks. When you have it all worked out correctly, put the transparency on top of your answers and make a photocopy of the sandwiched pages.

Printing on Small Pieces of Paper

Another problem that often comes up is how to print on small pieces of paper. Most printers can handle an envelope without trouble, but when you get down to a 3×5 file card or something smaller, some printers just can't get hold of the paper or feed it through the paper path reliably.

The answer to this one is a Post-it or equivalent. (See Figure 5.10.) In addition to serving as handy bookmarks or littering your telephone with all the important calls that you have to make today, these little slips of paper can help you with your printer as well—thanks to their easily placed and removed adhesive.

Figure 5.10 Use Post-its or similar labels to hold small pieces of paper on larger ones for printing.

Just use two labels (on each side) to hold your smaller piece of paper in place on a letter-size sheet of paper. Place the labels so that the adhesive strip goes through the printer first. Also, you may get the best results using the closest thing your printer has to a "straight-through" paper path; this varies among printers, but in general it means using a manual feed slot or tray and a face-up output tray.

When Labels Get Stuck Inside

Finally, there are labels. When Avery and other paper product suppliers started making self-adhesive labels for computer printers—especially lasers—it sure made life a lot easier. Now it's a simple matter to create labels for mailing, disks, return addresses, file folders, and even audio cassettes. It's wonderful. It's a great timesaver. It's really convenient. And it's fun . . . until one of them little suckers decides to depart the carrier sheet as it wanders through your printer, and the label takes up permanent residence wrapped tightly around a roller or other essential item. (And all other pages that you try to feed through decide that they just can't get past this new occupant of the paper path, and they jam.)

Ooops!

Hey, I can write about this because I've been there, done that. It's no fun, and I admit it, but this is something that you may be able to fix yourself if you're willing to take a chance. If you're not comfortable taking things apart without directions and then getting them back together again, skip this procedure and call the repair service.

If you're feeling brave, however, you can carefully start to take apart the pieces of the paper path where the label is located. (Keep track of the pieces—I find that taking Polaroid instant photos helps a lot in knowing where stuff goes again when reassembly time comes. I don't have a video camera here in the Electronic Cottage, but that might be a good way to document the process, too.)

When you find the label, you probably will discover that it will not unwind itself and come along peacefully. It will tear and stick and wad up, and even when all the paper is removed, a gunky adhesive residue will be left behind. This is not good, and subsequent sheets of paper are more than likely to accept this obstacle no better than they did the complete label.

Tossed label salad   The answer is vegetable oil. Put a few drops on the adhesive, rub a bit, and the adhesive should come off fairly easily. It may take a few cycles of oil and rubbing, but you should be able to get the sticky stuff off. If you don't have salad oil handy, a penetrating oil like WD-40 also works well. (I have been told that physicians have towelette-type pads with a solvent that they use to remove bandage adhesive, and that these are very effective on stuck labels, but I haven't tried them myself.)

Be careful not to fling oil around in other parts of the printer, and remove as much of the oil as you can when you're finished. A few wipes with rubbing alcohol may help with the clean-up operation.

UPGRADING

Not many upgrades are available for printers. Some of them are not particularly attractive. For example, some companies offer upgrades that claim to increase the resolution or print speed of a given printer. In my experience, these upgrades do not perform as well as a printer designed to have those attributes from the start, and they don't save you much money compared with selling the old printer and buying the new one with the improved features.

The Few Upgrades That Are Worth It

The upgrades that make the most sense are the ones that increase your existing printer's capacities. These make sense because you'll know when you need them, and you'll be able to see their impact right away.

For example, most printers come with a minimum memory configuration. This is sufficient for most users, but if you print large, complex images or the printer is shared among a number of busy users, more memory will make it possible to print the images or keep all the users busy.

The other category of capacity upgrades is paper handling. Some printers are built as though they were made out of Legos. You can get all sorts of options that plug in or hang onto the base model: larger input and output capacity trays, bin sorters, duplex printing features, and envelope feeders. Keep in mind that few printers have output trays that are equal to their input capacities, so just because a printer can hold more paper with a new input tray doesn't necessarily mean that it will be able to operate for a longer time without operator attention.

Some functionality add-ons and upgrades are worth consideration, such as additional I/O ports (especially network connections), the addition of PostScript language support (if you have a need for it), or plain-paper fax functions. This last item lets you receive incoming faxes right on your printer (and, in some cases, send outgoing faxes from your computer as well, just as if you were printing them on your printer). Compared with thermal-paper faxes, plain-paper fax is much easier to read, handle, and file. This capability is available as an option for some printers or as an external device from third-party sources.

Buying a New Printer

> Avoid making irrevocable decisions while tired or hungry. N.B.:
> Circumstances can force your hand. So think ahead!
>
> Robert Heinlein
> *The Notebooks of Lazarus Long,* 1973

In general, however, if you're not satisfied with your existing printer (or if it should suddenly give out completely), you will need to buy a replacement instead of upgrading the existing unit. Here are a few key points to keep in mind.

Resolution

Higher resolution improves graphics output (especially for photographs and other continuous tone images) because it permits the use of a finer halftone screening, which in turn means that more shades of gray can be produced in a given space. Newspaper photographs are printed with a lower halftone screen, making them look coarser than those printed in a news magazine.

Enhanced resolution features greatly improve the smoothness of text and numbers and of line art. They do not improve photographic images and, in some cases, can actually result in a poorer result. At 600 dpi, enhanced resolution is noticeable—even without magnification, in some cases—but at resolutions higher than that, it does not make much difference.

For personal and business correspondence use, 300 dpi is probably sufficient, especially if there is an enhanced resolution feature. For good-quality output, an enhanced 600 dpi is better; this also works well for average desktop publishing output. You only need to consider resolutions higher than this if you need professional-level graphic arts output.

Interface

The high-speed, bidirectional parallel port remains the best bet for performance and low cost. Serial ports are often in short supply on a PC, and they are not as fast. Network interfaces can be fast—especially when a printer is shared—but LocalTalk is outdated and slow and should be avoided where possible.

Language

PCL5 (HP LaserJet III-compatible or better) is all most people need. If you have to create output files to be sent to a different device, PostScript has some advantages, but recognize that this does not guarantee that your page will look the same coming out of both devices.

Color or Not

Color is the next great thing in personal computing. If an ink jet output is good enough for your needs, consider getting a color ink jet. You're bound to find all sorts of uses for color that you don't think you'd use now. If text quality is paramount, go with a laser printer. If money is no object, get a color laser printer. (And whether you get the printer or are just thinking about it, get David Stone's *Underground Guide to Color Printers* in any case.)

Fax Capability

More printers are offering this as a built-in feature or an option. There are advantages to getting a unit designed for your particular printer, but if you find a printer that you really like without this as an option, you can always add it with a third-party device.

More Windows 95 Plug and Play

If you are running Windows 95, be sure to get a printer that supports the Plug and Play feature. This lets you plug the printer in, turn it on, and start Windows 95, and the computer configures itself for the printer.

The way that this works is that the printer sends a notification to Windows that it is connected, and Windows then searches its files for a matching device ID. If it finds an exact match, Windows installs a driver for the printer. If it does not find an exact match, Windows searches for a compatible driver. If it finds one, Windows offers to install that driver, or lets you provide a disk with a matching driver instead.

6 Multimedia Stuff

It is a tale
Told by an idiot, full of sound and fury;
Signifying nothing.

> William Shakespeare
> *Macbeth,* 1605

"Multimedia"—the marketing term that launched millions of copies of Windows 3. What is it? I surely don't know.

I think it is old wine in a new bottle. Break down the term and you get "multiple types of media," which could be interpreted to mean an interface that uses text and sound and graphics. Well, stretch the sound to include "beeps," and we had multimedia back with Lotus 1-2-3. If you want to add animation to the mix of requirements, I had that with a package called "The Executive Briefing System," which was a presentation graphics program for the Apple][. (This program is notable because it was the first product from a new startup venture from Boston, named Lotus Development Corporation.)

So multimedia may be hard to define, but we all seem to know what we mean by it. To paraphrase the old chestnut, "I don't know what I like, but I know multimedia when I see it."

One fact is clear: The release of Windows 3.0 opened the floodgates of demand for multimedia on desktop computers. This resulted in explosive growth in the sales of sound cards and CD-ROM drives. Today it's getting difficult to find a computer system for sale that *doesn't* include multimedia support. Why did this happen?

The answer is that Windows did the same thing for multimedia equipment that it did for printers and displays. Once you have configured Windows to work with your hardware, any Windows program should then be able to use it without any reconfiguration. This is a far cry from DOS apps where every program had to include support for every hardware device, and you had to configure each program separately.

Windows makes multimedia happen.

159

To help reduce the confusion over the definition of multimedia and what you need to run it, an industry group—the MPC Marketing Council—was founded by Microsoft and other major manufacturers to create the specification for a Multimedia PC. The first level specification was set in 1990, but as software demands grew and equipment became more capable, a new MPC2 specification was released in 1993 (Table 6.1).

Table 6.1 Multimedia PC (MPC) specifications.

Component	MPC Level 1	MPC2
RAM	2 MB	4 MB
Processor	386SX, 16 MHz	486SX, 25 MHz
Hard drive	30 MB	160 MB
CD-ROM drive		
Sustained data transfer rate	150 KB/sec	300 KB/sec
Maximum average seek time	1 second	400 milliseconds
Other		CD-ROM XA ready, Multisession capable
Sound	8-bit digital sound, 8-voice synthesizer, MIDI playback	16-bit digital sound, 8-voice synthesizer, MIDI playback
Graphics display adapter		
Resolution/colors	640 x 480, 16 colors	640 x 480, 65,536 colors
Ports	MIDI I/O, joystick	MIDI I/O, joystick

It's difficult to buy a new computer these days that does not exceed the MPC2 standards; even most notebook computers have more power and capacity than this standard requires. If your system does not measure up to the MPC2 specifications, you might want to consider upgrading to match or exceed them.

 **Already the wheels of progress have turned, and a new MPC3 specification is out, although not many multimedia programs require this level of performance. The new specification calls for at least a 75 MHz Pentium CPU, quad-speed CD-ROM, wave table sound card support, and other details that you can expect to find in most new multimedia systems.**

But all is not skittles and beer in the land of multimedia. According to some sources, more than half the multimedia upgrade kits purchased each year are returned for refunds because the buyers could not get them installed and working properly. No other cluster of add-on products creates as much confusion and frustration. So let's try to shed some light on the darker side of multimedia.

NEED TO KNOW

A multimedia system involves three main pieces of hardware: the sound card, the CD-ROM drive, and the speakers. There are also implications for processor, hard disk, memory, and graphics adapter (especially for digitized video), but these are more or less covered already in the previous chapters. So I'll focus on the three main components.

Sound Card Features

> Music hath charms to soothe the savage beast.
>
> James Beamston
> *Man of Taste*

From a typical multimedia computer system, you can get three different kinds of sounds: digitized, MIDI, and Audio-CD. Each has its own purpose, and each works in its own way. Most—but not all—sound cards can support all three.

Digitized Sound (Wave Files)

Sound is an analog phenomenon; it occurs as waves of pressure in the air. (Okay, the waves can occur in some other medium—such as water—but since we spend most of our time in the air, I'll stick with this generalization.) We sense these waves in a number of ways, but mostly with tiny hairlike nerves inside our ears. These nerves sway back and forth in response to the waves, and our brains take those signals, and the music comes out here. Music, voices, sound effects—all make waves in the air.

But our computers are digital girls living in an analog world (to paraphrase Madonna), and they don't do waves. They do bits: on or off, one or zero, high or low. The trick is to convert the original sound wave signal into digital data, and then convert it back again. If the conversion is done with enough fidelity, the resulting sounds sound just like the originals: music, voices, sound effects, or whatever. The problem is getting that fidelity.

Consider a simple wave as shown in Figure 6.1. By measuring the wave at regular intervals, we can come up with numeric values for the wave at each point. The smaller the interval between measurements, the more accurate our re-created wave will be.

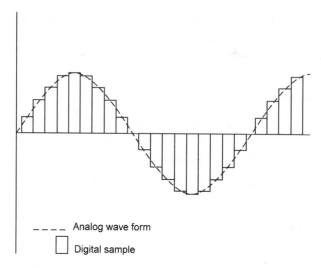

Analog wave form

Digital sample

Figure 6.1 Digital sampling converts sound waves into discrete data points.

One problem with this approach is that it cannot measure waves that go up and down faster than our measurement interval. Figure 6.2 shows two sound waves that would result in the same data points at the measurement interval used in Figure 6.1. The computer would see either of these waves as the same in the first figure, and thus would not accurately record the information of the smaller waves.

You get more and smaller waves in a given length of time, which is another way of saying that they have a higher frequency. So, to be able to reproduce higher frequency sounds, you need to take more measurements in a given length of time.

Sampling rate In digitized sound terms, the number of measurements per second is called the **sampling rate.** The range of sounds audible to human hearing is from about 15 Hz to about 20,000 Hz (or 20 KHz). As we get older, the top limit of the range tends to fall off, making us less sensitive to dog whistles and other "ultrasonic" devices that younger ears can hear.

As a rule of thumb, you need to have a sample rate that is at least twice that of the highest frequency you wish to reproduce. This is why audio CDs—the ones you play on your stereo—have a sampling rate of 44.1 KHz, so that they can capture the highest range of sounds that we can hear.

There's another dimension to digital sampling of sound, and that is the question of what scale you will use to measure the height of the waves. If you only used a 1-bit scale, you wouldn't get much useful information; all you could record was whether there was sound (on or one) or not (off or zero). When you tried to reconstruct the waves, they would all have the same height, so the volume would be the same for all the waves.

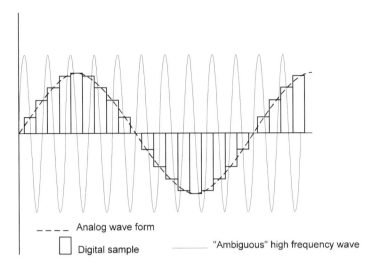

_ _ _ _ Analog wave form

[ ] Digital sample   ———— "Ambiguous" high frequency wave

Figure 6.2 If your measurement interval is too small, you will not be able to accurately measure higher frequency waves.

If you use an 8-bit scale (one byte), you can have 256 different volume levels separating the loudest and most quiet sounds. This may seem like a lot, but it isn't. In audiophile terms, this is a very flat dynamic range. But 16-bit samples—2 bytes per measure—provide a much greater range; the 65,536 levels result in a much richer and realistic sound.

Sample size

And then we have stereo sound; most music is recorded in stereo, which means that separate tracks are recorded for the left and right channels. When played back through a pair of speakers, you get the impression of sounds coming from different locations as if the musicians were spread across the front of your room.

People want high fidelity sound from their audio CDs. As a result, the original sounds are digitized at a high sampling rate—44.1 KHz—with a broad dynamic range—16-bit samples—and in stereo. This adds up to a lot of data per second; 2 bytes times 44,100 samples per second times two channels equals just over 170KB/sec. That adds up quickly. At this rate, a minute of music takes up more than 10MB of storage space.

The storage problem

A "single-speed" CD-ROM drive is rated at just 150KB/sec data transfer rate, which is slightly more than 20KB/sec slower than the rate required to play back an audio CD, yet these drives are capable of playing audio CDs. This apparent paradox is actually easy to explain. The "data" on an audio CD is just a constant stream of information; if the player misreads some of that information, the "error" probably won't make an audible difference in the sound. On the

other hand, a single bit out of place in a computer program can have disas-
trous results, so CD-ROMs have extra information included to provide for error
checking and error correction. For every 2KB of data (2048 bytes) stored on a
CD-ROM, there is an additional 304 bytes used for these overhead functions. If
you include the overhead data in the total data transfer, a single-speed CD-
ROM does in fact transfer more than 170KB of data every second. The more
familiar 150KB/sec rating is more useful, however, because it refers to the
amount of usable data that gets transferred.

You can use lower sampling rates to digitize sounds, and these take up less
storage space though the audio quality is lower. Choosing mono (one channel)
instead of stereo (two channels) cuts the storage requirements in half. And you
can use 8-bit samples instead of 16-bit samples to cut the requirements in half
again, though you will lose dynamic range when you do.

Table 6.2 shows some different sampling rates and sizes, the amount of space
required for a minute of sound, and the quality you can expect to get from the
result.

Table 6.2   Storage requirements increase rapidly as digitized
sound quality improves.

Sampling Rate	Sample Size	KB/min	Quality
11 KHz	8 bit	645	telephone
22 KHz	8 bit	1289	AM radio
22 KHz	16 bit	2578	FM radio (one channel)
44.1 KHz	16 bit	5156	Audio CD (one channel)

For a symphony, you may want to use the best quality digitized sound, but
for the little sounds that play for Windows events, you may want to save some
disk space at the price of sound quality.

**Three-
dimensional
sound**

Stereo sound is more or less limited to moving the perceived source of a
recorded sound to your left or right. In recent years, however, new technologies
have been created to move the sound up and down, and back and forth as well,
so that the sound can appear to come from just about anywhere in the room.

Dolby Pro Logic surround sound started it all. It was designed originally for
home entertainment systems. Pro Logic uses additional channels that are encoded
in the stereo signals that can then be decoded to provide a center channel and a
"surround" channel.

Since then, some companies have developed ways to get similar effects from
just two channels of sound. By adjusting the timing of the portions of the sounds
by tiny fractions of a second, the source of the sound can be made to seem farther

away or closer, even with just two speakers. Some of the leading products in this category are QSound, Spatializer, and SRS.

The most common file format for digitized files have a .WAV file extension and are called **wave files.** These are the ones used by most Windows applications. Some programs use a similar file format with a .VOC extension, and you can find programs that can convert one format to the other. For example, SoundBlaster cards come with VOC2WAV.EXE and WAV2VOC.EXE that let you convert back and forth between these two digitized sound file formats. Most sound cards also come with utilities that let you record your own digitized sound files.

Making waves

MIDI

This FLA (four-letter acronym) stands for Musical Instrument Digital Interface. Primarily designed as a way to control musical instruments from a computer, it is a different way to record music with a computer. Most sound cards include support for MIDI file playback, even though most people don't have MIDI instruments that they can use with them.

The reason that MIDI is so popular is that the sound files take up much less space than digitized sound files. If a digitized sound file is like a photograph of a scene, then a MIDI file is like a paint-by-number diagram of the same page. Each instrument in the musical arrangement is assigned a number, and the sound card re-creates the sounds for those instruments according to the instructions in the MIDI file. (These same instructions can be sent to a MIDI instrument such as an electronic keyboard, and the instrument will re-create the desired sounds.)

The information required is much more compact than digitized sound files. For example, a 30KB WAV file holds only a second and a half of mono sound at a 22 KHz sampling rate, but a similarly sized MIDI file can hold as much as two minutes of sound. That's about ten times as much music in the same amount of storage space.

The re-creation of the instrument sounds is often accomplished through a process called **FM synthesis.** The FM is for frequency modulation, and the synthesis refers to the fact that the sounds are created from mathematical tables. The way that these sounds are created is what gives MIDI playback its "synthesizer" sound—you can tell what instrument it is trying to be, but it doesn't sound like the real thing.

Tin can alley

Early sound cards had limited ability to synthesize instruments, and the result was a flat, tinny, and monotonous sound. All MIDI files sounded more or less the same. Some cards also were limited in the number of different instruments that they could create at one time.

Today the FM synthesis is performed by more sophisticated chips, and many boards are capable of generating 16 to 32 different instruments at once—the specifications often will list this either as the "polyphony" specification or as the number of voices the card supports.

General agreement
One problem with MIDI is that any instrument can be assigned to any channel. To take the paint-by-number metaphor one step farther, you could decide to make the number 2 orange instead of blue in your picture and get an orange sky. MIDI composers can assign any instrument that they want to any channel, and so playing some files back can sound strange if your MIDI driver is configured with a different set of instruments.

You can also have some fun with this feature if your sound card includes a MIDI editor that lets you change the assignment of instruments. My favorite trick is to change the background instruments to some sort of drum or percussion instruments, and then change the lead instrument to "Tubular Bells." The net effect is what I expect you would hear if you turned a tribe of musically inclined monkeys loose in a junkyard filled with oil drums and scrap steel.

To make sure that MIDI files play back with the same instrument arrangement that was originally intended, the industry has come up with a General MIDI specification. This assigns 128 MIDI channels to certain instruments, which ensures that the playback sound will be what the developer intended. You can configure your MIDI settings using the MIDI Mapper applet from the Windows Control Panel (Figure 6.3).

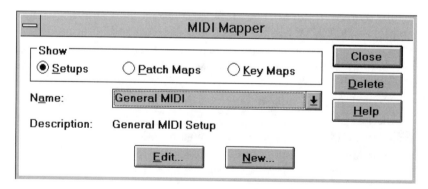

Figure 6.3 Use the MIDI Mapper applet in the Windows Control Panel to configure your MIDI settings.

Sounds like the real thing!
Many sound cards today have another MIDI feature that makes the resulting sound more realistic than before: **wavetables.** Instead of synthesizing the instrument sounds from a few simple mathematical curves, these boards actually have

stored samples of digitized sound from the actual instruments. Some synthesis is still involved—the pitch and duration of the notes are changed mathematically as required—but because the sound is based on the actual complex curves created by the real instruments, the result is much more realistic than the tinny FM synthesis that we normally associate with MIDI files.

Some cards even have on-board memory (either standard or optional) in which you can store your own digitized samples. This lets you add your own instruments (or sound effects, or whatever you want) to your palette of MIDI instruments.

Windows 95 adds one more new feature to the MIDI mix: **polymessage support.** This refers to an ability to send multiple instructions to the sound card at one time. As a result, the CPU has to spend less time waiting to see if the sound card is ready for its next instruction and thus is freed up to carry on other processing tasks in the interim. This should make it possible to have even more complex graphics and other events take place while MIDI files are played back than we've had with other versions of Windows.

More MIDI messages

CD-Audio

The third type of sound that you can get out of a multimedia computer system is **CD-Audio.** This is sometimes referred to as **Red Book Audio,** named for the specification book that describes it. It simply means the kind of audio that you get when you put a music CD in your home stereo system.

Your CD-ROM drive knows how to play audio CDs; most of them already have headphone jacks and volume controls on their front panels, and a few even have play/stop/skip buttons as well. What you may not realize is that a number of CD-ROM titles include CD-Audio tracks in addition to data. In most cases, the CD-Audio sounds are simply piped through your sound card and out to your speakers. Aside from starting and stopping the drive, your computer isn't involved at all in the process, making it practical to listen to audio CDs on your computer while you work.

CD-ROM

> Oh! I have slipped the surly bonds of Earth
> And danced the skies on laughter-silvered wings
>
> John Gillespie Magee
> *High Flight,* 1941

This brings up the larger topic of CD-ROMs and the drives you need to access the data on them. In many ways, they are like the CD player on a stereo system, though there are some important differences.

Interfaces

A CD-ROM can hold more than 500MB of data. Compared with the 1.2MB capacity of a floppy disk of similar diameter, that's a lot of data. Like any other disk drive, the data has to get from the disk to your computer, and like hard disks, you have a number of choices for interface.

Many people connect their CD-ROM drives to their sound boards. Years ago, sound boards had their own proprietary CD-ROM drive interfaces, and you had to get the right type of drive in order to have it work correctly. Then sound card makers started putting all the possible proprietary interfaces on their cards, and a forest of dual-inline pin connectors appeared.

Now, the whole issue of CD-ROM drive interface is simplified. You can choose either a SCSI drive or an ATAPI model (which connects to an IDE interface). And although most sound cards still sport at least one type of CD-ROM drive connector, you are generally better off if you connect your CD-ROM drive to the same type of interface as your hard disk.

The reason that you should use your hard disk controller is performance—especially if you have a local bus controller. At best, your sound card will use a 16-bit ISA expansion slot, running at 8 MHz. In contrast, your local bus hard disk controller operates with a 32-bit connection at speeds up to 33 MHz. Data can be moved much more quickly to your CPU for processing.

Features

There are a number of important features to consider when comparing CD-ROM drives. Perhaps the most important aspect is the speed—which refers to the data transfer rate. A **single-speed** CD-ROM is capable of a 150KB/sec sustained data transfer rate, which is the rate required for audio CDs. Watch out for old, bargain CD-ROM drives because the first drives were not capable of even this speed.

The most common drives right now are **dual-speed** drives. For computer data, they can transfer data at 300KB/sec, and then they slow down to 150KB/sec to play audio CDs. **Quad-speed drives** (sometimes referred to as **4x drives**) have a data transfer rate of about 600KB/sec, and we have just begun to see 6x and 8x with 900KB/sec and 1200KB/sec transfer rates.

Another feature is the number of disks that the drive can hold. Most drives hold one disk, either in a tray or using a caddy, but disk changers are becoming increasingly popular. Although they are a bit more expensive, they can hold three to seven individual disks, which they can change automatically when you want to access a different disk.

Windows 95 Autoload

Although it is not a feature of the disk drive itself, the new Autoload feature in Windows 95 is handy. If the disk has been prepared to take advantage of this function, Windows recognizes the disk when you insert it in the drive and automatically starts the associated application. Stick in a clip art disk and your graphics editor launches. Stick in a game CD and the game begins. This process includes all the setup and installation procedures automatically. No longer do you have to manually install a new CD-ROM on your system. And stick in any audio CD and Win95 starts to play it. It may take a while before all new CD-ROM titles are Win95-aware, but this feature should save a lot of time and headaches.

If you have Windows 3.x and would like to have a feature similar to the Win95 Autoload, shareware programs are available that can do just that. One example is AutoCD. When this program is running and you insert a CD in the computer, the program recognizes that a new disk is in the drive. If it's an audio CD, it will start to play it. If it's a data CD-ROM, you must register the program in the AutoCD database the first time you insert it, but after that, AutoCD automatically runs the associated program for that disk. The program is from Industrial Software, P.O. Box 50334, Provo, UT 84605-0334, and is available for downloading from online services including CompuServe and ZD Net.

Speakers

> True merit, like a river, the deeper it is, the less noise it makes.
>
> Lord Halifax

When it comes to computer speakers, you get what you pay for—never more, and sometimes even less. If you have a stereo sound system nearby, consider running the output from your sound card through it and its speakers. If you don't, figure on getting the best speakers that your budget will allow.

The cheapest speakers have tiny little speaker cones—typically only one cone per speaker—and little in the way of controls or engineering. They are the modern equivalent of the 1960s Detroit dashboard speaker; they make noise and that's about the best that can be said for them.

More expensive speakers add multiple cones (or drivers) to provide better response at different sound frequency ranges, and more carefully engineered housings that reduce unwanted sounds and boost low-frequency response.

You need two speakers for stereo sound—one for each channel—but if you listen to much music or are a game player, you'll also want to get a subwoofer to fill in the bass range.

Amplification Issues

One important cost factor is whether or not the speakers have their own amplification. Most sound cards include circuitry to drive speakers directly, but these tend to have only minimal power—5 watts or less—and can only drive the cheapest, most efficient speakers. Quality speakers require more power, and you can either provide this amplification from a third source (such as a stereo set) or you can get self-powered speakers that have amplifying circuitry built in. If the speakers have a volume control, they have a built-in amplifier.

@#%$%@!

> It is good to learn caution by the misfortunes of others.
>
> Publilius Syrus

I admit that I have spent my share of time struggling with sound cards and other multimedia equipment, but I have to say that I expect the return rate on multimedia kits to drop substantially in the coming years. The last kits that I installed went in without a hitch, and I expect that most users would be able to follow the directions and get an equally successful result.

Of course, the easiest way to beat most of these problems is to simply purchase a new system with all the multimedia hardware already installed, but I realize that this is not always the most practical option for many budgets. So here are some of the most common problems (and a few less common ones as well) that I have run across.

Sound Card Problems

Leading the list of high-blood pressure elevators are sound cards; they can be maddeningly frustrating. Some careful experimentation can often help eliminate the problems, so don't give up hope.

Configuration Problems

Once a sound card is installed and running correctly, chances are that you'll never have to think about it again. Unfortunately, getting it to that pleasant state is sometimes problematical. Sound cards typically have three settings: an I/O address, a DMA (Direct Memory Access) channel, and an IRQ. Finding values for these three that are not already taken in your system is the biggest source of trouble with sound card installation.

Fortunately many sound cards come with installation routines that test different settings *before* you install the card so that you can configure it correctly from the start. If your card does not include such a utility, many other hardware analysis programs provide a similar function. For example, WinSleuth Gold has a feature that inspects your computer system and reports on the status of the various options.

DMA channels are numbered 0 through 3 and 5 through 7, with 2 typically assigned to your floppy disk controller. The channels numbered up through 3 are 8-bit channels, and the other three are 16-bit channels. Most systems have plenty of DMA channels available; all you have to do is make certain that the one you assign to the sound card is not already in use.

IRQs are sometimes in scarcer supply. Table 6.3 lists the default assignments for the IRQ settings.

Table 6.3 Default IRQ assignments in a typical AT-compatible PC.

IRQ	Default Assignment
IRQ0	System Timer Tick
IRQ1	Keyboard Event
IRQ2	Cascade
IRQ3	Serial Port COM2
IRQ4	Serial Port COM1
IRQ5	Parallel Port LPT2
IRQ6	Diskette Controller
IRQ7	Parallel Port LPT1
IRQ8	CMOS Real-Time Clock
IRQ9	Software Redirected to IRQ2
IRQ10	Not used
IRQ11	Not used
IRQ12	Not used
IRQ13	Math Coprocessor
IRQ14	Hard Disk Controller
IRQ15	Not used

As you can see, things can get a bit crowded. If you do not have a second parallel port installed in your system (as is often the case), you can use IRQ5 for your sound card. Better yet, use one of the free IRQs numbered 10 or above if your card will support that assignment.

Some cards make this process even more difficult. The Pro Audio Spectrum cards from Media Vision required two sets of settings: one for the Media Vision portion of the board and another for the SoundBlaster-compatible portion. These boards can be especially difficult to shoehorn into a crowded system.

If you have an original PC- or XT-compatible system, you will not have the IRQs higher than 7, and you may well not have any available IRQs. These older systems do not have the processing power to handle multimedia tasks, however, so the problem of configuring a sound card is moot.

When you do find a combination of settings that works, be sure to write them down someplace so that you know how the card is configured. You will need to know the information when installing some software packages, especially games. In Windows, make sure that the required drivers are installed in the Drivers applet of the Control Panel, and that they are configured correctly for the settings you have used.

In fact, it's a good idea to write down all your IRQ and DMA assignments and keep a copy in your computer. Tape a plastic bag to the bottom of the case or inside somewhere, and while you're at it, add copies of your CMOS configuration settings and any other information you might want the next time you need to troubleshoot or upgrade your system.

Compatibility/Emulation Issues

A less frequent problem is that your card may not be compatible with some software. If you do not see your particular brand of card listed among the program's choices, try SoundBlaster for the digitized sound and AdLib for the MIDI settings, as most sound cards are compatible with these two standards.

No CD-Audio Sound

Another common problem is that you play a CD-ROM title and discover that you don't hear anything when you should, even though you know that you can play digitized WAV files and MIDI files without a problem. What can make the sound go away like this?

The answer is that your CD-ROM program is probably using a CD-Audio sound track instead of WAV or MIDI. This is not very common, but it does happen. One way to find out if the CD has CD-Audio tracks is to use an audio CD player utility. Most multimedia systems and kits come with one, or you can use the Windows Media Player to play audio CD tracks. These utilities display the number of tracks on the disk. The program data (if there is any) is stored in the first track, so if there is more than one track, the remaining tracks are almost certainly audio tracks. If you have a pair of Walkman-style headphones, plug them into the front of your CD-ROM drive and see if you hear anything through them when the program is running. If you do, you are definitely dealing with a CD-Audio track.

Now for why you don't hear these tracks when they play. Chances are good that the signal isn't getting to your sound card. If you have an external CD-ROM drive, you need to have a patch cable that takes the left and right channel signals (typically a pair of RCA jacks) to the sound card (typically a stereo mini-plug jack that is marked "Input"). If you have an internal CD-ROM drive, you need a special cable to connect it to your sound card (such as the one in Figure 6.4).

Figure 6.4 To connect an internal CD-ROM drive to your sound card, you will need a special cable similar to this one.

All multimedia kits include such a cable, so you shouldn't have this problem if the kit was installed correctly. Most "bare" CD-ROM drives include one or more sound cables, but since different sound cards use different connectors, the one that comes with a drive may not fit your card. It used to be difficult to find the right cable, but now many companies stock all sorts of CD-ROM drive and sound card combination cables, making it much easier to find what you need. Just make certain that you specify which drive and sound card you have so that you get the right cable.

CD-ROM

CD-ROM disks and drives are reliable, and I have not encountered many problems with them once you have the drives installed and working correctly.

One relatively rare problem you may encounter is a CD that will not read reliably on one drive, but will on another. Sometimes this occurs with an older title that works fine on a single- or dual-speed drive, but fails to read correctly on a quad-speed drive. This may be the result of errors in the disk mastering process, where the data tracks may have been created slightly outside the range of normal specifications. The fact that one drive can successfully read the data and another cannot may be due to a combination of differences in rotation speed, the design of the data-reading laser and optics, and the head-tracking mechanism used in the drive. If you encounter such a problem and the CD title is still in print, contact the publisher and see if they have a more recent pressing that might correct the problem.

Dust

If your drive has problems reading all disks, dust may be at the root of the difficulty. The read head of a laser uses precision lenses to focus the laser beam and channel the light to various sensors. If this light path is obstructed by dust, you may get read errors.

Check your CD-ROM drive manual for any information about cleaning the head, but if there is no information on the subject, try using a CD drive head cleaner from a stereo store. Since the mechanism is essentially the same as for audio CD drives, the same cleaning disk should work fine for your data CD drive.

Damaged Disks

If you have a CD that won't read on any drive, the disk itself may be damaged. Figure 6.5 shows a schematic cross-section of a CD-ROM disk.

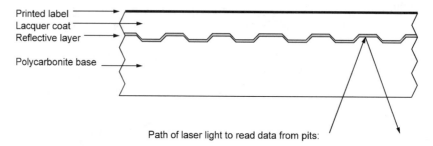

Figure 6.5 A magnified cross-section of a CD-ROM disk.

As part of the CD mastering process, a metal plate is created with the bumps that convey the stored data. This is used to stamp the pits into a polycarbonate plastic blank disk. The top surface is covered with a thin aluminum layer to provide a reflective surface for the laser beam, and the aluminum is protected by a hard lacquer coating. The CD's label is then printed on top of the lacquer layer.

If the clear bottom layer of the plastic disk gets minor scratches, it will probably still read successfully. This is because the laser beam is focused at the top layer of the plastic and can "look past" minor surface flaws just as you can see outside through a screen window. If the scratches get too severe, however, the laser may not be able to read the data reliably.

If you have a CD that is badly scratched on the bottom side, you may be able to gently polish the plastic and make it clear enough that it can be read again. Try rubbing the scratch with toothpaste; it is a gentle abrasive. After you smooth the worst of the scratch, you can finish by buffing the disk with a cloth.

Scratches on the top of the CD—the label side—are much more devastating. If the scratch goes through to the aluminum layer, the damage to the data may be permanent and unrecoverable.

The best way to avoid scratches is to handle your disks carefully in the first place. Always keep them in a case when they are not in use. Some people prefer to use drives that use disk caddies. Despite the extra cost, caddies protect the disks when they are out of the drive. A CD-changer that holds more than one disk at a time can also reduce the amount of CD handling. If you don't have enough cases for your CDs, you can use the Tyvek sleeves from 5.25 floppy disks to provide ample protection.

If you must place a "naked" CD down on a surface without protection, there is an honest difference of opinion about which way to place them. Some say to put the label side up because minor scratches on the bottom won't hurt the disk, but scratches on the top surface can be fatal to the data. I take the view that the lacquer layer is much tougher than the softer bottom plastic layer, and if I'm careful to put the disk on a smooth surface (like a clean sheet of paper), there is less risk involved in placing the disk label side down. But the best procedure is to not do it at all. Take your pick.

Speaker Problems

Speakers are also reliable components, although you may run into a few problems.

Magnetic Shielding

At the back of a speaker's cone, there is a magnet. The bigger and better the speaker, the larger this magnet is likely to be. Magnets can deflect streams of electrons. In fact, the average CRT has little magnets glued all over its surface to correct minor defects in manufacturing. So if you place a big speaker magnet right next to your computer screen, you might expect an undesirable result.

The fact is that, in the worst cases, speakers can cause a psychedelic distortion of your monitor's colors. The speaker magnets deflect the electron beams inside the tube, causing them to strike the wrong color phosphors, resulting in a rainbow where you expected to see a solid color. Better quality speakers designed for use with computers are carefully shielded to prevent any such interference, using other sets of magnets inside the speaker housing to counteract the effects of the cone's magnet.

If your speakers are distorting your monitor's image, the easy fix is to simply move them a bit farther to the side of the monitor. The permanent fix, however, is best achieved by upgrading to better quality speakers.

Signal Interference in Cabling

Did you have classmates in high school who could receive radio broadcasts on their braces? Well, a similar problem can arise with computer speakers.

Behind most computers is a mare's nest of tangled wires. When you run a current through a wire, it creates an electromagnetic field around the wire. Turn the current on and off—as happens with data flowing through a cable—and you can create radio waves. After all, that's what happens at your local radio station broadcast tower, but on a larger scale. And if radio waves are around and they strike a wire, an induced current can be created in the wire as the electromagnetic waves push and pull the electrons in the wire. Again, that's what is going on inside the antenna on your radio.

The problem is that if you have poorly shielded cables in the back of your computer, one may be "broadcasting" interference that is picked up by another. If you are using your sound card's amplifier to drive small speakers, these tiny signals will more than likely be drowned out by the amplified signal. But if you are using amplified speakers or are running your sound card output through a stereo system, the weak interference signals may also get amplified to the point where they are noticeable and objectionable.

The first fix to try is rerouting your cables. Try to arrange them so that they are not bundled together and instead run separately from each other. If this does not solve the problem, you may have to invest in some better quality cables that are more thoroughly shielded.

UPGRADING

> All things must change
> To something new, to something strange.
>
>   Henry Wadsworth Longfellow

If you have no sound card or CD-ROM drive and want to add one, multimedia kits are certainly a reasonable way to go. Despite their reputation, they are generally straightforward to install and configure. Some do represent an excellent value over purchasing the components separately.

Not always a bargain   One of the big attractions to these kits, however, is the long list of bundled utilities and CDs that are included in the box. This aspect of these kits reminds me a bit of the conversation between two little old ladies on a cruise ship. "The food's not very good on this trip, is it?" said the first one, to which her companion replied with a happy smile, "No, but they do give such nice large portions!"

In many cases, the best that can be said about the bundled disks and utilities is that at least the portions are large. Before you're swayed by an impressive and endless list of "free" software included in a kit, see how many of the titles you'd be willing to pay $30 for if you had to buy them separately. Chances are that the disks may not add all that much actual value to the package.

In addition, kits cut corners that you may not want to cut. For example, most kits come with the absolutely cheapest speakers that they can get. How much sound do you think you can get from speakers that sell separately for $20 a pair?

So if you don't need all those "free" disks of outdated CD titles or you plan on getting better quality speakers, you might want to skip the kits and go *à la carte* with separate components.

Sound Cards

If you already have a sound card, you might consider some upgrade options and additions.

Many sound cards have a feature connector that you can use to add wave table support to your existing MIDI functions. Wave table MIDI does not have the plastic, tinny sound of regular MIDI, thanks to the sampled real sounds that make the overall effect much more life-like. If your card has the ability to accept such an upgrade, it can be a worthwhile investment if you play MIDI sounds. (Many popular games use MIDI for their musical soundtracks.)

Adding wave table

You also might want to add a MIDI device to play with your sound card. You can use a MIDI keyboard to compose music that your computer can then record and play back. (And with a MIDI editing program, you can do everything from "clean-up" your composition to print out sheet music of your creation.) Most sound cards have a connector that you can use to hook up MIDI devices; the connector is the same 15-pin connector that you use to plug in a joystick to the card. You'll need a connector kit to provide the connections between the DIN connectors used by MIDI devices and the 15-pin connector on your sound card. These adapters are available from most sound card companies, as well as third-party sources for $50 or less.

MIDI devices

Reasons to Replace Your Card

There are some good reasons to consider replacing your sound card completely. If you have an older card, it may not provide support for 16-bit sound samples, or it may not have the ability to accept a wave table upgrade for the MIDI. Some older cards also have very limited polyphony specifications—the number of simultaneous instruments that can be created for MIDI tracks.

CD-ROM

Whether you have an older CD-ROM drive or none at all, there are good reasons to think about getting a new one.

Speed choices   One of the biggest choices to make is what speed to get. As I write this, the "sweet spot" in price/performance seems to be the quad-speed drives. Prices are around $200, and you get sufficiently better performance than you'd get from the dual-speed models that sell for about half that price. The faster (6x and 8x) drives cost a lot more and don't deliver that much better performance at this point.

Interface choices   As I mentioned earlier, the best way to go in most cases is to get the same kind of CD-ROM interface as your current hard disk uses. If you have a choice, I tend to favor SCSI because you can hang more devices on the one chain than you can with EIDE, making it more flexible if you want to add scanners or other devices.

If you are running Windows 3.1 or later and you want to connect your CD-ROM drive to an IDE interface, you should get an EIDE interface, if you don't already have one, because it has two channels that can handle two devices on each channel. You should put your CD-ROM on the secondary channel, not on the first channel with your hard disk, because a CD-ROM drive does not support the Windows 32-bit disk access feature, and if a CD-ROM is on the same channel as your hard disk, you won't be able to use this feature with your hard disk, either. To avoid this performance loss, put your CD-ROM on the secondary channel and you will be able to retain the 32-bit disk access for your hard disk on the primary channel.

Single drive vs. changers   The other choice is whether you want a single disk drive or a disk changer. If you're like me, you have several CDs that you use on a regular basis. (For example, while working on this book, I have three different titles that I consult frequently.) A changer lets you leave from three to seven disks loaded at all times, and it only takes a matter of seconds for the drive to swap from one to the next. Changers cost relatively little more than a single drive, making them attractive and affordable choices.

And while I'm on the subject of alternative drives, let me again mention a new technology from Panasonic. Their new phase change PD/CD drive takes 680 MB read/write optical disk cartridges that you can use for backup or for storing "live" data. The same drive also acts as a quad-speed CD-ROM drive, giving you two functions in a single drive mechanism.

Speakers

If you got your speakers as part of a multimedia kit, you're probably thinking about replacing them. (If you aren't thinking that yet, either you got a really good kit or you'll be thinking about this sooner or later.)

There are lots of quality speakers out there to choose from, in a range of prices. If you listen to audio CDs much, you might want to consider getting an Altec Lansing ACS500 Sound System (Figure 6.6). These two mini-tower speakers and subwoofer are self-powered and include electronics to decode Dolby Pro Logic surround sound information from your audio disks, giving you a home-theater sound in an amazingly compact package.

Figure 6.6   The compact Altec Lansing ACS500 speaker system can decode Dolby Pro Logic surround sound information from stereo signals.

Like the other chapters in this book, this topic could fill a book on its own. And in fact, it has filled lots of books, including one in particular. If you want to get more detail on this topic, check out *Troubleshooting Your Multimedia PC* by fellow *Underground Guide* author John Montgomery (published by Addison-Wesley).

7 Input Devices: Keyboards, Mice, Joysticks, Scanners

Watson, come here. I want you.

Alexander Graham Bell
March 10, 1876

To this point, we have concentrated mainly on the pieces required to get a computer to perform useful work (well, we hope that at least some of it will be useful) and to convey the results of that work as some form of output. But how do you tell the computer what to do and what information to do it to in the first place?

Science fiction writers have had a long-standing love affair with a spoken interface. An entire generation has grown up looking forward to the year 2001 when we could simply say "Open the pod door, HAL," and an understanding computer would respond to our spoken command.

Say what?

It looks as though 2001 won't bring an affordable and reliable spoken language interface for computers—at least not personal computers. One reason is that the task of understanding natural language is far more difficult and complex than it might appear at first glance. Obviously you have to cope with homonyms. "Show me your bear skin" and "Show me your bare skin" have distinctly different meanings, and the correct one can only be discerned by context.

But context plays a much larger role in spoken conversation. I once heard or read of a fairly normal conversation that went something like this:

He said: "What's for dinner?"
She said: "I have some coupons for McDonald's."
He said: "Have you seen my car keys?"
She said: "Did you look on your dresser?"

As humans with an incredible facility for pattern matching and interpretation, we can easily understand the negotiation and agreement that takes place in these four short lines, but just imagine how much a computer would have to know in order to be able to determine that the man does not intend to use his car to avoid being fed slips of paper by his wife.

Then throw in the fact that we speak "continuous speech" (no break in the sound between words), that we speak with changing inflection and volume, and that each of us has our own voice qualities and accents, and you begin to see why computerized voice recognition is so difficult.

There are good voice recognition systems for PCs that use a limited vocabulary, that often require extensive training (though it's often questionable whether it is the computer or the user who is being trained!), and that you can use for simple tasks. They typically require that you enunciate each command word separately. There are computerized dictation systems capable of recognizing continuous speech for a relatively large yet specialized vocabulary, but these remain prohibitively expensive for most users.

So I'm sorry to say it, but it looks like we won't have voice recognition as a major source of input and control of computers until some time off in the future. It will come, but don't hold your breath.

NEED TO KNOW

So what can we expect to use for data input and control for our computers? In this chapter, I'll cover four major categories: keyboards, mice, joysticks, and scanners.

Keyboards and Compatibility

> Thou hast the keys of Paradise!
>
> Thomas De Quincey
> *Confessions of an English Opium-Eater,* 1822

In 1867, Christopher Sholes and colleagues invented the first practical typewriter (later to be manufactured by Remington). About 65 years later, this invention helped a cash register company branch into a new product line, a move that enabled IBM to dominate both the electric typewriter and later the computer markets. So we owe a lot to the keyboard aside from its demented letter layout.

Basic designs   Computer keyboards have undergone a surprising number of changes just since the introduction of the first IBM PC. The original IBM PC came with a keyboard (Figure 7.1) that had ten function keys along the left side and an "embedded" numeric keypad. The keypad keys did double duty as number and cursor control keys. This keyboard is often referred to as an **83-key layout,** based on the number of keys. There were a lot of complaints about this layout. Even though its Selectric typewriters were the industry standard, for its PC, IBM decided to use a totally new layout, which included a backslash key (\) where your left little finger

Figure 7.1 The original IBM PC keyboard also was used on the IBM XT.

would expect to find the Shift key. (It was easy in those days to spot who was using a computer instead of a typewriter because I'd get mail addressed to "Alfred \poor".)

This keyboard used a standard 5-pin **DIN** (Deutsch Industrie Norm—a German national standard) **connector,** which is a circular connector about a half inch in diameter with the five pins arranged in a semicircle around half of the circle. The keyboard was designed to send data from the keyboard to the computer in series, so only a single data line was required. The other four connections provide a ground, +5 volts DC to power the keyboard, a keyboard-reset signal line, and a keyboard clock timing signal.

Engineers find that the 5-volt line is a handy power source for some peripherals that don't need much electricity. As a result, you'll find that some devices plug into your keyboard connector instead of a separate AC power outlet.

When IBM came out with the AT, the keyboard looked a lot like the PC keyboard, but there were some important differences (Figure 7.2). It had 84 keys (adding a SysRq that few people ever used), and the numeric pad was separated by a slight space from the rest of the keys.

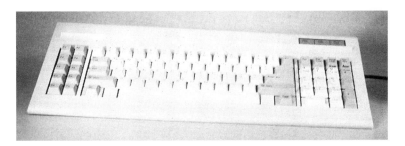

Figure 7.2 The IBM AT keyboard had more changes inside than outside.

The big difference, however, was inside. The keyboard was programmable, which meant that the keyboard could accept commands from the computer. This made the new keyboards incompatible with the original PC and XT keyboards, even though both used the same DIN connector.

For a while, third-party keyboard makers put a switch on the bottom of their products so you could choose PC or AT compatibility modes. (Many keyboards from this period also had a switch to let you choose whether you wanted the Control key above or below the left Shift key—people felt strongly about keyboard layouts.)

Keyboards changed again when IBM came out with its line of PS/2 computers. (See Figure 7.3.) The numeric keypad could still do double duty, but most people left it in numeric mode because the cursor controls and other special functions were set aside as their own dedicated keys. Two more function keys were added, and all twelve were moved to a row along the top of the keyboard instead of the two-column layout on the left edge.

Figure 7.3   The 101-style keyboard arrived with the IBM PS/2 and is the most popular layout.

The connector changed as well; a new mini-DIN connector with six pins was used instead. Four of the pins have the same function as the pins in the larger DIN keyboard connector (minus the keyboard-reset line); the other two pins are not used. If you have a keyboard and computer that use the different DIN connectors, don't fret—it's easy to get a short adapter that lets you plug one into the other. Today you have a wide range of choices for keyboards, as we'll discuss later in this chapter.

Mice

He took Miss Mousie on his knee,

Said, "Miss Mousie will you marry me?" A-huh, a-huh.

"Froggie Went A'Courtin"
Traditional American folk song

Until Windows took off, mice were not a popular PC accessory. (In fact, mice in computers were downright undesirable; a friend of mine in Connecticut had his computer motherboard ruined by a family of field mice that took up residence inside the case one winter . . .)

Nowadays you get a mouse automatically with just about any computer. Some programmers seem to have forgotten about the keyboard almost completely; in fact, some Windows programs have features that can only be accessed by mouse clicks. (I like the mouse, don't get me wrong, but I get more work done more quickly if I can keep my hands on the keys without interrupting my train of thought to go grab a plastic soap bar when I need to change something.) By and large, mice are fairly simple creatures compared with other computer peripherals, but they still have some interesting details.

Interface

Mice come in three varieties: serial, PS/2, and bus. They are closely related, but have some important differences.

Serial mice are probably the most common, but there are good reasons not to use one if you have an alternative. As described in Chapter 5, you are limited to four serial ports (COM1 through COM4) and these four ports must share two IRQ settings. Furthermore, the Microsoft Windows 3.x mouse driver doesn't recognize a mouse on a serial port other than COM1 or COM2.

Serial mice

This means that if you have a modem and a second serial device (such as a printer, file exchange cable, or serial-port scanner), you may run into IRQ conflicts when you try to add a serial mouse to the mix.

When IBM came out with the PS/2 series of computers, the engineers added a new port: a **PS/2 mouse port.** This port uses the same 6-pin mini-DIN connector as a PS/2-style keyboard (Figure 7.4). It also has its own IRQ and I/O port assignments that do not conflict with any serial port settings. The PS/2 mouse port uses IRQ 12 (one of the "16-bit" IRQ settings that were introduced with the IBM AT), and I/O address 060h.

PS/2 mice

If your computer does not come with a PS/2 mouse port, but you don't want to use a serial port for your mouse, there is an alternative. You can add a **bus mouse port** to your computer. Microsoft has its InPort line of bus mice, and many

Bus mice

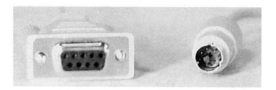

Figure 7.4 Most mice use a 9-pin serial connection (left) or a 6-pin mini-DIN PS/2-style connection (right).

other major mouse manufacturers also have bus mouse configurations available. Even ATI has included a bus mouse port on some of its graphics adapters. The interface options vary with a bus mouse port, but these typically give you a choice of IRQ settings (including some that are not used by serial ports) and I/O addresses that do not conflict with standard serial and parallel port assignments.

Features

Aside from the differences in interface, there are also significant differences between mice in terms of features. Some of these traits are aesthetic—you can get mice in a wide range of colors, including one that looks as if it were made of marble. Other features are ergonomic—early mice were rectangular blocks, but now you have a choice of hand-fitting designs that look more like Brancusi sculpture than a piece of computer equipment. There are even left- and right-handed mice (although most mice also have utilities that let you swap the functions of the left and right mouse buttons).

And what do you get when you flip a mouse on its back? A trackball, such as the one shown in Figure 7.5. These are functionally the same as a mouse, but in-

Figure 7.5 A trackball, such as this one from CH Products, is essentially a mouse on its back.

stead of moving the mouse around, you roll the ball with your fingers. As countless air traffic controllers and video arcade players have discovered, trackballs are an excellent alternative to a mouse, especially in cramped quarters.

A more functional difference is the number of buttons. The Macintosh went for simplicity and limited its users to a single mouse button; if you want to click the mouse, there are no choices to make. When Microsoft came out with a mouse for Windows, it had two buttons—never mind that the second button didn't really do anything in most programs, it was there all the same. Not to be outdone, Logitech made a name for itself by shipping mice with three buttons.

Who's got the button?

When the Microsoft Office suite shipped, many of the Microsoft applications were finally making use of the right mouse button; in general, the button pops up a context-sensitive speed menu that gives you quick access to frequently used commands.

Windows 95 has institutionalized the right mouse button. For example, the right mouse button opens menus in many situations, starting right with the Start button and objects on your desktop. It's worth experimenting in Win95 and within the applications themselves to see what the right button will do.

The other way that mice differ is in their tracking mechanisms. Almost all mice and trackballs have a ball that can roll in any direction; the difference lies in how the device senses the ball's rotation. As the ball turns, it turns two rollers—one for each of the two axes of rotation—which in turn cause disks to turn. A device then senses the spinning of these disks. Some mice use mechanical devices that have electrical contacts, and the turning is measured as metal strips on the wheel make and break the electrical connection. Other mice use optical encoders that have a light sensor that looks at a light source through the rotating disk. The disk has small holes cut through it so it alternately breaks the beam of light and then lets it strike the sensor.

Like a rolling stone

There have been mice made with no moving parts, but these required you to use a special reflective mouse pad. Based on the relative lack of success of these designs, I can only conclude that many other people out there have the same innate ability that I have to cover a desk with a hopeless layer of clutter.

Joystick Features

> Speak softly and carry a big stick.
>
> Theodore Roosevelt
> Speech, September 2, 1901

Whereas mice are digital creatures—marking their movement with a series of electrical on and off signals—joysticks are analog devices. The computer reads the position of the joystick as a pair of voltages, one for each of two directions. These voltages are created by running a current through a pair of variable resistors, known as **potentiometers,** or **pots** to the ham radio crowd, but you can think of them as being similar to the volume control on a radio or the dimmer knob on a light switch.

Joysticks plug into a D-connector with 15 pins. Table 7.1 shows the pinouts for the typical PC game port.

Table 7.1 Pin out assignments for a game port

Pin	Signal
1	+5 volts DC
2	Joystick A, Button 1
3	Joystick A, X Axis
4	Ground
5	Ground
6	Joystick A, Y Axis
7	Joystick A, Button 2
8	+5 volts DC
9	+5 volts DC
10	Joystick B, Button 1
11	Joystick B, X Axis
12	Ground
13	Joystick B, Y Axis
14	Joystick B, Button 2
15	+5 volts DC

If you look at Table 7.1 in two sections, dividing it between pins 8 and 9, you can see that (aside from an extra ground line) there are two sets of connections, one for Joystick A and one for Joystick B. Each half has two 5-volt inputs, which are then read at the x and y axis lines. When the joystick is moved all the way to one side, the voltage passing through the pot is at its lowest level (similar to turning the volume on the radio all the way down). Move the joystick all the way in the other direction, and the passed-through voltage is at its maximum (loudest volume).

There's a problem with this system, however. Because joysticks are based on an analog measurement system, you don't get the benefit of an absolute *on* or *off* position. And because different pots have individual characteristics, there's no absolute way to know where the joystick is positioned, simply based on the voltage coming in through the game port. This is why you need to calibrate joysticks before you use them.

To make matters even more complicated, the range of voltages changes as the joystick wears and changes temperature, so the calibration settings can "drift" over time. This means that the computer won't think the joystick is centered when in fact it is, and you have to calibrate the joystick again.

There's a whole new joystick technology on the scene, thanks to Windows 95. Microsoft has built its new SideWinder 3D Pro (shown in Figure 7.6) to act as a standard analog device for DOS games, but under Win95, it uses its optical sensors to produce digital control. The result is much more accurate and responsive controls. The SideWinder Pro supports control for all four axes and has four buttons and a four-way hat switch that lets you control the view direction in many games.

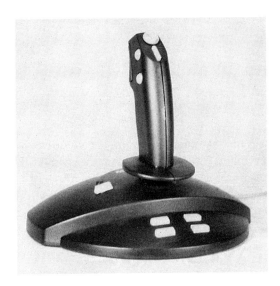

Figure 7.6 Microsoft's SideWinder 3D Pro joystick uses optical sensors to create digital controls under Windows 95.

One part of the design that does work well is that you can hook up two joysticks to the one game port. Some games support head-to-head competition using two joysticks, but more often, the second joystick's controls are used for other functions. For example, many flying simulators support a throttle and rudder pedals in addition to the standard yoke (aileron and elevator) controls (Figure 7.7). These extra functions are supported through the two "extra" axes provided by the second joystick connections.

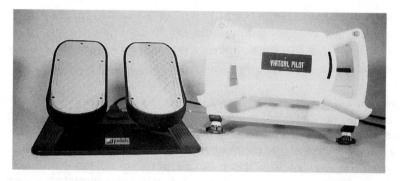

Figure 7.7   Flight simulator pilots often fly with yoke and pedal controls, such as these from CH Products, which use all the axes and buttons for both joystick channels on a game port.

Scanners

> Isn't life a series of images that change as they repeat themselves?
>
> Andy Warhol, as quoted by Victor Bokris
> *Warhol,* 1989

The paperless office remains a distant dream. (I bet you're reading this on paper, right?) And there are many times that we wish that something printed on paper could be stuffed into our computer—*without* us having to rekey it (if it's data) or redraw it (if it's an image). For many of us, our typing and drawing skills are such an impediment to success that the chances are next to nothing that the results of our efforts will bear even a close resemblance to the original. Thank goodness we can go out and buy a scanner!

Types of Scanners

There are a bunch of different categories of scanners. The three main types are: hand, personal, and flatbed.

Hand scanners

Hand scanners look a bit like a mouse with a window at the top. Their biggest attraction is that they are inexpensive. I suppose that if you do a lot of research in a library with a laptop computer, their portability might also be a favorable feature as well. But hand scanners are fussy to use, and the output is not always great. If you don't pull the scanner across the page smoothly and straight and at the correct speed, the resulting image suffers. And if you want to scan something wider than your hand scanner, things get even stickier.

Personal scanners

For not much more money, you can buy a **personal scanner** such as the unit shown in Figure 7.8. These tend to take just one sheet at a time (though a few models do take more) and scan them into your computer. Most of these include

Figure 7.8   The Hewlett-Packard ScanJet 4s is a single-sheet personal scanner. (Photograph courtesy of Hewlett-Packard)

the ability to scan grayscale images, such as black and white photographs, and convert scanned pages into text files using **OCR software.** (OCR is a TLA for **Optical Character Recognition.**) Many of these scanners also come with programs that make it easy to store scanned images in a virtual filing cabinet on your computer's disk.

The next step up—in price and quality—is a **flatbed scanner,** such as the one shown in Figure 7.9. At the lower end of the price range, you can get units that have relatively low resolution and grayscale support. As the prices rise, you get color scanning at higher resolution. Most color scanners now scan an image in a single pass; older models had to take three passes. Less expensive models produce 24-bit color images at 400 dpi resolution, whereas the best models have 30-bit color support at resolutions up to 1200 dpi resolution.

Flatbed scanners

Figure 7.9   The Hewlett-Packard ScanJet 4c is an affordable, mid-priced color flatbed scanner. (Photograph courtesy of Hewlett-Packard)

Flatbed scanners have a few important advantages over the less expensive models. Perhaps the most important one is that they can easily handle both single sheets (like a photograph or a letter) and bound items (such as pages in magazines and books). They are the only way to scan a part of an oversize document, such as a part of a newspaper, without cutting or photocopying the original first. And if you have to scan lots of pages, such as when converting a printed report to a text file using OCR, you can get an **automatic document feeder** (**ADF**) that feeds a stack of pages through, one sheet at a time. For color scanners, you can even get a special transparency adapter that lets you scan copies of overhead projection sheets or photographic slides. Although a flatbed scanner takes up the most space, it is also the most versatile.

Interface Choices

Less expensive scanners plug right into a serial or parallel port. A few come with their own proprietary interfaces. And the more expensive models tend to have a SCSI interface.

The parallel and serial solutions are certainly easy to install, but they may not be the most convenient in the long run. As described in Chapter 5, you can run into conflicts if you have more than two serial devices in use at a time. With a serial mouse and a modem, adding a serial scanner can lead to IRQ conflicts.

As for parallel port connections, not all scanners include a pass-through for a printer connection, which means that you need to have a separate parallel port for the scanner. Most computers only have one parallel port, but it costs $10 or less to add a second parallel port if you have an open expansion slot. Even if the scanner does have a pass-through for the printer, you probably won't be able to use the scanner and printer at the same time.

The proprietary cards are often a variation on either parallel or SCSI connections, but they are limited in that they can only be used with that particular scanner. These cards may also have requirements for I/O addresses or IRQ assignments that could conflict with other ports and devices already installed in your computer.

This leads to the SCSI interface, which is clearly the one I prefer. If you're going to be adding a scanner to your system, chances are that you've also got a bunch of other devices in mind as well: hard disk, backup device, and CD-ROM drive. All of these can be run off the same SCSI card, with minimal chance for configuration conflicts and better data transfer rates than you can expect to get with either a parallel or serial interface. If your system already has a SCSI interface installed, I strongly recommend getting a scanner that attaches to it. Even if your system does not currently have SCSI, but you're thinking of upgrading or adding other components in addition to a scanner, I recommend that you consider adding a SCSI card and getting a SCSI scanner.

TWAIN Support

The last point to consider about scanners is the matter of TWAIN support. TWAIN is purportedly an acronym for Technology Without An Interesting Name. Despite its name, the standard refers to an interesting solution to a common problem. Just as each older DOS program had to be configured separately for your computer's display adapter and printer, so did all programs have to be configured to work with a specific scanner. Windows solved the first problem by providing a universal program interface that works with the display adapter and printer that you specify in the Windows configuration. Unfortunately Windows does not provide the same function for scanners.

Catching the TWAIN

TWAIN was developed so that scanners and programs that can use scanners would have a common middle ground where they could meet without requiring special configurations. The TWAIN driver for a scanner provides a standard way to access the scanner and its features, and any TWAIN-compliant program can then work directly with the scanner. Many graphics and OCR Windows packages support TWAIN.

@#%$%@!

An ounce of action is worth a ton of theory.

Friedrich Engels, quoted by Reg Groves
The Strange Case of Victor Grayson, 1975

Since we must rely on our input devices in order to communicate with our computers, it can be especially frustrating when they let us down. Fortunately the problems you are most likely to encounter are fairly easy to diagnose and resolve. And although the resolution often involves replacement, it's often an inexpensive answer.

Keyboards

The first place to start is the keyboard. It is rare, but keyboards do break down and wear out. In the past eight years, I have had two fail on me, and I spend a *lot* of time pounding on my keyboards.

It is not difficult to fix some problems on a typical keyboard. You can pry off the key cap of a key to clean underneath it or replace a spring that may have broken or become misaligned. You can generally take a keyboard apart by removing a few screws if the cable needs replacement. And if the problem is serious, there are services that can repair your keyboard for a flat fee. And, in general, it's probably not worth the effort to do any of these things.

Let's face it: Keyboards are inexpensive. You can buy a new one for as little as $15. Even a brand name model such as Keytronics can be found for $50 or less. And you can get genuine Microsoft or IBM keyboards for $90 or less. So how much is your time worth? You'd probably spend more time trying to take your keyboard apart and put it back together than it would cost for a replacement. And if it should turn out that there is a busted switch or failed component on the keyboard's circuitry, it will almost certainly cost more to fix than the keyboard is worth.

So if your keyboard breaks, I recommend that you either chuck it in the dumpster or give it to a deserving 6 year old and let him or her dismantle it to see what's inside. Besides, this will give you an opportunity to go out and find a keyboard that has just the touch that you want.

Maintenance

Now, it is possible to extend the life of your keyboard and thus postpone the moment when you have to decide whether to choose the dumpster or the dismantler. Like so many other computer components, the secret boils down to three words: Keep It Clean!

Different keyboards use different switch mechanisms and, as a result, have varying degrees of sensitivity to dirt, dust, and liquids. Most keyboards can actually tolerate a fair amount of dust and debris below the keycaps, but it is a good idea to try to keep it to a minimum. Periodically take the time to vacuum the keyboard, or pop off a few keycaps and blast out any dust or dirt with a puff of air.

Now, I don't want to cause any trouble, but you might be interested to know that the keycaps on most keyboards are interchangeable from one position to another (except for the oversize ones like Enter or Backspace). If you have a colleague or friend who is not completely familiar with the keyboard layout, it *would* be possible to rearrange the layout of the keycaps and thus give them at least a few moments of confusion. Or you *could* scramble the keycaps entirely, turning the keyboard into a giant cryptography puzzle. However, since I don't take part in practical jokes of this sort, I think it would be best if you simply forgot that I brought this up in the first place.

Testing a keyboard

If you should suspect a problem with your keyboard, first check that the cables are properly seated. IBM PS/2 keyboards have a cable that detaches at both the keyboard and the computer ends, so be sure to check *both* ends. Next check that the scan codes for the various keys are being sent correctly to the computer. Many computer systems come with diagnostic programs that include a keyboard test, but if yours didn't, you can use a third-party diagnostic. System Sleuth and WinSleuth from Dariana Software (see Appendix A) have such a test that tests every key on the keyboard. And if you find a bad key that you can't fix with some simple attempts at cleaning under the keycap, consider replacement instead of repair.

Mice

> The gods had condemned Sisyphus to ceaselessly rolling a rock to the top
> of a mountain.
>
> Albert Camus
> *The Myth of Sisyphus,* 1942

As with keyboards, most mice don't cost enough to make it worth bothering to   **Maintenance**
get them repaired if they fail. Every few years, I buy a pair of cheap mice to have
on hand in the event that one of my existing mice should roll over and play dead.

As with keyboards, the best repair strategy is to keep problems from occur-
ring in the first place. Depending on your housekeeping habits, the soft rubber
roller in your mouse may find lots of dust and debris to be picked up and distributed within the casing.

Aside from keeping your mousepad as clean and dust-free as possible, you
can also prolong your mouse's lifespan by cleaning the ball and rollers every once
in a while. Different mice work in different ways, but in general, there is a hatch
that you turn in one direction or another to open the cavity where the ball is
housed. Take out the ball and clean it—a little rubbing alcohol on a lint-free cloth
works well. Then clean the two rollers inside the housing. You'll probably find a
build-up of grime in the center of each roller where the ball makes contact.

You can also clean your mousepad, which will reduce the grime build-up on
the rollers. Some mousepads have a porous cloth surface which is harder to clean,
but the hard-surfaced pads can be cleaned easily with a little alcohol or glass
cleaner. Test a small spot first to make certain that the cleaner won't remove the
color or any printing on the pad first.

Sometimes even a clean, new mouse may behave erratically or not at all. If   **Trouble-**
you're using a serial mouse, the first step is to make certain that you don't have   **shooting**
any configuration conflicts with other serial ports. (See Chapter 5 for a description of the potential problems of having serial devices on both COM1 and COM3,
or both COM2 and COM4.) It is also possible, though less likely, that you can have
conflicts between a PS/2 mouse or some other bus mouse and some other component in your computer (most often a sound card).

Optical Mouse Goes Haywire

Some problems take a bit of sleuthing to diagnose and solve. I had one reader
write to me about a problem he had with his mouse. Every afternoon, it would
start going crazy, with the mouse pointer jumping all over the screen. This would
happen when he was using an optical mouse (one that uses optical sensors to detect movement instead of a mechanical sensor), but never with his mechanical
mouse.

What was the problem? It turned out that in the late afternoon, the sun would shine across his desk at a very low angle. It was low enough to get under the optical mouse, and then illuminate the inside of the mouse cavity. The optical sensors would "see" this light intermittently as he dragged the mouse around, sending false signals about the mouse's motion. The solution was as simple as closing the blinds on sunny afternoons.

Mouse Won't Work in DOS

A more common problem occurs when a mouse works under Windows but doesn't work for DOS programs. Fortunately this one also has a fairly simple solution.

In order for the computer to receive input from a mouse, it must have a driver loaded to communicate with the mouse. Most mice are Microsoft-mouse compatible and thus can use a standard driver, but some mice have added features and require a proprietary driver.

Windows relies on the configuration information established in its SETUP program, and if you specify that the system includes a mouse, Windows loads its own appropriate mouse driver when it starts. When you run a DOS program, however, the driver is not available. For DOS programs to have access to the mouse, you must run a DOS-level driver.

DOS mouse drivers typically come in one of two forms. They can be drivers that load in your CONFIG.SYS file in a DEVICE= line—such a file typically has a name like MOUSE.SYS. The alternative is an executable file that you can run from the DOS prompt or have load automatically as part of your AUTOEXEC.BAT file—MOUSE.COM and MOUSE.EXE are typical names for this type of file.

Using AUTOEXEC.BAT or CONFIG.SYS to automatically load the driver makes the mouse available to most DOS programs that can use a mouse. It will also be available to DOS programs run under Windows.

If you don't want to give up the memory required for the mouse driver, you can also use the executable version only when you want to load it. If you run MOUSE in a DOS window under Windows, the driver is removed from memory when you close that window. Note that not all versions of the Microsoft mouse driver work in this way.

Finding a Mouse Driver

Your mouse should come with DOS drivers on a disk, but unfortunately this is something that many computer manufacturers fail to provide. Chances are excellent, however, that if your mouse is Microsoft compatible (and most are), you already have a driver at hand.

DOS 5.x, DOS 6.x, Windows 3.1, and Windows for Workgroups 3.11 all include a copy of MOUSE.COM on their distribution disks. The Windows versions include MOUSE.SYS as well. These files may be installed automatically on your system, but unless you already have a mouse driver loaded in your AUTOEXEC.BAT or CONFIG.SYS, they will not. You'll have to do it yourself.

This technique is actually useful for a lot of reasons, and not just for getting a mouse driver from your DOS or Windows disks. Microsoft compresses the files on the distribution disks, in much the same way that the shareware program PKZIP can compress files. Microsoft uses its own software compression tools, however, and provides its own utility to uncompress them. This program is called EXPAND.EXE. The actual program varies from one version of DOS or Windows to another, so you generally have to use the same version as the file you are trying to expand. Chances are that the current versions of the program for your version of DOS and Windows were installed in your DOS and WINDOWS directories when you installed those programs.

Expanding compressed Microsoft files

To use EXPAND, change to the directory where you want the uncompressed files to go. Search through the DOS or Windows disks for the MOUSE.CO_ or MOUSE.SY_ file (depending on whether you want the executable or device driver version). Assuming you have the DOS disk with MOUSE.CO_ on it in Drive A, at the DOS prompt you can type:

```
\DOS\EXPAND A:MOUSE.CO_ MOUSE.COM
```

Note that you should specify the path to the DOS directory so that you execute the correct copy of EXPAND. (If you are getting the mouse file from a Windows disk, use the copy of EXPAND in your Windows directory.) The first filename is the source file; you must include the full path to it, including the disk drive. The second filename is the destination file; you must add the last letter of the extension for the full filename, to take the place of the underscore character at the end of the compressed version of the file. (Most files that end in an underscore are probably compressed Microsoft files.)

You can also just run the EXPAND program without filenames at all, and the program will prompt you for the source file and destination file names. You can use EXPAND to uncompress any of the compressed files on DOS or Windows distribution disks.

Switching Under Windows

There is one problem that cannot be solved easily under Windows 3.1 or Windows for Workgroups 3.11. Some people like to use a mouse for some functions and a trackball or other pointing device for other functions. These devices typically require different drivers, and therein lies the problem. For Windows 3.x, you can only specify a single pointing device at a time. To switch from one to another, you have to run the Windows Setup program and then restart Windows. This is a pain, to be sure, but I'm not aware of any way around the problem. Even if the two devices use the same driver, switching two pointing devices using a switch box does not work reliably.

Windows 95 has new protected mode drivers for mice and other pointing devices. One advantage of these drivers is that they make the mouse available to DOS applications running either in a Window or in full-screen mode, without having to load a mouse driver in your CONFIG.SYS or AUTOEXEC.BAT first (as you do for Windows 3.x). An additional advantage, however, is that Win95 now also supports multiple pointing devices; you can have a serial mouse and a PS/2 mouse connected at the same time, and both will be active. This means that you can have both a mouse and a trackball installed on a single computer at the same time.

Joysticks

Joysticks are probably some of the most heavily tested products in the industry. Fire buttons are rated at millions of presses. The handles are built to withstand the violent maneuvers of a fighter pilot struggling to clear his or her six. But, eventually, they break. They may be built ruggedly, but they are also the most abused pieces of hardware on a typical computer system.

There is not much to do to repair or maintain them, though the more expensive models may be worth sending back to the factory for repair rather than replacement. (It's easier to spend more on a good joystick than it is on a keyboard!)

Joystick port problems

However, you may encounter a situation where the joystick doesn't work at all. There are a number of possible causes for this.

Most computers rely on a sound card to provide a game port for a joystick. Since this same port can be configured for use as a MIDI port, the card can be configured to disable the game port functions. The Pro Audio Spectrum cards from Media Vision have this feature, for example. If you are installing a joystick for the first time, you may want to double-check your sound card documentation to make certain that the game port is enabled and properly configured.

In some instances, an inexpensive game port may not work reliably with today's high-speed processors. In these cases, you may want to purchase a special game port adapter that is designed to work with processors of different speeds. Both CH Products and Thrustmaster (Figure 7.10) make game port expansion cards.

Figure 7.10   Dedicated game port expansion cards, such as this one from Thrustmaster, are designed to work with high-speed computer systems.

About the most common problem is the need for calibrating your joystick. You need to do this for each game, and for reasons described earlier in this chapter, you may have to calibrate before each session—sometimes in mid session as well. You can tell when your joystick needs to be recalibrated; it will act as if you were pushing it in one direction or another even though it is centered. Check your program documentation for instructions on how to calibrate the joystick.

Calibrating the joysticks for your programs

Scanners

Scanners are rarely used so much that they break down, but people have plenty of other complaints about using them. Scanners can be painfully slow, and although they are much easier to install these days, you can still run into snags when first trying to get one to work. Fortunately these are all problems that you should be able to resolve without too much trouble.

The most common complaint is getting the scanner working in the first place. Hand and personal scanners that use parallel or serial ports tend not to have these problems (aside from the standard conflicts encountered with more than two serial ports).

Configuration problems

Proprietary interfaces can cause configuration headaches, however. If you run into configuration problems, try removing the card and running a third-party installation advisor to make sure that you have IRQ and I/O address (and DMA channels, if necessary) that are available for the configuration choices on the interface card.

SCSI interfaces used to create the biggest problems, but now they tend to be fairly easy to configure and install. In fact, it is not a big deal to have two SCSI interfaces installed in the same system. The key points to get right are:

- Each device on the SCSI chain, including the interface card itself, must have its own ID number (0 through 7).

- The SCSI chain must terminate at the two ends of the chain—and *only* at the ends.

When adding a scanner to an existing SCSI installation that does not have any other external SCSI devices, you may need to change the termination settings on the interface card and make certain that there is a terminator at the scanner. (See Chapter 3 for more details on the SCSI interface.)

Bottleneck problems

Once you get your scanner working, you may find that your scanner isn't performing quite as fast as you'd like. Several features and configuration choices besides your scanner can affect performance.

To begin with, serial and parallel port connections are not nearly as fast as SCSI. If speed is important, you may want to consider upgrading to a SCSI scanner. Some units are able to take advantage of the new high-speed enhanced parallel ports, so you may be able to get a significant performance for a parallel interface scanner if your system is only outfitted with older parallel ports.

The CPU and its clock speed can also have a major impact on scanner performance. If you can get your scanner working off a local-bus (VL-Bus or PCI) SCSI interface, it can take advantage of faster communications with the CPU and system memory. Also, the data from the scanner has to get spooled onto the computer's hard disk in most cases—especially for large image files such as 24-bit true-color images—so a high-speed hard disk with a large software cache can result in a significant performance boost.

You can also improve scanner speed by reducing the amount of information in the image file. Reducing the resolution of a scan from 400 dpi to 200 dpi shrinks the size of the resulting file to one-fourth its original size; this takes one-fourth the amount of time to send from the scanner to the computer. And if your picture is simply black-and-white line art, or you plan to print it on a black-and-white laser printer, there may be no need to scan it at anything higher than a 1-bit black-and-white setting. Scanning the same image at 256 levels of gray increases the data stream size by eight times, and choosing 24-bit color results in a file that is 24 times larger than the simple black-and-white one. So consider shrinking the resolution and color depth of your images when you make your scans, and you can save a lot of time (not to mention disk space).

Optimizing quality and accuracy

There are other reasons why you may want to scan at less than the highest resolution or color depth. Using settings that are too high can actually reduce the image quality of your printouts.

In general, for a grayscale image like a photograph that you are going to print on a black-and-white laser, scan the original at about one-third to one-fourth the printer's resolution. So for a 300 dpi printer, try 75 to 100 dpi for the best results. The finer the dithering pattern used by the printer driver, the fewer shades of gray it will be able to represent, so you should choose a grayscale setting that is matched to the dither pattern. For a very fine dither setting, a 16-level grayscale scan may look as good as a 256-level scan. And even with a fairly coarse dither pattern that can represent lots of shades of gray, there's no reason to scan at more than 256 levels of gray; don't waste the time and space on a 16-bit or 24-bit color scan.

For color printers, the consensus seems to be that you should scan at the same resolution as the printer and at a color depth that is commensurate with the printer's abilities.

The time when higher resolutions and grayscales can make more sense is when you are doing OCR work. Check the documentation for your OCR software to find out what settings should work best for it, but some programs work best at high resolution settings with grayscale. This takes longer to scan and process, but it may pay dividends in terms of higher accuracy in the converted results.

UPGRADING

> A disposition to preserve, and an ability to improve, taken together, would be my standard of a statesman.
>
> Edmund Burke
> *Reflections on the Revolution in France,* 1790

For all these input devices, upgrading means replacing. Few products in this chapter can be improved through an upgrade. Instead, the focus is on getting a new component instead.

Different Keystrokes for Different Folks

If your keyboard breaks down, it typically makes more sense to replace it than try to repair it. Inexpensive keyboards now cost $15 or less. Even if your keyboard is working fine, you may want to change some aspects of it and replacement may be an affordable solution.

Not everyone is satisfied with the standard keyboard layouts and features. Over the years, companies have come up with an incredible range of variations on the theme. There are keyboards with:

- Trackballs
- Touchpads in place of the cursor controls

- Four-function light-powered calculators
- Function keys along the left, along the top, or both
- Stereo speakers mounted in their corners

There are also compact keyboards, ergonomic keyboards, adjustable keyboards, and keyboards with infrared interfaces so you don't need a cable connecting it to your computer.

The right touch   In addition to features, there is also the matter of feel. Choosing a keyboard is like picking a mattress; individual tastes vary a great deal. Some people like a soft touch on the keys; others prefer more resistance when they type. The best keyboards include tactile feedback, where the resistance gradually builds as you press down on the key and then releases at the point where the electrical contact is made. This feedback makes it easier to type more rapidly because it provides an indication of when the computer has registered the keypress. It also makes typing less tiring because you don't have to mash the keycap all the way to the bottom of its travel as you type.

Finally, there is the question of noise. Some folks prefer to hear a little click when they press a key—perhaps this is a holdover from the days of working to the clickety-clack of a typewriter—and this sound can be created in two ways, mechanically and electronically.

Some keyboards have a mechanical click built into each key. Some are pronounced, and some are more subtle. It's a matter of taste, but I found that the early PS/2 keyboards were a bit obnoxious in their sound profile; each key had a spring that would go *boing* as you typed, but the pitches of the sounds varied from one key to the next. As a result, rapid typing sounded like a symphony played on pogo sticks.

Other keyboards produce their clicks electronically, with a small speaker built into the keyboard housing. One advantage of this approach is that you can often control the volume of the clicks (not to mention that you can turn them off altogether if you want).

Some people prefer a quieter keyboard. Although I have not encountered a totally silent keyboard (aside from membrane-surfaced models designed for harsh environments), some are fairly quiet. When looking for a quiet keyboard, don't focus just on the sounds of pressing the keys. Many keyboards may be quiet when you press the keys, but the keys themselves are mounted loosely on the keyboard and any side-to-side movement can produce an undesirable rattling noise. One of my favorite tests is to brush my hand lightly across the tops of the keycaps to see how much horizontal play there is in the keys and how much noise they make when you move them this way.

There's a new key on the PC-compatible scene, thanks to Windows 95. Similar to the Command key on the Macintosh keyboards, Windows keyboards such as the Microsoft Natural Keyboard have a new Windows key. Table 7.2 shows the different keystroke combinations available with this key under Win95.

Table 7.2 Windows 95 supports a new Windows key, which can be used in combination with other keys to issue these commands.

Key	Command
Windows+F1	Help
Windows+E	Run Windows Explorer
Ctrl+Windows+F	Find Computer
Windows+M	Minimize all
Shift+Windows+M	Undo minimize all
Windows+R	Open Run dialog box
Windows+Tab	Cycle through Taskbar buttons
Windows+Break	Open System Properties dialog box

Building a Better Mouse

As mentioned earlier in this chapter, mice now come in a wide variety of shapes and sizes. For a traditional mouse, look for one that fits your hand and makes it easy to click either button quickly and with control. Remember that more and more programs will be making good use of the right button, thanks to Windows 95, so you'll want to pay attention to both buttons.

If you have a cluttered desk and can't seem to find the mouse (or even the mouse pad) when you need it, consider a trackball. It is bigger, stays in one place, and with a little practice, is just as easy to use as a mouse—some people even prefer it.

Other, more exotic choices are available. For example, there are keyboards with tiny joystick-style pointers in the middle, like the IBM TrackPoint design. These originally appeared on notebook computers as a space-saving design, but many users decided that they wanted them on their desktop keyboards as well. Even though they are mounted on keyboards, however, these pointing devices still need a PS/2 mouse or serial port to connect to, in addition to the keyboard connector.

Then there are the touchpads, such as the GlidePoint. You use these by dragging a stylus or your fingertip across their surface. You can find this type of pointer control either as a separate component, or integrated into a keyboard.

More Than a Joystick

It used to be that a joystick was a joystick, and that was that. Now there are dozens of different designs with different types of controls. Some don't look like joysticks at all.

The most common kind of joystick looks like an original model on steroids. Bristling with buttons and switches, you can control just about every aspect of many games without ever touching the keyboard. To control everything, these joysticks often need more than just the four axes and four buttons offered by the standard pair of joystick circuits, and as a result these devices often also connect with the keyboard port, sending some commands as if they had been typed into the keyboard. Some companies, such as CH Products and Thrustmaster (Figure 7.11) have companion controls that handle throttle and weapons functions for many combat flight simulation programs.

Figure 7.11 The Flight Control System and Weapon Control System from Thrustmaster resemble the controls in a real jet fighter, and are some of the most popular controls for combat flight simulation games.

Other kinds of controls   If you want to fly a simulated Cessna or Ferrari, you won't want a joystick at all because that is not the type of control you'd find in the real vehicle. As a result, companies have built flight yokes/steering wheels and pedal controls such as those from CH Products (Figure 7.12). With a throttle lever on the yoke using a third joystick axis, the fourth is available for the pedals.

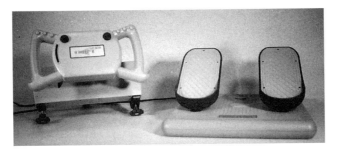

Figure 7.12 The Virtual Pilot Pro and Pro Pedals are favorites of driving and flying simulation enthusiasts for their realistic control.

With all these specialized joystick controls available, it is easy to see how you might want to use different ones for different games. It can be a pain to have to connect and disconnect cables from your computer's game port, reaching around in back into a cramped tangle of wires so that you can plug in a cable to a connector that you cannot see is more of a challenge than most people want. Fortunately you can now get switch boxes that let you plug in two or more sets of joystick controls and connect them to a single game port.

Joystick switches

Picking a Scanner

When choosing a new or replacement scanner, the most important point is to pick one that is well suited to your needs. Don't discount color too quickly; most color scanners are often very good at grayscale scanning as well, and they don't cost too much more than the grayscale models. Since more and more people are getting color printers, it can be handy to have a color scanner on hand.

Another approach, however, is to get a full-size grayscale scanner for black-and-white images, OCR, and document management, and then an inexpensive color scanner that can handle snapshot-size photographs. The combination may cost less than a full-size color scanner and is almost as versatile unless you are a professional graphic artist.

As for the interface, chances are good that SCSI may be the most flexible, fastest, and most cost-effective in the long run, especially if you already have or plan to add other storage devices. The serial and parallel ports are convenient and are best suited for systems that only have a modest number of components installed.

8 Portable Stuff

> Where a calculator on the ENIAC is equipped with 18,000 vacuum tubes and weighs 30 tons, computers in the future may have only 1,000 vacuum tubes and perhaps weigh only 1½ tons.
>
> *Popular Mechanics*
> March 1949

They say "you can't take it with you," but portable computers are proof that the old sayings are not always true. Osborne started the portable movement with an arm-stretching, AC-powered behemoth that was about as portable as a sewing machine, but that was all it took to get peripatetic Americans hooked on computing *à go-go*.

Today you no longer have to choose between full-featured power and portability. Given a big enough budget, you can get everything from Pentium processors to complete multimedia systems all in a package that weighs no more than a big city phonebook.

NEED TO KNOW

> Reasons for not keeping a notebook: 1) the ambiguity of the reader—it is never quite oneself. 2) I usually hate the sight of my handwriting—it lives too much and I dislike its life—I mean by "lives," of course, betrays too much!
>
> Lionel Trilling
> *Partisan Review,* 50th Anniversary Edition, ed. by William Philips, 1985

There are still some essential differences between desktop systems and portables, however, which can play a huge role in what you buy in the first place, how you approach troubleshooting and repair tasks, and what your choices are when it comes to consider upgrades. You pay a price—and not just with dollars—when you choose a portable solution.

Notebooks

The first popular notebook computer was the Radio Shack Model 100 (Figure 8.1). Although it was programmable (it included a built-in version of the BASIC programming language), it had no disk operating system and was not compatible with any other computer systems such as the IBM PC. It also had a limited monochrome LCD display: 8 lines of 40 characters, text only.

Figure 8.1   Weighing in at just 4 pounds, the Radio Shack Model 100 was the first popular notebook computer.

Almost all portable computers sold today fall into the notebook category. True, you can still buy the old "lunchbox" style units with hinged LCD displays, and even the "portable sewing machine" style that includes a real CRT display like the old Osborne and original Compaq portables, but these represent such a tiny portion of the market that they can be dispensed with quickly. These older designs—more accurately called "transportables" or "luggables"—typically run only on AC power (no batteries), but do let you install expansion cards. This makes them attractive to niche markets where special adapters need to be installed in a system that must be transportable but is only used in places where AC outlets are readily available.

So when we talk about portable computers, we almost invariably mean a notebook computer: battery powered, weighing about 8 pounds or less, and with length and width dimensions that are slightly larger than an $8\frac{1}{2} \times 11$-inch sheet of letter paper.

TANSTAAFL

"There ain't no such thing as a free lunch." Life is a series of choices, trade-offs, and compromises, and nowhere is this more apparent than with portable computers. Variations in processor, display, and optional features have direct and significant effects on battery life and weight. The interrelations of these factors is complex, but it all boils down to the fact that you can't have a big, bright, colorful screen and a large keyboard with a powerful processor backed by a huge hard disk and lots of memory in a small, lightweight package that will run for hours and hours without recharging—no matter how much you are willing to spend. So you must consider your options carefully.

Processors

Not long ago, there were two separate classes of CPU chips: one for desktops and one for portables. The reason for the split was that the portable processors had additional circuitry built in that would reduce the power consumption during normal use, which in turn would extend battery life.

Early into the run of the 80486 chip, however, Intel decided to add power management to all their chips in the line, simplifying production. (This also was supported by the Energy Department's efforts at promoting the Energy Star standard for power-saving devices.) As a result, all Intel 486 chips have "SL technology" included in their circuitry. These features let the CPU slow down its processing—or even stop it almost altogether—during periods of little or no activity. Much of a computer's time is spent waiting for the user to do something, such as press the next letter while writing with a word processor. Letting the CPU take quick naps during these periods can dramatically reduce power consumption.

Since most processors incorporate power management, the issue becomes one of size. The more complex and powerful a CPU is, the more power it will draw while operating (which means you either get less running time on the battery or have to increase battery capacity, which in turn adds weight).

Screens

A color LCD (the TLA stands for Liquid Crystal Display) panel doesn't weigh much more than a monochrome panel, but it can add pounds to the overall weight of the computer. The reason is power consumption.

Several different LCD panel technologies are commonly used for notebook displays. The simplest is a **monochrome passive matrix** design, which makes it the least expensive to manufacture. LCD panels create an image by blocking light as it passes through the liquid crystal layer. The problem is that even when a pixel is set to let the light pass through, a large portion of light is absorbed by the liquid crystals and other filter layers that make up an LCD panel. Monochrome passive matrix panels absorb about 75 to 85 percent of the light that passes through them, so only less than one-fourth the light from the backlight reaches your eyes when displaying a white image.

Monochrome passive matrix

Passive matrix panels have some limitations. If too strong a current is sent to an individual pixel, it can affect other pixels in the same column on the panel; this causes the familiar ghosting that is seen on these displays. Because the amount of current that can be applied is limited, there is a limit to how fast the pixels can turn on or off. This not only limits the display's effectiveness for animated images such as digitized video clips, but it also limits the number of colors that the panel can display. Because an LCD cell can only be on or off, shades of colors are created by turning a cell on and off rapidly to create a dimmer shade of that color. Finally, the viewing angle of passive matrix screens is limited. You more or less have to view the image straight on, and the image disappears if you move up or down or to the side.

Color passive matrix

Color passive matrix screens have the same limitations as a monochrome panel, except that they transmit even less light because some is absorbed by the colored filters for each pixel.

LCD designers have come up with an approach that retains most of the low-cost production aspects of a standard passive matrix panel, while improving the response time of the individual cells. This design is called **dual-scan** and it essentially divides a standard panel into two horizontal pieces. Each half is driven separately, which makes it possible to drive each cell with a stronger current. This makes the cells respond more rapidly and also makes it possible for the panel to produce more shades of colors.

The top of the line in LCD panels is **active matrix.** In a passive matrix panel, the transistors that switch the current (controlling which pixels are turned on or off) are separate from the panel. On an active matrix panel, each individual LCD cell has its own transistor, which controls whether that individual cell is on or off. This makes it possible to create very responsive displays that have a wider viewing angle and can produce nearly as many colors as a CRT can. The problem is that the manufacturing process is extremely more expensive than for passive matrix, especially because the failure of a single transistor at one of the LCD cells results in a panel that has a permanent flaw. Because each panel has thousands of transistors, product yield becomes a major factor in the manufacturing cost.

Another major limitation of active matrix panels is that they absorb much more of the transmitted light—95 percent or more. Thus you need something like a car headlight behind the panel to get sufficient brightness, but then the backlight must draw more power, which in turn puts designers in the bind of choosing between shorter battery life or an increased battery capacity, which of course adds weight.

There is an enormous pent-up demand for new flat panel technologies that provide brighter displays with more colors and faster response times at lower power consumption rates. Several promising technologies are nearing production, but the most promising of all is the field-emitter display (FED) . This design produces what amounts to hundreds of tiny CRTs at each pixel, but in a panel no thicker than a typical LCD panel. Electrons are shot directly at individual phosphors, so there is no light transmission loss, and the huge number of electron-emitters per phosphor dot eliminates the yield problems of active

matrix LCDs. (Even if a quarter of the emitters do not function, the pixel still works normally.) FEDs have the potential to be much cheaper to build than active matrix LCDs, yet they provide an image that is nearly identical to a CRT display. Although no commercial products are available with this technology as I write this, pre-production panels have been demonstrated at industry conferences, and it looks as though it is only a matter of time before they become available.

Batteries

Fortunately for notebook users, there have been many recent advances in battery technology. Designers now have options that can provide increased power capacity at lower weights than was possible with older batteries.

The first popular rechargeable battery for electronic devices was the **nicad** (which is a contraction of nickel-cadmium, the two basic elements used in their design). These were relatively lightweight and could be used to power devices such as video cameras and portable phones. The problem with nicads is that they have a "memory"—if you recharged one without fully discharging it first, it would only "remember" the recharged portion of the power and would run out of power before using the remainder. Newer nicads have less problem with this memory effect, but most still have it to some degree.

Nicad

It's always a good idea to completely discharge a nicad battery before recharging, but this is not always a practical procedure. Make plans, however, to fully discharge any rechargeable battery on a regular schedule. Some older batteries may take two or three discharge cycles to be fully reconditioned, especially if they often have been partially recharged.

The next technology to be widely used was **nickel metal hydride (NiMH).** These provide 10 to 20 percent more power per pound than the best nicads, have less of a memory effect than nicads, and are popular with current notebook computer designs.

NiMH

The next most likely candidate to dominate the portable battery market is **lithium-ion** technology. These batteries are expected to produce as much as 50 percent more power per pound than NiMH units and, as an added bonus, may have manufacturing costs that are far lower than even those of nicads.

Lithium-ion

Some wildcard technologies are also out there, such as the zinc-air battery. These batteries "breathe" oxygen, absorbing it as they discharge and emitting it as they recharge. The batteries have a fairly good power-to-weight ratio, but because their efficiency is directly related to the total surface area of the battery, they tend to be large and bulky. Although some notebook manufacturers have taken advantage of this technology, it remains to be seen whether or not they will be a significant player in the market.

Zinc-air

Battery packaging

Many notebooks use batteries of proprietary shape and specifications, which can limit the number of sources available for replacements. Early battery-operated computers, such as the Radio Shack Model 100, ran on standard penlight batteries. Manufacturers are now trying to settle on some standard battery sizes and shapes, and there are even some low-power notebooks that are using standard household battery types such as AA penlight batteries. This approach can be handy in an emergency. If your rechargeable battery should run out of power, you can always dash into a newsstand or drug store and buy a handful of standard alkaline batteries to tide you over until you can recharge your main battery.

Storage

Everything about computers has become smaller, faster, with larger capacities at a lower price. Nowhere is this more visible than with hard disks. The original IBM XT hard disk was amazing because it managed to pack a full 10MB into a single 5.25-inch full-height storage device. Now we have hard disks with platters that are only 2.5 inches in diameter and smaller, less than an inch tall, and yet with capacities greater than 1GB—more than 100 times greater than the original XT drive.

By shrinking the size of these drives, their power consumption is greatly reduced, making them practical components for a battery-powered computer. Most notebook computers come standard with at least a 500MB hard disk these days.

PC Card (aka PCMCIA)

> If you are going to build something in the air it is always better to build castles than houses of cards.
>
> G. C. Lichtenberg (1742–1799)
> *Aphorisms*

One feature that most new notebooks have that you won't find on a desktop is support for **PC Cards.** These are also known as **PCMCIA cards** (which is an SLA for Personal Computer Memory Card International Association), but mercifully, the association is now trying to get people to call them PC Cards instead.

There is no truth to the widely held belief that PCMCIA stands for "People Can't Memorize Computer Industry Acronyms," despite the accuracy of its self-referential assertion.

The original PC Cards are known as Type 1 cards, and were originally designed as memory cards (Figure 8.2). They were used for a variety of memory types, including nonvolatile or battery-powered units that could retain their stored data when removed from the computer.

Figure 8.2 The first PC Cards were designed as removable memory for portable computers.

The PC Card interface was not limited to just memory, however, and soon other cards appeared on the market. The Type 2 specification allowed for thicker cards, which made it possible to create communications devices such as modems and network interface cards. Then came the Type 3 specification, designed to accommodate tiny hard disks mounted in a PC Card. These were significantly thicker than Type 1 or 2 cards, and most computers that have a Type 3 slot can also take two Type 1 or 2 cards in the same space instead.

Just because PC Cards are designed primarily for notebooks doesn't mean that you can't use them on your desktop computer. Several companies, including SCM Microsystems, make PC Card devices for desktop systems. Their SwapBox line of products even includes a device that combines a 3.5-inch floppy disk drive with a PC Card slot in a single unit the size of a standard 3.5-inch floppy disk drive. This Classic Combo unit (Figure 8.3) accepts one PC Card, Type 1, 2, or 3. Now that many notebook computers do not include internal floppy disk drives, PC Card support on your desktop can make it easier to move data back and forth between desktop and notebook systems.

Printers

A portable printer is certainly handy, but it's hardly a necessity for most people. Chances are excellent that, no matter where you're headed, you can get access to a printer. Many hotels now have office centers where you can rent time on printers, computers, and other equipment.

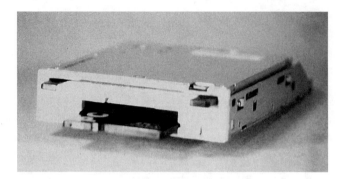

Figure 8.3 Devices such as the SCM Microsystems Classic Combo SwapBox let you use PC Cards on your desktop computer.

If you need a portable printer, however, lots of excellent choices are certainly available. Just as with the desktop printer market, ink jet technology has taken a dominant share of the portable market. Both monochrome and full color ink jet models are available from manufacturers, including Hewlett-Packard and Canon, at prices that are not much different than similar desktop units. The main difference is that the portable units tend to have smaller ink capacities and slower print speeds, but they can be a handy addition to your traveling hardware kit.

On the road? Don't have a printer? Don't have access to a printer in your hotel and you need to have a hard copy of a proposal to hand to your client in 30 minutes? If you have a fax modem, you're all set. Simply call down to the front desk, find out the hotel's fax number, and fax yourself your document. (And if you don't have a fax modem, but have a regular modem and access to an on-line service such as CompuServe or an electronic mail service such as MCI Mail, you can send yourself an email message to be sent to the hotel's fax machine.)

Modems

> Well, if I called the wrong number, why did you answer the phone?
>
> James Thurber
> Cartoon caption in the *New Yorker,* June 5, 1937

Portable modems come in a wide range of prices, sizes, and features. The main decision that you have to make is whether to buy an internal modem (that comes as part of your portable computer), a PC Card modem (the most popular use of all for PC Card slots in notebooks), or external "pocket" modems.

The internal modem is not always the best way to go. They are completely proprietary and can be difficult or impossible to replace or upgrade when communications standards or your needs change. Internal modems can also put an added strain on battery power, and if you forget to turn off the modem (or your notebook doesn't have such an option), your battery life can be severely reduced.

The pocket modem is the only other choice available to people with notebooks that don't have a PC Card slot. Few of these modems actually fit comfortably in your pocket, but they are smaller than a typical desktop external modem. An external modem means that you'll also have to carry a separate cable so you can connect the modem to your computer's serial port, but most pocket modems come with the required cable.

Another disadvantage of some pocket modems is that they can draw a fair amount of power. This means that their battery power will not last long, and you may end up plugging them in to a power outlet when you want to use it. This can be an added hassle that most portable users don't want to face.

The one big advantage of an external pocket modem is that most have indicator lights. This makes it easier to see (and if it has a speaker, hear) what is going on when your computer is trying to make a connection. If your connection goes smoothly, you won't need this; but if it doesn't, the lights can help you troubleshoot the situation by indicating whether you're communicating with the modem, with the phone line, or with the other computer at all.

PC Cards (Figure 8.4) are popular as modems for many reasons. They are relatively inexpensive (ranging from about $150 on up) and are tiny (you could slip a few of them in your shirt pocket and still have room in your pocket protector).

Figure 8.4   PC Card modems such as this one from AT&T are popular with notebook users.

A PC Card modem doesn't draw much power, and you can remove it when you're not using it. No data cable is required, and some even have very compact phone jacks that retract into the card case when not in use.

Another advantage with PC Card modems is that you can also get models that serve multiple functions. Several cards, for example, provide both modem features and an interface for local area network connections.

Fast talkers

Once you have decided which type of modem you want to get, you need to consider its features. One important feature is the data transmission speed. You can get lost in the alphabet soup of "vee-dot this" and "vee-dot that" (such as V.32 and V.32bis and so on). I've listed the major standards in Table 8.1, but the important thing to know is that most modems you can buy today will run at least at 14.4 Kbps (kilobits per second). The best modems run at 28.8 Kbps. These speeds can be effectively increased through the use of data compression; depending on your data, it can be shrunk to as little as one-tenth its original size for transmission and then decompressed at the other end by the receiving modem. Both modems at each end have to support this feature in order to take advantage of compression's gains.

Table 8.1 Some of the common standards for modem features

Standard	Function
V.32	Supports data transmission up to 9600 bps.
V.32bis	Supports data transmission up to 14.4 Kbps.
V.FC	Also known as V.FAST, supports data transmission up to 28.8 Kbps; an interim standard created by modem manufacturers before the V.34 standard was finalized.
V.34	Supports data transmission up to 28.8 Kbps.
V.42	Error correction protocol.
V.42bis	Data compression protocol with up to 4:1 compression ratio.
MNP-3	Error correction protocol.
MNP-4	Error correction protocol.
MNP-5	Data compression protocol with up to 2:1 compression ratio.
MNP-10	Adverse channel enhancements (helps with poor line conditions, as with a cellular phone connection).

Keep your fax straight.

Most modems also include fax support. Even if you don't think you need this feature, it's still a good idea to get it anyway. Documents sent from a fax modem come out the other end looking far better than the same document printed and then scanned by a typical office fax machine. There are no stray marks or errors, so the received copy looks crisp and clear.

The fax modem features are also easy to use. If you're running Windows applications, most fax modems include software that makes sending a fax as easy as printing your document on a printer instead. Fax modem features add little cost to the total package, so it makes sense to get them from the start.

Pointing Devices

As with desktop systems, you have a lot of choices for pointing devices on notebook computers. Many notebooks have built-in pointing devices. Some have trackballs; others have little buttons that don't move but instead respond to pressure (such as the TruePoint pointing device) or a touchpad where you trace the pointer's movement with your finger.

These built-in devices are convenient and generally make it easy to move the Windows pointer around the screen, but pay close attention to how these devices provide the equivalent of the left and right mouse buttons. Trackballs and pressure buttons often have special keys or buttons that provide the equivalent of the mouse buttons, but they are not always placed conveniently. Some are designed in such a way that it takes a second hand to operate the buttons, which some users may find to be inconvenient or awkward. And some touchpads require that you use taps to trigger mouse button presses. This can be a tricky skill to master because this feature may not work as expected if you are too slow or too fast with the taps.

You often can use any external pointing device that you might want, such as a standard mouse or trackball. Special trackballs that are small and designed to be held in your hand have also been designed for use with portables. These are particularly handy for people making presentations with their notebooks because most Windows presentation software can be controlled by mouse button clicks (such as left button to go forward one slide, right button to go back one). A hand-held trackball can work much like a tethered remote control on a slide projector, making it easy to stand at a podium or move around, without having to go over to the notebook each time you want to advance to the next image in your presentation.

Most airlines do not allow the use of "tethered" devices such as mice, detached trackballs, and other external pointing devices on notebook computers while in flight. This is because the electrical signals passing through the cable set up electromagnetic fields, and if the cable is improperly shielded, these fields can be broadcast from the cable as radio waves. I am not aware of any studies that show that such devices actually cause problems with aircraft navigation equipment or electronic controls, but there is certainly strong anecdotal evidence that indicates that it can happen. To be safe and to avoid possible confrontations with airline employees, you may want to pick a notebook with an integral pointing device.

@#%$%@!

> The shortest answer is doing.
>
> English proverb: collected by George Herbert
> *Jacula Prudentum,* 1651

Problems with portables are the same as those with desktop systems, only different. They are the same in that a notebook computer has all the same *functional* components as a desktop system. The difference is that where a desktop has modular, standardized, interchangeable components—such as hard disk controllers, display adapters, and keyboards—notebook computers have highly integrated, proprietary parts that are difficult to separate for diagnosis or replacement.

Some problems you can handle in more or less the same way as you would on a desktop. The first line of treatment for hard disk problems would be the use of the same software tools for diagnosis and repair as you would use on a desktop.

Other problems are clearly beyond the scope of the skills of most users. If the keyboard breaks down or there is a memory failure, you probably won't be able to do much about it. Even the advice of reseating socketed chips or cables is hard to apply with notebooks. Most units are assembled as such a puzzle-box of circuit boards and connecting cables that it can be nearly impossible for an untrained person to disassemble them successfully . . . and nearly twice as hard to get the pieces all back in their appropriate places again when you're finished.

So unless you're very adventurous or you don't really care what happens or you're already resigned to purchasing professional service and just want to take a chance that you can fix the problem without making the problem worse, my advice is don't try to open your notebook's case.

Just because one of these highly integrated, proprietary components fails, you may not be stuck with a dead computer until the repairs are made. Most notebooks have ports for external displays and keyboards. If the LCD panel or keyboard fails, you may be able to carry on using an external keyboard or monitor instead. This is certainly not a portable solution, but it can help you finish some high-priority work before you send the system off for repair. And just because the hard disk fails doesn't mean you're stuck; you may be able to boot from a floppy disk and use an external hard disk attached to a parallel port as a stopgap measure.

Problems with Notebooks

There are a few problems with a portable computer that you can address.

Battery and power maintenance

Notebook computers are running longer on a battery charge than ever before, in spite of larger hard disks, more memory, faster processors, and bigger and brighter displays. Part of this increase in running time is due to batteries that can store more power per pound, and part of this is due to more energy-efficient components, but a major part of the gains can be attributed to more intelligent power-savings systems. The problems are that you must use these systems intelligently to maximize battery life and the default settings are not always the best.

Different computers have different power-saving features implemented in different ways. Some older systems require special software drivers loaded in the CONFIG.SYS file; more recent models accomplish the same functions through features in their BIOS software. Your notebook's documentation should include information on power-saving features and how they are implemented.

Some power-saving drivers can cause conflicts with some programs. If you are having problems with software crashing, start by removing any power-saving drivers from your CONFIG.SYS file. Then edit the file and put the letters REM and a space before any line with a power-saving driver. If this eliminates the problem, you may have to choose between longer battery life and that software.

Another problem you may encounter is that some software may produce an error message stating that the disk is not ready. This can happen when the hard disk powers down after it has been inactive for a length of time. When the software tries to read or write to the drive, it takes a few moments for the drive to get back up to speed. You may be able to prevent this from happening by specifying a longer delay period before the drive shuts down.

Some notebooks have a keystroke combination that automatically shuts down all the computer systems, maintaining just enough power to keep the contents of the system memory intact. In many cases, when you press the keystroke to wake the system back up again, the hard disk remains powered down until the next read or write request. If you are working with a program that makes infrequent disk accesses (such as a spreadsheet or word processing program), you can greatly extend battery life by putting the system to sleep after a disk access, then waking it up right away after the disk has stopped. This shuts the hard disk down sooner than it would using the automatic shutdown feature, and saves power. Remember to turn off any automatic save feature of your software if you want to minimize how often the disk is powered up. Also keep in mind that software cache programs such as SmartDrive automatically flush any cached writes to the drive after a short delay—about 10 seconds or so—so wait for that to happen before you put the computer to sleep, or you'll just have to do it twice in a row.

In addition to adjusting the power-saving features to settings that work best for you, you can also extend your battery charge by taking care of your rechargeable batteries. As mentioned earlier, these work best when you completely discharge them before recharging. If a battery has developed a reduced capacity due to the memory effect, you may need to run through a few cycles of deep discharging and recharging in order to recondition the battery.

It also makes good sense to pack a spare battery, and if it's available, a separate charger. This lets you charge one battery while using the other, and it also provides you with a spare in case the first should fail.

Storage issues   Notebooks have hard disks that are as large as those on your desktop, but you can't install a tape drive attached to your notebook's floppy drive interface like you can on a desktop system. So how are you going to protect yourself from a storage meltdown?

The best answer is to get either a second hard disk (which you can use to make a mirror of the notebook's contents) or a removable media device that connects to your notebook through either the parallel port or a PC Card interface. There are PC Card SCSI interfaces available, making it easy to use an external SCSI device such as an optical disk or removable disk. The advantage of the removable media approach is that you could use the same device to back up other computers (especially if you got one that uses a parallel or SCSI interface, and your other computers have that interface).

Of course, not everyone has critical data on his or her notebook; lots of people use notebooks more or less as electronic scratch paper for drafts and notes and sketched ideas that will later be polished on a desktop system. If you have a floppy disk for the notebook, and you are careful to back up all your data files onto floppies as you create them (which is not a big ordeal if you're going to use the floppy to transfer the files to the desktop anyway), then you may not really need to back up your entire notebook system at all. I know that this is a heretical position, but it's a pragmatic one that recognizes how people actually use these things.

Synchronizing files with your desktop   The remaining problem with a notebook is not so much a troubleshooting or hardware maintenance problem as it is a data management problem. If you're using the notebook as your only computer, you can skip this.

But if you're using the notebook as an adjunct to a desktop system, you face the problem of synchronizing the data on the two systems. At its simplest, this means that new files created on one system need to be copied to the other. A deeper level is figuring out which version of a given file is the most recent, and then updating the other system. And at the deepest level, there is the situation where changes have been made to a file in both systems (such as names and addresses in a contact management program), where you want both lists updated with the other's changes.

Some applications can handle even the deepest level of this problem for themselves. If you have a contact management program and you're not familiar with its data synchronization capabilities, you might want to check into it more before you make a commitment to work on two systems at once.

In order for synchronization features to work correctly, make certain that you have the date and time set accurately on both machines.

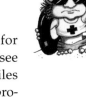

For the simpler, file-level tasks, file exchange programs can handle this for you. LapLink from Traveling Software and FastLynx from Rupp Technology (see Appendix A) are two examples of programs that make it easy to exchange files across a parallel or serial port connection. These programs can identify which programs have been created on one machine but not the other, which files exist on both but only one has been updated, and which files exist on both machines and both have been modified since the last time the program was run.

A utility like this can save hours of poking through disk directories and the frustration of trying to locate the latest version of a file.

Windows 95 comes with everything you need to synchronize files without the need for any extra software. A new feature called Briefcase lets you set up a set of files on each computer. These sets are called Briefcases, and you can synchronize the contents of the files in Briefcases in separate computers. This feature can delete files, create new ones, update one file from changes in another, and in some cases, make changes to both files when both have been changed since they were last synchronized. This process can be done with a floppy disk to move the files between computers, but it also works across local area network connections or direct serial port connections using the Win95 Direct Cable Connection.

UPGRADING

> Yield to temptation; it may not pass your way again.
>
> Robert Heinlein
> *The Notebooks of Lazarus Long,* 1973

Buy your notebooks carefully. Making changes to a notebook's features can be an expensive proposition, and the choices may be limited, so try to get what you want from the outset. Changing details such as the processor or display adapter circuitry is almost always more expensive than it is worth, if the change is even possible in the first place.

Fortunately quite a few upgrade and expansion options are worth consideration. Memory is the easiest, though it often costs more than standard SIMMs used in desktop systems. It is available from the manufacturer or from third-party sources for the more popular models.

Hard Disk Upgrades

Aside from memory, the other most common feature that notebook users want to upgrade is the hard disk capacity. This task is more difficult than it is with desktop units because there are rarely open disk drive bays, and it is not easy to get at the hard disk controller connections (unless you have one of the newer designs that uses modular hard disks in special bays, but even then you are limited to whatever hard disk models and capacities the manufacturer offers).

External   One approach to increasing hard disk capacity is to add an external hard disk. As mentioned earlier, there are models that attach to a parallel port, but for best performance, you may want to use a PC Card drive or a SCSI device connected to a PC Card SCSI adapter.

Third-party upgrade services   If you simply want a larger hard disk inside your computer, however, this is also fairly easy to achieve—though you probably won't be able to do it yourself. Most notebooks do not have the BIOS entries for hard disks other than the few that the manufacturer offered. Several third-party services, however, are experts in upgrading notebooks with larger hard disks. They can provide either a revised BIOS or a software driver to accommodate the larger disks, and they have the experience to remove the old disk and install a new one.

Adding Exotica

If notebooks are to be the functional equivalent to a desktop system, you must be able to add all the components that you can add to a larger system. Fortunately there are products that do just that.

Joysticks   People play games with computers, and some games just can't be played with anything less than a joystick. Face it: There was no keyboard or mouse in a P-51 Mustang World War II fighter cockpit.

You can add a game port to your notebook in several ways. Some machines have docking stations that can take regular expansion cards, and because joysticks aren't all that portable in the first place, a docking station is not that bad a limitation. If you have a PC Card slot, however, there are multimedia add-ons that will add a game port.

If you don't have either of these, you may still be able to use a joystick on your portable. The Notebook Gameport from Colorado Spectrum (Figure 8.5) attaches to a serial port and lets you connect a joystick while leaving the serial port active for a mouse or other device. Note that this is not the exact equivalent of a game port; the device requires a special driver for each application in order to pass along the joystick position information to the program. If the Gameport does not include a driver for your favorite game, you won't be able to use it.

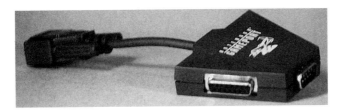

Figure 8.5 The Notebook Gameport from Colorado
Spectrum adds joystick support to portable computers
through a serial port.

Multimedia

Just because notebooks are small doesn't mean that you can't have full multimedia support. Some notebooks offer everything, including sound card and CD-ROM, right in the notebook's case. Others offer it as an optional upgrade, either as a separate "layer" that attaches to the bottom of the notebook or as a docking station.

Several add-ons are available for PC Card slots. Some cards combine a SCSI interface for a CD-ROM drive and a 16-bit stereo sound card, all in one device. You can even buy complete multimedia add-on units—CD-ROM drive, sound card, and amplified speakers—with a single PC Card as its interface. These devices can be a little temperamental to set up, but they do provide portable, affordable multimedia support for notebooks.

There are also sound devices designed for parallel port interfaces. In general, these devices do not have the same sound quality or performance of the PC Card devices. They often are single-channel (not stereo) devices and are not capable of the higher sampling rates or 16-bit sound samples required to reach CD-Audio standards. These simpler devices can be fine for business audio uses such as recording voice annotations, but they are not sufficient for more complex multimedia applications such as full-blown presentations with music backgrounds.

Scanners

Hand scanners are a good match for notebook computers. They are easy to install and configure and can be handy to make copies of documents when working away from your base, such as in a library or on site at a client's. They can even be used for OCR applications, making it easier than retyping printed text.

Security Issues

> Secrecy is the first essential in affairs of the State.
>
> Cardinal de Richelieu
> *Testament Politique,* 1641

The remaining upgrade issue to consider is that of security. Many notebook computers have a password protection feature that you can activate. The machine then requires that you enter the password every time you power up before it will boot up. This is a double-edged feature, however, because it can lock you out just like everyone else if you should forget the password.

A password also can't prevent someone from simply walking off with your notebook, which unfortunately is all too common an occurrence. There are lots of physical security devices that you can purchase, and many notebooks now have special locking tabs that you can secure with a cable or padlock so you can lock the unit to a piece of furniture or other large object that might deter a light-fingered fellow.

A password also can't prevent someone from reading over your shoulder as you work. I know a number of people who no longer do any serious work while on train rides or airplane flights because they are concerned about nosy neighbors. At least one product is designed to combat this problem, however. InvisiView is available from Man & Machine (see Appendix A) for most popular notebook computers, and it works by removing the top polarizing layers from the notebook screen. The company then provides a removable panel with the same filters that you can slip into place when you are working in private or want others to see the screen. When you want to work in public, however, you remove the panel, and the screen's image will be solid white. Slip on a pair of the sunglasses provided by the company—which have the precise polarizing characteristics required for that screen—and then only you will be able to see the image on the screen.

Appendix A
Sources

It has long been known that one horse can run faster than another—but *which one?* Differences are crucial.

Robert Heinlein
The Notebooks of Lazarus Long, 1973

There are tons of products and resources on the market. Most of them are good. A few of them are awful. A very few are really excellent. Here are some of the sources of programs, peripherals, components, and other products that I think are good. Most of them are excellent. None of them are awful. And almost all of them are mentioned in various places throughout the book.

I have listed them here in alphabetical order by category, which is probably only slightly more helpful than listing the categories in random order, but it was the best I could come up with at the time. If you have a better idea how to list these, let me know and I'll try it in the next revision.

I have not listed prices for any of these products or services. This book will be out of date soon enough without doing something silly like listing prices, so call or write the company (at least *that* information shouldn't change as quickly as prices) for the latest details.

BENCHMARK UTILITIES

Ziff-Davis Benchmark Operation, One Copley Parkway, Suite 510, Morrisville, NC 27560

Winstone, WinBench, PC Bench, and others

These benchmark tests on CD-ROM are free for the asking; be sure to include your name, address, and phone number. You can also download WinBench and PC Bench from the ZD Benchmark Operation forum on ZD Net (see *Online Services*) or from the World Wide Web at http://www.zdnet.com/~zdbop/.

CABLES AND COMMUNICATIONS PRODUCTS

Black Box Corporation, P.O. Box 12800, Pittsburgh, PA 15241; 800-552-6816; 412-746-5500

DIAGNOSTIC AND CONFIGURATION UTILITIES—MONITORS

Sonera Technologies, P.O. Box 565, Rumson, NJ 07760; 908-747-6886; fax 908-747-4523

Displaymate

DIAGNOSTIC AND CONFIGURATION UTILITIES—SYSTEMS

DiagSoft, 5615 Scotts Valley Drive #140, Scotts Valley, CA 95066; 800-342-4763, 408-438-8247; fax 408-438-7113

QA Plus

Dariana Software, 5241 Lincoln Avenue, Suite B5, Cypress, CA 90630; 800-892-9950; 714-236-1380

WinSleuth
System Sleuth

Landmark Research International Corporation, 703 Grand Central Street, Clearwater, FL; 800-683-6696, 813-443-1331; fax 813-443-6603

Landmark WINProbe

Touchstone Software Corporation, 2130 Main Street, Huntington Beach, CA; 800-531-0450, 714-969-7746; fax 714-960-1886

CheckIt Pro

FILE EXCHANGE PROGRAMS

Rupp Technology Corporation, 3228 E. Indian School, Phoenix, AZ 85018; 800-844-7775; 602-224-9922; fax 602-224-0898

FastLynx
WinLynx

Traveling Software, 18702 N. Creek Parkway, Bothell, WA 98011; 800-343-8080, 206-483-8088; fax 206-487-1284

LapLink

HARD DISK AND SYSTEM UTILITIES

Central Point Software Inc., 15220 N.W. Greenbrier Parkway, #150, Beaverton, OR; 800-228-5651, 310-782-8190; fax 310-328-5892

PC Tools

Symantec Corporation, 10201 Torre Avenue, Cupertino, CA 95014; 800-441-7234, 503-334-6054; fax 503-334-7474

Norton's Utilities for DOS
Norton's Utilities for Windows

Gibson Research Corporation, 35 Journey, Aliso Viejo, CA 92656; 714-362-8800; fax 714-362-8808

SpinRite 3.1

LAPTOP SCREEN SECURITY, LAPTOP REPAIRS AND UPGRADES

Man & Machine, 3706 West Street, Landover, MD 20785; 301-341-4900; fax 301-341-4079

InvisiView

MEMORY-MANAGEMENT UTILITIES FOR WINDOWS

Connectix, 2655 Campus Drive, San Mateo, CA 94403; 800-950-5880; 415-571-5100; fax 415-571-5195

Ram Doubler

Helix Software Co., 4709 30th Street, Long Island City, NY 11101; 800-451-0551; 718-392-3100; fax 718-392-4212

Hurricane

Quarterdeck, 5770 Roosevelt Boulevard, Clearwater, FL 34620; 800-683-6696; 813-523-9700; fax 813-532-4222

MagnaRAM

ONLINE SERVICES

America Online, Inc., 8619 Westwood Center Drive, Vienna, VA 22182-2285; 800-827-6364; 703-448-8700

CompuServe, 5000 Arlington Centre Boulevard, Columbus, OH 43220; 800-848-8199; 614-457-8600

Prodigy Services Co., 445 Hamilton Avenue, White Plains, NY 10601; 800-776-3449

ZD Net, 800-895-4596

This is the service for the Ziff Davis magazines, including *PC Magazine, Computer Shopper, Computer Life,* and others. It is arguably the best source of technical information and has one of the largest and best collections of software for downloading anywhere. It's also where you can ask me your hardware questions online—you'll find me in the "Alfred's Cures" section on the Computer Shopper forum, which you can reach with the "GO COMPSHOP" command.

POWER SUPPLIES AND COOLING FANS

PC Power & Cooling, Inc., 5995 Avenida Encinas, Carlsbad, CA 92008; 800-722-6555; 619-931-5700; fax 619-931-6988

REFERENCES ON HARD DISKS, I/O CARDS, AND MOTHERBOARDS

Micro House, Inc., 4900 Pearl East Circle #101, Boulder, CO 80301; 800-926-8299; 303-443-3388; 303-443-3323 fax; 303-443-9957 BBS; HTTP://WWW.MICRO-HOUSE.COM

The Hard Disk Technical Guide
The Technical Library on CD-ROM

USED, REFURBISHED, AND SURPLUS EQUIPMENT AND REPAIR SERVICES

CompuMart, 899 Presidential, Suite 110, Richardson, TX 75081; 800-864-1177

Computer Hot Line, 15400 Knoll Trail, Suite 500, Dallas, TX 75248; 800-866-3241

Processor, P.O. Box 85518, Lincoln, NE 68501; 800-334-7443

WINDOWS DRIVERS AND PATCHES

Microsoft Corporation, One Microsoft Way, Redmond, WA 98052; 800-426-9400, 206-882-8080; fax 206-936-7329

Microsoft Software Library:
America Online: keyword MICROSOFT
Compuserve: GO MICROSOFT
GEnie: prompt MICROSOFT
Microsoft Download Service (MSDL): 206-936-6735
Internet FTP: ftp.microsoft.com

Appendix B

CPU Comparison Table

> Everything that is beautiful and noble is the product of reason and calculation.
>
> Charles Baudelaire
> *L'Art Romantique,* 1869

Some people call the tangled mess of computer specifications "confusing"; I call it "job security"—it seems that there will always be a need for someone to explain what these companies are really selling.

Perhaps the single most-confusing feature of a computer is its central processor chip (the CPU). At first glance, there seems to be some pattern to the conventions used to name the different models, but a closer examination quickly reveals the uncomfortable truth that the model names are of little help in determining the comparative features of the various chips.

The list of CPUs that follows is by no means comprehensive, either for models or features. I have tried to include only those CPUs that you are most likely to encounter. For each model, I have listed the most important features that provide some indication about relative performance.

For more detail about what these features mean, see Chapter 1. Here are brief explanations of the different features.

Chip   This is the model name that you are most likely to see used to identify the chip. In many real-life references (such as advertisements), the manufacturer's initials are omitted. I have sorted the list alphabetically by manufacturer and then by chip model. This order is totally arbitrary, but should make it easier to locate and compare different chips.

Data Bus: Internal and External   The data bus refers to the number of bits of information that can be handled at one time. The internal number refers to the bus width used within the chip for calculations, and the external number refers to the bus width used to exchange data with the system memory. A wider bus results in faster performance.

Clock Speed: Internal and External   The clock speed governs how quickly operations occur. The internal number refers to the speed used for operations within the CPU, and the external number indicates how rapidly operations occur between the CPU and the rest of the system components. The advent of clock-doubled and -tripled chips have made it necessary to make the distinction between internal and external speeds. Many chips show a range of times for these speeds; the range indicates the minimum and maximum available in different versions of that model chip. A faster clock speed results in faster performance.

Internal Cache: Data and Instruction An internal cache on the CPU chip can speed processing operations by holding recently used data or instructions. The use of this feature is a relatively new development in CPU design. The latest designs have two separate caches: one for data and one for instruction. In the chart, a number in just the data column indicates a cache that is used for both data and instructions. Internal caches do increase performance and a larger cache is better, but for fastest results you will want an additional system cache (L2 cache) on the motherboard as well.

Coprocessor A math coprocessor speeds certain types of calculations. Many CPU designs rely on an optional, separate chip to provide this function. Some include floating point (FP) coprocessing circuitry on the chip, while others provide a more limited integer (I) coprocessing capability. The integer feature provides limited performance gains, but the floating point feature can accelerate performance dramatically with many applications—particularly computer-aided design (CAD) programs.

CPU Comparison Table

Company	Coprocessor	Chip	Data Bus (bits) Internal	Data Bus (bits) External	Clock Speed (MHz)[1] Internal	Clock Speed (MHz)[1] External	Internal Cache (KB) Data[2]	Internal Cache (KB) Instruction[3]
AMD	Am386DX	32	32	16–40	16–40	0	—	N
AMD	Am386DXL	32	32	20–40	20–40	0	—	N
AMD	Am386SX	32	16	16–40	16–40	0	—	N
AMD	Am386SXL	32	16	20–40	20–40	0	—	N
AMD	Am486DX	32	32	33–40	33–40	8	—	FP
AMD	Am486DX2	32	32	50–80	25–40	8	—	FP
AMD	Am486DX4	32	32	99–133	33–44.3	8	—	FP
AMD	Am486SX	32	32	33–40	33–40	8	—	N
AMD	Am486SX2	32	32	50–66	25–33	8	—	N
AMD	Am80286	16	16	8–20	8–20	0	—	N
AMD	Am8086	16	16	5–10	5–10	0	—	N
AMD	Am8088	16	8	4.77–10	4.77–10	0	—	N
Cyrix	Cx486D	32	32	40	40	2	—	N
Cyrix	Cx486DLC	32	32	25–40	25–40	1	—	I
Cyrix	Cx486DLC2	32	32	50–80	25–40	1	—	I
Cyrix	Cx486DRx2	32	32	32–66	16–33	1	—	I
Cyrix	Cx486DX	32	32	25–50	25–50	8	—	FP
Cyrix	Cx486DX2	32	32	66–80	33–40	2	—	N
Cyrix	Cx486DX2	32	32	40–80	20–40	8	—	FP

CPU Comparison Table *(cont.)*

Company	Coprocessor	Chip	Data Bus (bits)		Clock Speed (MHz)[1]		Internal Cache (KB)	
			Internal	External	Internal	External	Data[2]	Instruction[3]
Cyrix	Cx486DX4	32	32	75–100	25–33.3	8	—	FP
Cyrix	Cx486S	32	32	25–50	25–50	2	—	N
Cyrix	Cx486S2	32	32	40–50	20–25	2	—	N
Cyrix	Cx486SLC	32	16	20–40	20–40	1	—	I
Cyrix	Cx486SLC2	32	16	50	25	1	—	I
Cyrix	Cx486SRx	32	16	16–33	16–33	1	—	I
Cyrix	Cx486SRx2	32	32	16–33	16–33	1	—	I
Cyrix	Cx586	32	64	50–120	25–40	16	—	FP
IBM	386SLC	32	16	16–25	16–25	8	—	N
IBM	486BLX	32	32	15–33	15–33	16	—	N
IBM	486BLX2	32	32	30–66	15–33	16	—	N
IBM	486BLX3	32	32	45–99	15–33	16	—	N
IBM	486DLC	32	32	33	33	16	—	N
IBM	486DLC2	32	32	66	33	16	—	N
IBM	486SLC	32	16	16–25	16–25	16	—	N
IBM	486SLC2	32	16	32–80	16–40	16	—	N
IBM	80486BLDX2	32	32	66–80	33–40	2	—	N
Intel	i80186	16	16	6–20	6–20	0	—	N
Inte	i80188	16	8	6–20	6–20	0	—	N
Intel	i80286	16	16	6–20	6–20	0	—	N
Intel	i80386DX	32	32	12–33	12–33	0	—	N
Intel	i80386SL	32	16	16–33	16–33	0	—	N
Inte l	i80386SX	32	16	16–33	16–33	0	—	N
Inte l	i80486DX	32	32	20–50	20–50	8	—	FP
Intel	i80486DX2	32	32	40–66	20–33	8	—	FP
Intel	i80486DX4	32	32	75–99	25–33	16	—	FP
Intel	i80486SL	32	32	25–33	25–33	8	—	FP
Intel	i80486SX	32	32	16–33	16–33	8	—	N
Intel	i80486SX2	32	32	25	50	8	—	N
Intel	i8086	16	16	4–12	4–12	0	—	N
Intel	i8088	16	8	4.77–12	4.77–12	0	—	N
Intel	Pentium	32	64	60–133	50–66	8	8	FP
NEC	V20	16	8	8–16	8–16	0	—	N
NEC	V30	16	16	10–16	10–16	0	—	N
NexGen	Nx586	32	64	60–66	60–66	16	16	FP
T.I.[4]	TI486DLC	32	32	25–40	25–40	1	—	I
T.I.[4]	TI486SLC	32	16	20–40	20–40	1	—	I
T.I.[4]	TI486SXL	32	32	25–40	25–40	8	—	N
T.I.[4]	TI486SXL2	32	32	40–50	20–25	8	—	N
T.I.[4]	TI486SXL2	32	32	40–50	20–25	8	—	N

[1] A range of speeds indicates the slowest and fastest models offered in the line of chips.

[2] CPUs with an entry in only the data column for internal cache used the same cache for instructions and data.

[3] N = None, I = Integer, FP = Floating Point.

[4] T.I. = Texas Instruments.

Epilogue

A motion to adjourn is always in order.

Robert Heinlein
The Notebooks of Lazarus Long, 1973

I loved *The Streets of San Francisco* and the way that it was divided into four acts and an epilogue. Everything got tied together neatly before the top of the hour (still leaving time for a few commercials).

I wish I could claim such a tidy wrap-up to this project, but the hard truth is that hardware is messy. The problems are intermittent, the clues are ambiguous, and the cast of characters is always changing as new technologies arrive on the scene and older ones get written out of the script.

But I hope that this book has given you enough reference points so that you can write in these new characters for yourself as they appear. There is no doubt that computers and their related components will continue to become smaller, faster, more complicated, cheaper, and more powerful as time goes on. The trick is to remember that these machines are built to work for us, and not the other way around. Keep your eye on the goal—getting a task accomplished—and not on how state-of-the-art your equipment may be. Do your best to make sure that your tools are appropriate to the job at hand; if they're not, then upgrade or replace them. But watch out for the technology driving your decisions; collecting the latest and greatest can be a fun hobby, but it also can wreak havoc on your ability to get meaningful work done in a reasonable amount of time.

The most important point to remember is to have fun with this stuff. Life's too short and complicated without making it more of a struggle. Computers can be a real kick, especially when they make it possible to do your work faster and better so you have more time for other parts of your world.

Enjoy.

Index